What people are saying about
BEYOND PATRIARCHY

"*Beyond Patriarchy* is an immensely timely and learned book. Timely, in that the issues of traditionalism in religious and secular life are now subject to great pressure by the new movements for sexual parity. Learned in that the subject deals with immensely complex cross-cultural issues with sensitivity and literary grace. The book provides the groundwork for Jewish continuity in a highly volatile gender environment. Above all, Fuchs is on solid ground developing the case for sexual and gender equity, not supremacy."

IRVING LOUIS HOROWITZ
Editor Emeritus, *Society* magazine

"Sure to be controversial! A daring answer to a big question—how to rear competitive, successful, but tender fathers."

WILLIAM J. GOODE
Author of *World Changes in Divorce Patterns*

"Larry Fuchs's central question—how do we end patriarchy without getting rid of fathers?—reflects his commitment to gender equality and to fatherhood. His ability to fuse intellectual arguments with his own passion for creating a just world is a mark of all of Fuchs's scholarship. The book's optimism that patriarchy is not inevitable and can change is encouraging while his focus on Jewish fathers will help us to move towards a model of gender studies that is inclusive of men."

SHELLY TENENBAUM
Coeditor of *Feminist Perspectives on Jewish Studies*

"Fuchs restores the ideal of fatherhood to its honored niche within Jewish tradition. His work will interest scholars and general readers alike in reconstructing the history of Jewish fatherhood, articulating a contemporary Jewish message that American society should value greatly."

STEVEN BAYME
Director, William Petschek National Jewish Family Center
of the American Jewish Committee

"In discovering the origin and persistence of patriarchy, Lawrence Fuchs analyzes Jewish history, medieval rabbinical writings, evolutionary psychology, cultural anthropology, popular literature, and American ethnic history, yet he does not leave us with merely a history: his book also offers the possibility of how patriarchy can be supplanted by parental partnership. It is a book in which conservatives, liberals, feminists, Jews, Gentiles, Promise Keepers, and Darwinians will learn much. *Beyond Patriarchy* is fair-minded, clear-headed, and lucidly written. Its subject and argument cry out for popular recognition."

CARL DEGLER
Author of *At Odds: Women and Family in America
from the Revolution to the Present*

"It is rare that a book of such ambitious reach achieves such impressive grasp. Fuchs challenges just about everyone who has ever thought about issues of gender and of parenting. His challenges, though always tough, are never harsh. The narrow-minded will take offense; the vast rest will learn and gain breadth, understand the world—perhaps even ourselves—better."

LEONARD FEIN
Author of *Where Are We? The Inner Life of America's Jews*

"Can we put an end to patriarchy that does not result in a large-scale flight from fatherhood? Lawrence Fuchs is cautiously optimistic that we can, even as he acknowledges the deep roots of the patriarchal model. In this superb study, drawing on a wide range of historical, sociological and literary evidence, Fuchs finds support for his thesis in the Jewish patriarchal paradigm, which diminished the absolute power of males over females and called upon Jewish fathers to nurture, teach, and discipline their children. He hopes that modern men will be prepared to go one step further, and surrender the power of patriarchy in return for the satisfactions of a partnership approach to parenting. This is a stimulating and sure-to-be-controversial book. Fuchs tells us where we need to go, but readily admits how hard it will be to get there."

RABBI ERIC H. YOFFIE
President, Union of American Hebrew Congregations

BEYOND PATRIARCHY

The Political Behavior of American Jews

Hawaii Pono: An Ethnic and Political History

John F. Kennedy and American Catholicism

Those Peculiar Americans

American Ethnic Politics

Family Matters

The American Kaleidoscope: Race, Ethnicity, and the Civic Culture

BEYOND

PATRIARCHY

JEWISH FATHERS AND FAMILIES

Lawrence H. Fuchs

Brandeis University Press

PUBLISHED BY UNIVERSITY PRESS OF NEW ENGLAND

HANOVER AND LONDON

Brandeis University Press
Published by University Press of New England,
Hanover, NH 03755
©2000 by Lawrence H. Fuchs
Printed in the United States of America

5 4 3 2 1

LIBRARY OF CONGRESS CATALOGING-IN-PUBLICATION DATA
Fuchs, Lawrence H.
   Beyond patriarchy : Jewish fathers and families / Lawrence H. Fuchs.
       p.   cm.
   Includes bibliographical references (p.   ) and index.
   ISBN 0-87451-941-1 (cloth)
   1. Patriarchy—Religious aspects—Judaism.   2. Jewish
families–Conduct of life—History.   3. Patriarchy—History.   4. Women
in Judaism—History.   5. Jewish families—United States—Social
conditions.   I. Title.
   BM627 .F83 2000
       306.85'8'089924—dc21

                                                        00–008426

Like a bird that strays from its nest,
so is the man who strays from his home.

PROV. 27:8, 9

Listen, my son, to your fathers's instruction,
do not reject your mother's teaching:
they will be a crown of grace for your head,
a circlet for your neck.

PROV. 1:8, 9

CONTENTS

Contents

ACKNOWLEDGMENTS

I am grateful to many people who have made this book possible, especially those who took the time to read portions of the manuscript and to give me their critical advice: Joyce Antler, Steven Bayme, Marc Brettler, Sylvia Barack Fishman, Chae-Ran Freeze, Betty Fuchs, Victor Fuchs, Carole Hooven, Reuben Kimelman, Shulamit Magnus, Jonathan D. Sarna, Chaim Waxman, Stephen J. Whitfield, and Richard Wrangham. Michael Fishbane read an early version of several chapters. Sylvia Fishman, Victor Fuchs, Betty Fuchs, and Stephen Whitfield read the entire manuscript and made detailed suggestions and criticisms. All of the above are exempt from any responsibility for mistakes of mine.

My thanks to Phil Pochoda, editor at the University Press of New England, for his extremely helpful conceptual and organizational suggestions; to April Ossman, Mr. Pochoda's assistant; and to my longtime friend and agent, Gerard F. McCauley.

I am indebted, as I have been for many years, to the administrator of the American Studies Department at Brandeis University, Angela Simeone, and over the past two years for the assistance I have received from a Brandeis undergraduate, Bailey Giesler. I began writing this book many years ago and received able assistance from a wonderful friend and secretary, Molly Krakauer. Her job was taken up fifteen years ago by Christine Stone. Ms. Stone is a person of high literary intelligence. She has provided me with sharply critical and constructive queries and suggestions on the material of this book, my previous book, and dozens of articles and essays. The word *invaluable* is overworked, but in this case she truly deserves it.

October 24, 1999   L.H.F.

A PERSONAL NOTE

Beyond Patriarchy: Jewish Fathers and Families holds considerable personal meaning for me. My grandparents on my mother's side came to New York City in the 1880s, where they lived the Jewish immigrant saga on the Lower East Side. My father came as an immigrant from Austria to the Lower East Side in 1909 at the age of nine and did not finish high school because he had to support his parents after his father became ill. I consider myself a religious Jew, one who prays and meditates almost every day. I was not raised in a religiously observant home, and my ritual observance remains thin compared to that of Orthodox and most Conservative Jews.

That this book is primarily about fathers is consistent with the tremendous respect I have for the millions of mothers who have been raising children with little or no help from those children's biological fathers. Children need loving adult caregivers, of whatever sex or sexual orientation, and they need a continuity of authoritative love if they are to have a good chance to become healthy men and women.

I am committed to the goal of sexual equality. That means living in a world in which women and men can work toward their personal goals without any discrimination against them because of sex or sexual orientation. I realize that the sexes, on the average, differ in important biological respects; but I also try to remember that every individual is in some ways unique.

This book is dedicated to the memory of my earliest caregivers: my mother, Frances; my father, Alfred; my aunt Rebecca; and my aunt Bertha, who died on October 25, 1998, the last survivor of my mother's seven siblings; and to my beloved illiterate immigrant grandmother, Pearl, who knew that love is the ultimate wisdom.

BEYOND PATRIARCHY

DILEMMAS OF PATRIARCHY

O F THE MANY DYNAMIC CHANGES IN FAMILY RELATIONSHIPS IN THE UNITED STATES DURING THE LAST DECADES OF THE TWENTIETH century, two stand out. The first is the erosion of patriarchy; the second is the large-scale flight from fatherhood and the growing incidence of children's physical and mental health problems associated with fatherlessness. Both generalizations are easy to document. Women of all classes, especially among those best educated, have broken through barriers of power and privilege with startling rapidity. With new choices regarding reproduction and wider access to education and remunerative work, the exclusive or near-exclusive male bonding systems of modern patriarchy have been breached. No longer will woman doctors and lawyers, business leaders, or even army generals, police officers, firefighters, or truck drivers be considered aberrations. For one example, women constituted over 40 percent of the admissions to medical schools in 1998. All this happened with stunning speed, in contrast to a few million years of hominid biological adaptation and at least ten thousand years of universal patriarchal conditioning.[1]

The large-scale flight from fatherhood has been caused by many things, one of which is the growing independence of women. The phenomenon of single women raising their children without the biological fathers present dramatically accelerated in the 1960s and 1970s. The link between fatherlessness and the growth in physical and mental health problems for children has been well researched and reported.[2]

Analysis by Sarah McLanahan and Gary Sandefur, examining data from many national research projects, demonstrated that adolescents—

regardless of income level—who lived apart from one of their parents during some period of childhood were twice as likely to drop out of high school, twice as likely to have a child before age twenty, and one and one half times as likely to be out of school and out of work in their late teens and early twenties as were those who have had a continuity of relationship with both parents.[3] Such studies do not account for the possibility that in many broken families the absent parent is not capable of sustained authoritative love for children and that some of those children might have been worse off if such a parent had stayed with them. Nor have researchers focused on the factors associated with children doing well in single-parent homes.

These phenomena—the growing movement toward the equality of the sexes, the flight from fatherhood, the growing child care deficit in many homes, and the acceleration of physical and mental health problems among children, particularly among the poor—were touched on in my book *Family Matters* (1972). Although fathers had become a popular topic by the 1990s, there was little discussion of how fatherhood relates to patriarchy. I became increasingly interested in that issue, reading widely on fathers in dozens of cultures as well as in biological anthropology to try to answer certain questions: What are the common characteristics of patriarchy? What is known about how deeply patriarchy is embedded in precultural hominid biology? What, if any, are the major variations in patriarchy among cultures? Under what conditions might sexual equality be established without sacrificing the care of children? These questions took on greater significance as I came to understand that patriarchy evolved everywhere as both a system of power and privilege on the part of adult males, and a system of incentives for post-biological fathering linked to power and privilege. The central issue became, how do we get rid of patriarchy as a system of power without getting rid of fathers?

I discovered that patriarchy everywhere had certain generic characteristics, including misogyny and quite often the brutal abuse of power by men against women. I also found that the only major civilization that had broken with or substantially modified those characteristics before the seventeenth century was that of the Jews. The story of the evolution and the transformation of Jewish patriarchy is worth telling in its own right, but it has general significance as an example of a major paradigmatic shift in the nature of patriarchy that illuminates possibilities for creating a society in which children can obtain a continuity of authoritative, loving care from fathers and mothers or other adults whom they perceive to be responsible for them—without males appropriating power and privileges for themselves.

PART I

GENERIC PATRIARCHY

At least one hundred thousand years ago, *Homo sapiens* developed the essential characteristics of all patriarchies: first, male domination of females, and second, the investment of energy by adult males as fathers beyond the act of procreation, accompanied by long-term bonding between biological parents. The first characteristic—male dominance—is generally found among primates. The second characteristic is a specialty of *Homo sapiens*. By the emergence of agricultural civilizations about ten thousand years ago and ever since, both characteristics of patriarchy have been elaborated through cultural myths, legends, customs, and rituals.

CHAPTER 1

THE BIOLOGICAL ORIGINS

OF PATRIARCHY?

THE FACT THAT HUMAN FATHERS ARE SO MUCH MORE INVOLVED IN THE CARE OF THE YOUNG THAN THE BIOLOGICAL FATHERS OF other primate species forces the question: Was there something adaptive for *Homo sapiens* about this behavior?[1] The investment of energy by human males in postbiological fathering contrasts sharply with the males of most species, which, from the fruit fly to the chimpanzee, are fathers in a biological sense only. They contribute sperm and little else. Consider the household cat. Biological fatherhood takes place in seconds. Then the male vanishes, sometimes even chased away by the female. She produces the young from her own body, nurses them, guards them from danger, and helps them learn how to find food for themselves. Wild cats, such as the leopards and the cheetahs, are like that. In almost all mammals, males invest almost nothing in postbiological fathering: rats, bats, deer, antelope, whales and seals, Indian elephants, giraffes, and so on.

The strategy used by males for increasing reproductive success is usually quite different from that of females. The males in some species, such as elephant seals, fight vigorously to gain access to females. Three or four dominant elephant seal males can father 85 percent of a herd's population, with one male fertilizing more than seventy females. The dominant bulls take charge of territory with overwhelming strength and reproduce their genes. After that task is finished, they drop out as fathers. The same is true of the black grouse, who jump and flap their wings to attract females. A female flies down and visits the territories of several males. She will make her choice and mate after showing her desire by crouching down. Then she leaves the territory, and the male's fathering is over, with one third of the males involved in as many as four fifths of the matings.

Compared to the vast majority of species, the tendency of human males is to establish long-term, continuing relationships, called pair bonds, with the females with whom they produce offspring. Systems of long-term bonding with those females can be monogamous, polygynous (several female partners with one male), and polyandrous (several male partners with one female), although polyandry is rare. Sexual activity often takes place outside the pair bonds, but it is usually within them that males assume some degree of responsibility for providing a continuity of care for their children.

Why did hominid males evolve in such a way as to give so much more of themselves as fathers than did males in nearly all other animal species? The short answer is that it was to their genetic advantage: Males who helped to provide for and protect their young would leave more surviving offspring than those who did not, because of the unusual dependence of hominid infants and children on learning from adult caregivers in order to survive.

A comparison with birds will help make the point. Once birds take to the air, their hollow bones will not grow any more. Separated from food and unable to fly, newly hatched birds are helpless and extremely vulnerable to predators. They must grow rapidly after hatching in order to fly quickly and improve their chances for survival. A fast growth rate requires a large amount of food, in addition to protection from predators, necessitating cooperation between male and female parents. Birds that cooperate effectively leave more surviving offspring than do those who do not. The male and female of the common city pigeon, for example, build their nest together. The female produces the eggs, and both parents sit on them and feed the young after they hatch. The male and the female each produce something called pigeon milk with which to feed the young. Both protect and care for them until they can fly, and a pigeon breeding pair remains together for as long as they live.

By helping to build a nest, sitting on eggs, and producing pigeon milk, the male pigeon makes a substantial biological investment in the production of a chick. It is not surprising that he should stay on to protect that investment. Consider the male phalarope (a small shorebird that breeds in northern Europe and the United States), whose biological investment in producing offspring is even greater than that of the pigeon. The female phalarope produces four large eggs, after which she leaves those eggs completely in the care of the male, who sits on them alone for about twenty days, leaving the nest only long enough to feed. When the eggs hatch, he leads the young around until they can fend for themselves.

The biological investment of human males, however, is slight relative to that of the phalarope or even the pigeon. Only a single human spermatozoon is needed to fertilize an egg. The rest of the spermatozoa—millions of them, compared to what is usually the female's one egg—die somewhere in the female passage. In relation to the biological investment of the human female in the production of offspring, the male investment seems almost insignificant. Yet the male investment in the care of the young has been considerable, compared to that of other primates and mammals. The fathers of baby wolves and foxes bring food to nursing mothers with whom they have paired and to their young; they also provide protection for them. Some male monkeys, such as baboons, will defend the group from predators and other monkeys, thereby benefiting the infant and juvenile members. But male monkeys do not appear to know their own young, even though they protect the offspring of the group. They have a sense of tribe but not of family.

Chimps, the primates that are extremely close to human beings genetically do not pair off following mating. The chimps, from which hominids split about five to six million years ago, show an interest in infants but have little to do with raising their offspring, probably because the adult chimp male is not necessary to protect them from predators or for feeding Indeed, the chimp infant, like the infants of other primates, is not nearly so dependent on adult care as are human infants. Not for six to nine months after birth does a human acquire the chemical responses of the liver, kidneys, immune system, and digestive tract, nor the motor reactions of brain development displayed by other primates shortly after birth. Human infants can cling, but not enough to support their own weight. Monkey infants learn to walk within a month and nonhuman apes within six months, whereas humans sometimes take as long as eighteen months. More than any other primate mothers, human mothers needed the help of other caregivers to feed, protect, and instruct the young to enable them to survive.

The extreme dependence of human infants and small children on adult care and teaching probably originated when *Homo erectus* began to walk upright, about 4.5 million years ago. Having to compete against faster, stronger animals on the ground, he or she adapted over time by developing a relatively large and complex brain. Hominid brains began expanding about 1.9 million years ago, a development that continued until about 500,000 years ago. Toolmaking, language, and social organization followed. About 130,000 years ago, the thinking hominid, *Homo sapiens*, emerged as a distinctive species whose infants and small children required an extraordinary degree of adult nurturing and teaching to exploit their competitive advantage as thinking and learning primates.

That hominid infants would benefit from being provided for and protected by their biological fathers as well as by their mothers seems obvious. But why did hominid males and females develop pair bonds that would enhance the survival chances of their offspring? Why did hominid males, who invest so little in the production of offspring, become their providers and protectors and bond in a continuing relationship with their mothers? Biological anthropologists have theorized for several decades about the origins of pair bonding in mating. The most widely held view has to do with the evolving nutritional needs of hominids. Once out of the forest and into the savanna, their nutritional needs were best met when males began to specialize in hunting small game. As with present-day hunters and gatherers, hominid females probably gathered the wild vegetable food that formed the main part of everyone's diet while males did nearly all of the hunting. Females and their children fared better if they could supplement their diet with meat; but hunting was always uncertain, and males who had a reliable source of other food were better off for it. The increasing male specialization in hunting probably favored the development of pair bonds. The male, by giving meat to a female, would indirectly help her offspring, with whom she would share the meat she received. If her children also were his, he would be increasing the chances that his own offspring would survive, thus optimizing the benefit of his genetic investment.[2]

Another theory explaining the development of pair-bonding mating strategies has been advanced recently by Richard Wrangham and four of his colleagues. They reason that the big transition to hominid pair bonding occurred between 2.4 and 1.9 million years ago, somewhat later than had been thought previously by theorists on the subject. The fossil record shows a marked improvement in hominid nutrition 1.9 million years ago, suggesting the beginning of cooking. Cooked food, especially meat, was extremely valuable because it could be stored. Also, it could be stolen. Females needed to have it and themselves protected from scroungers. In competition with each other, they sought alliances with the male guardians of the food. The most desirable females, whatever the criteria of desirability, obtained the best food guards.[3]

It does not matter for my purposes which theory best explains how and when pair bonding became so important to hominids and later to *Homo sapiens*. What matters is that according to any of these explanations, hominid females needed effective providers of protein and protectors against sexual predation and theft of food. Given the uncertainty of hunting, hominid males needed a reliable supply of grains and vegetables, cooked or not, and reliable, accessible sexual partners (which was facilitated by the elimination of estrus in hominid females). Infants needed a huge investment of care by adults. Pair bonding emerged as the mating strategy for satisfying all those needs.

But does it follow that pair-bonding mating practices and male dominance were inextricably linked? The answer is that no one really knows. We know only that male dominance and pair bonding have been linked from hominid times until quite recently. Male dominance exists in all of the other primates, except for the bonobos, without the pair bonding that characterizes human societies.[4] There is no logical reason that hominid pair bonding should have changed the usual practice of male primates in establishing hierarchies of dominance.

On the average, hominid males were much stronger than females. They developed much larger lung and red corpuscle capacity, greater speed afoot, and higher ratios of muscle mass to body weight than did females, in addition to greater body size.[5] Females, pregnant much of the time and relatively slow afoot, needed protectors as well as providers for their offspring to do well.[6] What is most distinctive about *Homo sapiens* males is not their dominance over females but the strong investment they make in postbiological fathering, even though, like the other primates, they make a tiny investment in the biology of fatherhood.

With the consciousness of paternity, whenever that came, *Homo sapiens* males developed an awareness of responsibility as fathers, stepfathers, grandfathers, and uncles, often with important tasks regarding the well being of the young. Then, over the past ten thousand-plus years (a wink of evolutionary time), males developed elaborate cultural rationalizations for their power in all clans, tribes, and civilizations, usually linked to their roles as primary custodians of the myths, values, and mores of their groups. Thus, patriarchy evolved both as a system of power of adult males over adult females and children and as a system of incentives for adult males to pass on the cultures of their tribes to the next generation. The question that remains—the one that is central to this book—is whether pair bonding and postbiological fathering can prosper without the system of male power and privilege called patriarchy.

CHAPTER 2

PATRIARCHY AND

CULTURAL FATHERHOOD

THE UNIVERSALITY OF PATRIARCHY IN HUMAN SOCIETIES IS NOW GENERALLY ACCEPTED BY ANTHROPOLOGISTS. AMBITIOUS SPECULATION concerning the existence of matriarchies in the past has gained audiences ever since J. J. Bachofen's *Das Mutterrecht* (1897), which hypothesized on the basis of an analysis of the mythologies of the Near East that matriarchies preceded patriarchies. Such speculation received a boost in a better known book by Robert Briffault, *The Mothers* (1927). But anthropologist Kathleen Gough's article "The Origin of the Family" (1971) persuasively demolishes those theories. She could not find a society in which women ruled over men, nor has anyone else since.[1]

Some controversy still exists on the point, partly because of the widespread confusion about the meaning of matriarchy and patriarchy. For a matriarchy to exist there would have to be evidence of rule by women as a class over men in society and in families. There are societies that are matrifocal, where activity revolves substantially around females and the mother is usually the focus of the household. Many of them are matrilocal, where a newly married couple moves in with the household or clan of the wife. A large number of societies are matrilineal, in which descent is recognized through the line of the family of the mother. But none of these equates with power. Some confusion exists also because it is obvious that even in patriarchies women may dominate one realm of activity or another, or several, within the framework of overall patriarchal rule. Male dominance rarely extends to all activities. But there is no question as to where ultimate power lies, more or less.

Susan Sered has written about women's religions, but female-dominated women's religions all exist within patriarchal cultures.[2] Some scholars have suggested that two small hunter-gatherer tribes, the Agta and the Imbuti, are exceptions to the general rule of the universality of patriarchy. Referring to work on women as gatherers, Cynthia Fuchs Epstein asks: "If women contribute to the food supply and have the authority to make decisions affecting their lives, why should they be less valued than men?"[3] But the fact is that they are. Aborigine women in Australia may often be breadwinners, yet they are beaten when they fail to live up to their husbands' expectations or demands. Whatever the biological basis for male power, gender is always constructed culturally to protect and maintain male privilege. Patriarchy has been and remains universal.[4]

By the time *Homo sapiens* began to establish agricultural communities a little more than ten thousand years ago, adult males had long since made the connection between the procreative act and paternity. Such a connection might induce in males ideas of continuing life through one's offspring. By that time, following the argument in chapter i, males had been wired toward pair-bonding mating strategies that involve them in a continuing connection with their biological children. Even before the settlement of large agricultural communities, children could add to the power of their fathers; the promise of immortality was another strong reason for feeding and taking care of one's own children. The drive of males for power, territory, and sex outside long-term pair-bonding relationships was not eliminated, but those drives were channeled to some extent into clan and tribal connections. The end result was that within the group, under patriarchal control, the reproductive success of the learning animal, *Homo sapiens*, would be enhanced. Confusion in progeny would be less likely. Stability of pair bonds would be encouraged. Males and their relatives would become involved in the care of children.

Perhaps patriarchy was strengthened by the introduction of the plow, which required great strength for farming. Much of the essential farm labor became men's work, with women perhaps losing their earlier, more critical roles in supplying food. In any case, there is ample evidence of women's subjugation in farming communities from the law codes of ancient Mesopotamia, in which women were described as chattel. Adult male investment in fathering beyond the act of procreation centered on their male children, as males appropriated to themselves bonding activities in which they often experienced camaraderie and competition and to which they attributed high prestige. The competition had to do with achieving high status—becoming alpha males in a cultural sense—within the society in which they lived.

Systems of male bonding still work pretty much that way. Monica Wilson described how in the 1940s the boys of the Nyakyusa, who lived in southern Tanzania, worked out hierarchical roles among themselves. They argued about who was performing best in herding cattle and fought until one of them beat his fellows and became the leader. Then he sent the others to turn back straying cattle, to fetch fire, and to collect firewood. Greatly respected as the leading male, he was called on to settle quarrels as an adult. Male bonding systems, whether based on work, religion, healing, toolmaking, or fighting, provided opportunities for leading males among the Nyakyusa to acquire considerable power in clans and tribes. Boys and young men were taught by older males what was appropriate work and play for them, as opposed to work and leisure activities for females. Most of all, they were taught what it meant to be a respected man in the culture, one who protected its myths and values from external attack and internal subversion.[5]

Male cultural dominance often is founded on tribal genesis myths that explain the supernatural origins of a tribe in a way that gives special cultural power to adult males. The founding myth of the Toda in India, a polyandrous tribe in which blood brothers married one woman, is an example. The Toda believed that the great god On brought forth sacred buffalo out of the earth. Since the first Toda man, and only a man, held onto the tail of the buffalo, only males, particularly dairy priests, were permitted to churn and clarify the butter of the sacred buffalo.

Perhaps the Toda emerged as a polyandrous society with female infanticide as the main method of birth control because they were forced to live on highly undesirable hills, where productive agriculture was extremely difficult. Whatever the reason, we see in the Toda the central characteristics of all patriarchies: the valuing of males as the primary protectors and custodians of the culture; the devaluing of females, who in this case were rented out by their husbands as consort-mistresses to non-brothers; and incentives for males to become cultural fathers, in a culture in which all of the brothers possessed the land—what little of it there was—and felt responsible for socializing young boys into the sacred dairying rituals.[6]

Similarly, in a vastly different society, the polygynous Baganda in Uganda, only males were allowed to serve in priestly functions as guardians of the culture. Only they could milk the cows. Polygyny, a much more common form of long-term pair bonding than polyandry, was and is more likely to occur with a substantial base of agricultural resources. Having access to wild game and good fruit, and possessing many domestic animals, Baganda men accumulated a fair amount of wealth to protect against enemy tribes. But frequent warfare killed many males, as did executions, priestly sacrifices, and even male infanticide, resulting in a high ratio of females to males: approximately three to one nearly one hundred years ago, when the Baganda were first studied.

But children were rarely without fathers. All brothers of a biological father, even if deceased, were also called "father." Successful males—probably the healthiest, strongest, and shrewdest—accumulated several wives and many children. Such males, like the king, who had hundreds of wives, would have the largest number of children subject to their guidance, teaching, and control. The value of wives, as is true of patriarchies generally, lay primarily in their ability to be biologically and economically productive. They had virtually no freedom of movement except within the compound of the family household; and women who were guilty of adultery could be beaten, perhaps to death, by their husbands.[7]

Even matrilineal cultures, where the newly born become members of their mothers' families, are patriarchal. The Hopi of North America, a small Native American group, also limit the performance of sacred rituals and the teaching of tribal law to males. There is also a strong sexual division of labor, in which the men, in typical patriarchal fashion, give high prestige to the activities that are male: herding, farming, weaving. The women grind corn, cook, care for the children, and make baskets and pottery. To mark their special status as males, boys sleep in a ceremonial house, paying visits to girls whom they are prepared to marry. But a boy must be acceptable to a girl's parents in this monogamous, matrilineal society. Although the husband is a guest in the wife's household and the ultimate authority for disciplining children lies with the brother of the child's mother, the biological father also provides guidance and discipline.[8]

A classic story of how patriarchy socializes young men to become respected elders comes from the autobiography of Sun Chief, a Hopi Indian who grew up in a village one hundred miles east of the Grand Canyon. His grandfather reminded him to obey his parents if he wanted to be seen as a good child and live to be an old man himself. The old man taught Sun Chief to get up before sunrise to bathe and exercise his body and find useful work to do. His mother's brother gave him frequent instruction, and his father's brother taught him to call him "father," just like his own father. His father's brother and clan brothers, also called "father," could whip the youngster when either of his parents asked them to. The boy was being socialized to be called a Hopi. It was a great disgrace to be called *kahopi* (not Hopi, not peaceful), and for a boy that meant being initiated into the Katinas society, where men masked and costumed as witches danced around him in order to drive the evil from him so that he could grow up to be a good and wise man. In fact, the dancers were his uncles, fathers, and clan brothers initiating him into a special male bonding society at the cusp of adolescence.[9] When Hopi men are initiated into the *katinas*, they learn secret, sacred knowledge and take on special responsibilities for the entire Hopi community.

Whether pair bonding took the form of monogamy, polyandry, or polygyny, patriarchy made fathers of adult males, involving them in teaching and disciplining their sons. Each culture had its ways of making males principal custodians of what is most valued—often sacred—in the culture, and of assigning to adult males the primary responsibility for inculcating in their sons the values and the rules of the culture and enforcing and defending those values and rules against outsiders. The Kikuyu, who inhabit the fertile highland country of central Kenya, are a typical example of a society that places considerable emphasis on the role of fathers as teachers and disciplinarians. The older boys stay with the men in their houses, where, far into the night, they listen to riddles and stories, socializing with adult men in recreational male bonding. There they learn the values of their tribe and to become custodians of those values for their children.[10]

All patriarchies have given young males models of manliness and male responsibility in the family. That has been true of small tribal cultures as well as major civilizations. Among the Aka, hunter-gatherer-traders of the tropical regions of south central Africa, economic necessity appears to have favored a high degree of cooperation between mothers and fathers. So important were fathers to Aka infants that most fatherless Aka children died within six months of birth.[11] The Ongee of the Little Andaman Islands in the Bay of Bengal regarded the birth of a boy as God's gift to the parents and that of a daughter as a debt incurred with God; but taking care of a child was seen as both a male and female duty. Among these Negrito hunters and gatherers, women and men did not work or socialize together, but men stayed back at the campsite to take care of children when women went out to a creek or forest to gather vegetables. Thus, Ongee boys were socialized to be nurturing fathers even as they were acculturated to an ideal of manliness that did not permit crying.[12]

Among the Hindu Brahmins, only men perform priestly functions. Upper-caste Hindu male children must make a ceremonial offering of water to the spirits of his deceased parents and ancestors, to assure that their souls will be at peace. A central task of adult males is to make certain that young boys will learn their responsibility to show respect for their elders and perform rites that demonstrate deep reverence for ancestors. In this way, Hindu fathers become involved in the teaching and disciplining of young boys and setting forth models for them as fathers in days to come.[13]

Ancestor worship played a central role in the evolution of cultural fatherhood in China. The Confucianist tradition developed the concept of *chun-tzu*, the superior man, the Chinese equivalent of the Jewish mensch. Who was such a man? He was the one who practiced *jen ji*—behaving with goodness or benevolence and in other things following male obligations, the most important of which was (and often still is) *hsiao*, filiopiety. Honoring one's ancestors led to many obligations among properly socialized Chinese males. Of vital importance was to show respect for one's mother as well as father. Another was to be a father who took care of daughters as well as sons. No father, for example, could commit a more serious departure from *jen ji* than neglecting a daughter's betrothal or failing to give instructions to a son in correct behavior. To fail in these matters would be a fundamental violation of filiopiety itself.

As a consequence, almost every Chinese child would grow up knowing by heart the twenty-four examples of filiopiety: Wu Mang, who let himself be eaten by mosquitoes so that they would not bother his parents; Wong Hsiang, who during the summer fanned his father's bed and during the winter warmed it with his body; and twenty-two other equally filial characters who were presented as models for children to imitate. In one of the stories, Kuo Chu is a poor man with a wife, mother, and child. One day he said to his wife: "We are so poor that we cannot even support Mother. Moreover, our child shares Mother's food. Why not bury this child? We may have another child, but if Mother should die, we cannot obtain her again." The wife does not dare to contradict him. Fathers come before mothers, but mothers come before children.[14] These precepts were passed on for centuries by Chinese fathers to their sons and are influential even today in the great Confucianist-influenced civilizations of the Far East. Chinese patriarchal civilization, like that of the Jews, has affected a large portion of the world's population. Both have emphasized the essential role of fathers as teachers, not just of work skills but of rules for moral and ethical living. Whereas Jewish patriarchy was grounded in a belief in God and, as we shall see, led to the formation of a people bound by a powerful religious identity, the Chinese developed a civilization that was based to a considerable extent on the power of dead ancestors to affect life in the present.

Like Jewish Torah, Confucianism produced a system of rules for ethical living, although the relationships between husband and wife and between the generations differed in important respects from the patriarchy of the Jews. What they had in common, among other things, was a body of doctrine that was written and could be taught from generation to generation, from father to son in patriarchal fashion. The written word became a subject of intense study, analysis, and disputation by males. In China, after the revival of Confucianism as a state philosophy under the Sung Dynasty (907–1279 C.E.), the educational system was directed toward teaching males the four classics of Confucianism, just as the Jewish educational system focused on males learning the Torah and Talmud. As was also true for the Jews, scholarship became a route to upward mobility, enabling a young man from a relatively modest Chinese family to become an official of the state.

Women in both cultures could not act independently, although, as we shall see, Jewish women were accorded certain rights two thousand years ago that were not available to any women in the Far East. Even until quite recently, a woman in traditional China could not act independently. On her wedding day her parents gave her final instructions: "Be respectful and cautious; do not disobey your husband." The husband was superior to the wife in much the same way that the ruler was superior to his ministers and the father to his son. Even after her husband's death, the widow's son or another male member of her husband's family succeeded to power. A daughter-in-law was expected to serve her parents-in-law as respectfully and carefully as she served her parents, and failure to do so was one of seven grounds for divorce. Many women who could not get along with their husbands but had no grounds for seeking a legal separation left them to return to their parents' house. But these women could never remarry and usually spent the rest of their lives caring for their nephews and nieces.

The most important responsibility for a Chinese wife was to become pregnant, to have happiness in the body, which is the meaning of "pregnant," *yu-hsi.* The Jewish commandment to be fruitful and multiply is directed toward men, but both cultures emphasized the importance of having sons, partly because in both only sons were given responsibility for saying prayers for dead parents. But there were major differences, too. Long after the Jews gave up concubinage, as we will see, Chinese culture still sanctioned it so that men could have sons that wives could not provide. Chinese wives typically had responsibility for helping to choose the concubines, as Sarah did for Abraham in Genesis. Along with permitting and even encouraging concubinage up until modern times, the devaluation of females by the Chinese was much more explicit than in Jewish culture, where it was modified by countering traditions and law.[15] The Jews, for example, as far as is known, never practiced female infanticide, something that still takes place in rural Chinese areas.

Confucianism provided a model for the ideal Chinese father, just as Torah and classic rabbinical teaching in the Talmud did two thousand years ago. The father who followed the teachings of those models was likely to be an honored man, one respected by others. In both cases, serious study of texts that provided guidelines for an honorable life was limited to men. By becoming fathers, Chinese and Jewish men—as is true of the men of other, less influential patriarchies—assumed roles as custodians of their cultures, becoming teachers of the founding myths, values, traditions, and rituals of their cultures. This has been the way of patriarchies, more or less. Typically, in addition to making cultural fathers out of biological fathers, patriarchies have given men as a class of people extraordinary power over females.

CHAPTER 3

PATRIARCHY AS A
SYSTEM OF POWER

THE POWER OF MEN OVER WOMEN OFTEN HAS LED TO ABUSE. WOMEN USUALLY ESTABLISH HIERARCHIES OF THEIR OWN WITHIN PATRI-archies, based on rank, class, lineage, and other factors, but women as a group are generally devalued. Female infanticide in China may have evolved as a form of birth control in resource-impoverished, famine-stricken areas. Yet it continues as a part of the cultural view of the importance of males compared to females in several Asian countries, where female children are fed less, pulled out of school earlier, forced into hard labor sooner, and given less health care than boys are. In one 1990 study of a major children's hospital in Pakistan, it was found that 71 percent of the babies admitted under age two were boys, suggesting that female infants are not valuable enough to receive hospital care.[1] Considering that females are more likely to survive birth and live longer than males, as they do in all of the developed countries, the male-to-female population ratios in Bangladesh, Pakistan, Afghanistan, and China are testimony to the way in which patriarchal cultures in the Far East and South Asia devalue females. Even after more than forty years of Communist rule in China, Swedish demographers estimated in 1991 that there were at least seven hundred thousand so-called missing girls among China's twenty million annual births.[2]

In many cultures females are seen as potentially contaminating to males. In Wogeo, New Guinea, the status of women was generally thought to be somewhat higher than among other nearby tribes, but men often criticized women "for undermining the perfection of male solidarity."[3] Among the Quiché Indians of Guatemala, where patriarchal rule, while strict, is not as abusive as among the other tribes in the area, young girls are taught to wash the men's clothes first and not to mix women's clothes with them because of the contaminating nature of women's menstrual periods. The Quiché are a good example of how the segregation of the sexes is nearly always linked to patriarchy. Quiché fathers would get the largest portion of the food, and mothers would keep little for themselves. Fathers, the women explained, could not afford to become ill or to get weak, and they needed encouragement. Patriarchy, to them, was connected to the grim necessity of the survival of their children, not just something imposed by males on females for no reason at all.[4]

Probably the apparent acquiescence of females in the dominance of males in so many cultures has to do with the perception that males are needed to feed them and to protect the group against outsiders. That case can be made in the hot, dusty, parched conditions of Sicily, Calabria, and other parts of southern Italy and elsewhere in the Mediterranean, where sons became co-guardians with the fathers of families and where the honored man was seen (and often still is) as protecting his blood by enforcing *l'ordine della famiglia* (the rules of family relationships). Families, it was believed, had to be ruled with an iron hand in order to survive.[5]

A tough and cunning protector of family was the man to be respected in the Greek mountain village of Sarakatsani, too, where a young man in the 1960s proved his manliness by his willingness to fight to protect his own blood. There, an older brother or father would buy a broad-bladed dagger for a young man when he reached the age of twenty or twenty-one.[6] In Sarakatsani, as in southern Italy, male members of the family constituted a little army who, giving each other unqualified loyalty, were also extremely distrustful of outsiders. Well into the twentieth century, brothers guarded their sisters against rape and insult and avenged any violation of their character, much as the brothers of Dinah did in the Old Testament. Sisters and mothers were to be protected at all costs, but wives were something less, as reflected in a southern Italian proverb: "Like a good weapon, she [a wife] should be cared for properly; like a hat, she should be kept straight; like a mule, she should be given plenty of work and occasional beatings. Above all, she should be kept in her place."[7] The ideal wife could be strong in the kitchen and sensual with her husband in the bedroom, but outside the home she must be subservient. Always, she must be loyal toward her husband.

In Sarakatsani, wives would walk two or three yards behind their husbands, as they have in many cultures. Husbands and wives did not eat together, and women ate what was left over by the men. Women were heard chanting: "When you are married, you are enslaved because God wills it so."[8] A new bride in Sarakatsani would be employed by her husband's family in the dirtiest of work. Even though she might never have seen them before, she began her marriage by calling her husband's brothers "master." Bent double under enormous loads, women often were seen staggering as far as a mile from the water well to the huts; carrying water in this culture was woman's work.[9] Segregation by work is a common expression of the subordination of females. So is the feeding of males ahead of females, as with the Quiché. In rural Hindu India today, a wife eats the leavings on her husband's plate, and wives wash their husbands' feet as well as their clothes, symbolizing the elevated status and power of the men. "Even when the husband is wrong, she is supposed to bear her lot meekly and submissively." When her husband dies, she wails: "Where is my master? Now, who will support me? The shield that protected me is gone; now I am helpless."[10]

The power and privilege of men has often led to physical abuse of women. The battering of adult females is a widely reported phenomenon, even in Western, democratic societies; but it is no longer sanctioned as appropriate behavior, as is still the case in many cultures. Ashanti husbands in West Africa are reported to cut the ears off women who overhear their private conversations.[11] Masai men in Tanzania and southern Kenya often beat their wives if the women are dilatory in doing chores.[12] Among the Aymara in Bolivia—about 25 percent of Bolivia's total population of seven million—a husband often hits his wife on the face and forehead if he does not like the way she keeps house.[13] Even among the Mbuti of Central Africa, where male hunters rely on their wives for the bulk of their diet, the men thought that a certain amount of wife beating was good for a woman.

Among the !Kung San foragers of southern Africa, women were given an unusual amount of respect. But in the well-known autobiography of a !Kung woman, *Nisa: The Life and Words of a !Kung Woman*, there are reports of jealous rages by her husband, who beat her ferociously with a stick. When her daughter resisted her husband's sexual advances, she was badly abused.[14] The men of the Yanamomo in South America routinely beat their wives. Whereas kinder husbands merely bruise and mutilate them for such offenses as failing to serve guests quickly and well, the fiercer husbands sometimes kill them. Wife abuse is so deeply sanctioned by the culture that women may even measure their status by the frequency of the minor beatings their husbands give them.[15]

One aspect of male power and privilege that characterizes generic patriarchy has to do with the control of female sexuality alongside the toleration or even approval of male sexual promiscuity. The preoccupation of males with sexual prowess has been described in many anthropological accounts. On the morning after a first sexual encounter, a Sarakatsani bridegroom would discuss his success or failure on the wedding night with his older brothers, who, when there had been some difficulty, tried to give the younger brother advice and encouragement.[16] If a husband in Sarakatsani surprised a wife engaged in sexual activity with another man, villagers believed that it was necessary for him to kill her and her seducer. Similar views can also be found in the Old Testament and in contemporary Myanmar (Burma), where in a recent survey males spoke openly of threatening wives with knives if they were sexually active with someone else, even though, as some of them said, a variety of sexual partners was important for themselves, like tasting various kinds of curry.[17]

The American press has reported widely on the practice of female genital mutilation, which affects at least twenty to seventy million women in more than twenty countries, according to a United Nations report. Yet in some tribes it is widely believed that genitalia must be cut or otherwise mutilated if a girl is to be marriageable. Many Kikuyu, successful in encouraging cultural fatherhood, as described in chapter 2, see the practice of genital mutilation as an affirmation of the value of women in traditional society, according to Jomo Kenyatta, Kenya's deceased national liberation leader, who wrote a description of the ceremony. It begins with the great dance on the day before the ritual. Then, girls walk to a sacred tree where, after much singing and dancing, the young females are privately circumcised by an elder woman. A *New York Times* journalist acknowledged that "there is little doubt that for the girls it was a joyous occasion," despite his perception of the practice as brutal.[18] Guarding the virginity of women and discouraging sexual intercourse outside marriage is commonly given as the reason for the practice, which the Bedouins call the ceremony of the "purification of women." But it is dangerous because it can result in uncontrolled bleeding, lead to tetanus and other infections, and even damage the Fallopian tubes. Nonetheless, it has been practiced among Christians and animists going back to the fifth century C.E.[19]

Among Sarakatsani men, as in Mediterranean and other cultures, women were seen as dangerously sensual, even though some Sarakatsani women reported their dislike of sexual intercourse.[20] In the eyes of the men, female sexuality made women unwilling agents of the devil. Thus, during their menstrual periods, women and girls did not approach sheep, which were thought to be God's special animals. Never would a woman milk a sheep, a taboo not unlike that found among the Baganda. After sleeping with his wife, a Sarakatsani shepherd had to wash his hands before milking sheep.[21]

Female child prostitution, frequently defended as a way to keep a family fed, is another expression of the denigration and abuse of females found in many cultures. The *New York Times* reported in 1996 on thirteen year old girls being purchased in Cambodia (some as young as eleven) by brothel owners, who then considered them to be their property. In the 1990s tens of thousands of children in Asia were slaves, working in brothels in Cambodia, India, China, Thailand, the Philippines, Taiwan, and other countries.[22] It can be argued that prostitution evolved as an outlet for male sexuality in ways that were compatible with maintaining cohesive families and a continuity of authoritative, loving care for infants and small children. Many cultures of the Far East developed elaborate codes of behavior for courtesans, procurers, attendants, and clientele that were consistent with pair bonding, cultural fatherhood, and cohesive extended families. The pattern, although not so elaborately prescribed and ritualized, can be found in nearly all of the patriarchies, although in this respect the Jews, for the most part, are an exception, as we will see.

In war, conquering soldiers often have been particularly vicious toward women whom they see as outsiders, as in the systematic rape of Bosnian Muslim women by Serbian soldiers in rape camps between 1991 and 1995 and of Tutsi women by Hutu troops in Rwanda in 1994. A notorious example of the sexual abuse of women was the rape of about twenty thousand of them in Nanking by Japanese troops in 1937 and the subsequent forcing of possibly as many as two hundred thousand girls and young women—Chinese, Filipino, and mostly Korean—to serve as sex slaves for Japanese soldiers. Even within nations, the sexual abuse of women who are perceived as outsiders, not in the family or tribe or clan or ethnic group, is not uncommon, as in the case of Peru's security forces, whose soldiers were reported in the 1990s to have raped women often, although not one soldier was punished for the offense.[23]

Sometimes rape is used as a culturally sanctioned system of internal control of women. In central Brazil the Mehinaku women were not allowed even to glance at the sacred flutes under the control of men. If one did, she could be raped by every man but her immediate kin. In the face of such behavior, it is not easy to recollect that patriarchy is anything more than a system of power often leading to flagrant abuse of females. Yet the male Mehinaku children, who became so abusive to wives as adults, were introduced to the responsibilities of fatherhood through a children's game played with girls in which the youngsters pretend that they are married and make babies out of mud. The chief's son says: "Two wives for you, and two for you. Make your sons. Say, 'my son,' to your children. Give him the baby. Cradle the baby in your arms. My son! Say, 'my child' to comfort it. Say your baby has died. A baby has died. Cry! Cry! All of you, cry!"[24]

In the Mehinaku game we can see the preparation of small boys to become fathers, especially to become teachers to their sons. In the male bonding system in which only they take care of the sacred flutes, we can see the way in which patriarchies devalue females. In the sanctioning of rape of those women who violate rules regarding the sacred flutes, we see the violence often perpetrated against women in patriarchies. Even if these behaviors have been sanctioned by cultural values considered to be sacred, the ending of patriarchal abuse has become a moral imperative in our time, one that was addressed by the rabbis of the Talmud two thousand years ago.

PART II

THE JEWISH
PATRIARCHAL PARADIGM

Most of the characteristics of generic patriarchy, including
the abuse of women and the denial of their most basic sexual
and economic rights, continued in all of the major civilizations of the world until the seventeenth and eighteenth centuries—except for that of the Jews. Two thousand years ago,
the rabbis, through ingenious and selective interpretation of
the Pentateuch, sharply modified the abusive practices of generic patriarchy. They acknowledged the dependence of husbands on their wives and extended to the wives certain fundamental sexual and economic rights.

The new Jewish model held fast to aspects of segregation
by gender in religious matters but profoundly reduced the
most abusive characteristics of patriarchy. Intense teachers
to their sons, Jewish fathers passed on a model of a husband-
father who could be nurturing and loving to children and
wives in what became a radically new patriarchal paradigm.

CHAPTER 4

YAHWEH'S INCENTIVES FOR

TAMING MALES

IN THE BEGINNING, THE IVRIM, THE PEOPLE FROM THE OTHER SIDE OF THE RIVER, WERE SHEPHERDS, ABOUT WHOM VIRTUALLY NOTHING IS known. Like other shepherds traveling across the dry waste of the Arabian desert, stopping awhile to live in goatskin tents and tending their tribal flocks and herds, they probably were tormented by demons and spirits who spoke through thunder and lightning and were in trees, springs, and even stones. Religion was practical: only results mattered. It was a gamble, betting on this god or goddess, building shrines to one or another in high places, usually a hill or a mountaintop, where a rock or tree stump served as an altar and where sacrifices, including human sacrifices, were made to the local *ba'alim* (the Hebrews called them *elim*) to whom tribes prayed for rain and fertility or victory in war. To gain favor with gods and goddesses, the shepherds made idols of wood and stone, which they worshipped as if they were the spirits themselves. To appease the idols, they sacrificed (burned) the firstborn of their flocks and sometimes even slew the firstborn of their children. Living in tribes or clans, they probably fought bloody wars against each other for control of desert springs. Women and children as well as sheep were stolen by enemy tribes, ownership and abuse of women by men was the rule, and sexual licentiousness and even incest were common.

These are not historical facts, but inferences drawn in part from stories told in the prehistorical books of the Pentateuch.[1] One of the stories became the central myth of the Jewish people to the present time. It is that some of the people from the other side of the river eventually wandered to Egypt in search of food, to a large tract of meadows called the Land of Goshen, where they were put to work by the Egyptian pharaohs, who were building high temples and monuments to themselves and their many gods. Perhaps it was in Egypt that the people who were to become the Jews first learned the idea of one God,[2] an idea they took with them when they escaped back to the desert and undertook a long, dangerous journey to the land of Canaan. It was in the desert that their leader, Moses, according to biblical legend, spoke to them of Yahweh, the *only* God, the source of all life.

The narrative of the sufferings of the Jews as slaves in Egypt and of their deliverance was subsequently celebrated in the Jewish holiday of Passover. The Israelites probably entered the land of Canaan between 1400 and 1100 B.C.E., where belief in the Exodus story undoubtedly helped to consolidate them (probably in the twelfth century) into the twelve tribes that waged war against the Canaanites. Abandoning their existence as nomads, the Jews ultimately created, under the leadership of David and Solomon, a small but prosperous kingdom that lasted about eighty-five years, from ?1010 to 925 B.C.E. Now there were ten tribes in the north, constituting the kingdom of Israel, and two in the south, Judah and Benjamin, forming the kingdom of Judah, with Jerusalem as its capital. The two kingdoms were beset by religious defections to the gods of the Canaanites, natural spirits that brought rain, fertility or success at war, as the gods of the nomadic Hebrews had done before they conceived of one God, Yahweh.

It was extremely difficult for many to hold onto the unusual idea of one God and not to fall back on the polytheistic pattern that was common in Mesopotamia. Later, the Hebrew prophets attributed the Assyrian conquest of the kingdom of Israel in 722 B.C.E. to the corruption of the Israelites in worshipping the *ba'alim* in ways, they asserted, that intermixed carnality with religion. Twenty years after the fall of Israel, when the southern kingdom of Judah was reduced to the state of a vassal kingdom under Assyria, the prophets explained its defeat by pointing again to the whoring of Jews after foreign gods.

Even after the kingdom was reestablished, seventy-five years later, they warned against seduction by the foreign cults that had been introduced into Israel.

Not much is known of the family life of everyday people in ancient Israel before the monarchy or during it, although Leo G. Perdue, Carol Myers, and others have made highly creative efforts to reconstruct a picture of what it was like from biblical and archaeological sources.[3] Myers believes that patriarchy was much less pronounced in the period prior to the monarchy, when male control was emphasized through kings, soldiers, bureaucrats, and priests.[4] Nonetheless, portions of the Pentateuch describe women as chattel, just as they were in other Mesopotamian societies. "You shall not covet your neighbor's wife, or his male or female slave, or his ox, or his ass, or anything that is your neighbor's" (Exod. 20:14). A woman was under the authority of first her father and then her husband (Num. 30:7–16). There were many legal distinctions between men and women in the Pentateuch. A wife could not initiate divorce. A husband could divorce her if he found fault (Deut. 24:1–4). The wife could not give legal testimony (Deut. 1:13). Daughters could inherit from a dead father only if there were no male heirs (Num. 27).

A little more is known about Jewish family life in the period of the Second Temple, beginning in 537 B.C.E., in which, as we shall see in chapter 6, protections for women were introduced in marriage contracts.[5] The Israelites were not unique in providing some protections in marriage for women. The code of Hammurabi provided that if a husband divorces a wife for improper reasons—that is, if she was not being divorced for neglecting the house or humiliating her husband or committing adultery—he would have to return her dowry. But Jewish protections came within a much larger context of a radically reformed patriarchy, which included growing respect for the sexual rights of women as well as their economic rights, a context that acknowledged the dependence of husbands on wives and encouraged expressions of affection between them within monogamous relationships. These changes in Jewish patriarchy reflected a vast shift away from the pervasive and blatant misogyny of the other cultures of Mesopotamia and the predatory sexual behavior of successful, powerful males within those cultures.

The Jews had been developing a tradition of oral law called the Mishnah (repetitions) from the tenth century to the second century B.C.E., much of which found its way into the Pentateuch (promulgated in the fifth century B.C.E.) and later was elaborated in great detail in the Talmud, which means "study" or "learning." The Talmud comprises the commentaries of rabbis, written between 200 B.C.E. and 500 C.E. The rabbis of the Talmud found 613 ethical and ritual commandments, addressed overwhelmingly to males. They proceeded to elaborate on them in the Talmud, which eventually consisted of 2.5 million words on 5,894 folio pages. The oral law was edited at academies in Palestine and Babylonia about 200 C.E. Then the rabbis prepared extensive commentaries on the Mishnah, called the Gemara, published two hundred years later in Palestine. There was no formal acceptance of the Babylonian Talmud, which closed in 499 C.E., but it grew in authority over the course of time, having been completed a century and a half after the Jerusalem Talmud. In four of its tractates—those called *Nashim* ("Women"), the Talmud codified many of the reforms that had been evolving over several hundred years regarding women's rights in betrothal, marriage, and divorce. In all, these changes represented a major uprooting of the almost unbridled power of males described in Genesis, a power that probably was characteristic of ancient patriarchies.

In interpreting the law so as to extend the rights of women, the rabbis found many commandments in Torah on which to build, commandments that, when taken together, represented a continuing concern of Jews, long before the Common Era, for the well-being of women as potential mothers as well as an acknowledgment of the importance to children of having fathers. A Jewish man who desires a woman taken in war is commanded to allow a month's warning for her mother and father and then to marry her: "be a husband to her, and she shall be your wife" (Deut. 21:10–14). Firstborn sons of unloved wives are to receive as much attention and care as those of wives who are beloved (Deut. 21:16–17). A man who lies with a betrothed virgin must make her his wife and never repudiate her as long as he lives (Deut. 22:28–29).

Some commandments were carryovers from ancient patriarchal rules against stealing another man's property. Hence, if a man is caught sleeping with another's wife, both offenders must die, not just the woman. But others are clearly a break from the unrestricted power of males. If a man falsely accuses his newly wed wife of not being a virgin, he is required to pay a heavy fine and be flogged for his calumny (Deut. 22:13–22). Ancient offenses against wives, such as offering them as hospitality or using them as bargaining chips (practices that may have been common at the time of the early patriarchs, when Abraham and Isaac both offered their wives to foreign rulers to buy peace) were abolished. Also, Jewish men were commanded that they must not send their wives away to become wives of other men and then take them back again, "for that is detestable in the sight of Yahweh" (Deut. 24:1–4).

The Deuteronomic code, under which these commandments are found, go back to more than a thousand years before the completion of Talmud, since Deuteronomy was promulgated in 621 B.C.E., not long before the fall of Judah and the destruction of Jerusalem by the Babylonians in 586. The rabbis of the Talmud—all men—interpreted the code to extend further the rights of women. Why would Jewish men acquiesce in these changes? Rarely does a group in power modify or attenuate that power unless threatened by a rebellious group under its control or by some outside force. Why would men allow themselves to be tamed? The religious view is that they did so because God commanded it. The historian's view incorporates religion, the power of faith in what is believed to be the will of God.

Some of the Israelites—the prophets, most notably—were God-intoxicated people who embraced the powerful ethical implications of one and only one God for all of life. Injustice against any class of people was an anathema to them. They would fight and die to defend their beliefs. They did fight and die against the Assyrians in 722 B.C.E., the Babylonians in 586, against the Romans in the Jewish war in 66–70 C.E. and again during the Bar Kokhbar revolt in 132–135. Only in the revolt of the Maccabees (167–142 B.C.E.) was their armed resistance to defend their religious beliefs successful. Those Israelites who became Jews during these hundreds of years of upheaval embraced ever more tightly the word of God as passed on through the oral law and, by the fifth century B.C.E.—for those to whom it was available and who could read it—the Pentateuch itself.

With the destruction of Jerusalem in 70 C.E., the Romans thought the Jews were finished, paying virtually no attention to the growing religious movement based on the life and death of a Jewish carpenter from Galilee. But Judaism lived in Torah and its interpreters, the rabbis. Now there were no kings or queens, no temple or priests, no bureaucrats or soldiers. The Jews carried with them in the diaspora a universal religion. The relationship to the land no longer defined their Jewish identity, although they would always dream of the day that it would. Only their observance of the behavioral requirements of Torah, now in the hands of the rabbis, provided their identity as Jews. And it was those guidelines, especially as codified in the Talmud, that tamed males into faithful husbands and devoted fathers, especially to their sons.[6]

Universal Judaism based on religion gave prominence to the central message of ethical monotheism: all life is precious to a genderless, faceless God, the source of all life. Thus, the early emphasis on the multiplication of children, which probably stemmed from the desire of Israelites to increase their numbers to fight the battles of Canaan, became an overarching ethical commandment: "Therefore, choose life, that your descendants might live" (Deut. 30:19). At the time of the Talmud, infanticide, child sacrifice, and rape in war were common among others (as they still are in much of the world, except for child sacrifice), but those who followed the Jewish God were forbidden to engage in them.

The new emphasis did not call on the Jews to abandon patriarchy. It did put major restraints on the abuse of patriarchal power, but it offered Jewish patriarchs many rewards if they obeyed the commandments set forth for them, including those that modified unbridled patriarchal power. If they obeyed God's laws, they would live and multiply; if they did not, they would perish. In addition to long life, Yahweh set forth in Deuteronomy other powerful incentives: relief "from all enemies that surround you" (Deut. 12:10–11); expansion of the territories promised first to Abraham and then to the twelve tribes of Israel (Gen. 12:7, Deut. 12:20); and happiness always in the sacred space promised to Abraham and his descendants (Deut. 12:28). But now they needed something more than the promise of the sacred space from which most of them had been driven. Positive rewards that would mean more in the diaspora are summarized in Psalm 112, "in praise of the virtuous," probably written some time around 450 B.C.E.:

> Happy the man who fears Yahweh
> by joyfully keeping his commandments!
>
> Children of such a man will be powers on earth,
> descendants of the upright will always be blessed.
>
> There will be riches and wealth for his family,
> and his righteousness can never change.
>
> For the upright he shines like a lamp in the dark,
> he is merciful, tender-hearted, virtuous.
>
> Interest is not charged by this good man,
> He is honest in all his dealings.
>
> Kept safe by virtue, he is ever steadfast,
> and leaves an imperishable memory behind him.
>
> with constant heart and confidence in Yahweh,
> he need never fear bad news.
>
> Steadfast in heart he overcomes his fears:
> in the end he will triumph over his enemies.
>
> Quick to be generous, he gives to the poor,
> his righteousness can never change.
> Men such as this will always be honored,
>
> though this fills the wicked with fury
> until, grinding their teeth, they waste away,
> vanishing like their vain hopes.

Yahweh's promises were reinforced by the warnings of the prophets. Moses had warned as he was about to die that Jews would vanish from the land if they should ever follow the gods and morality of the Canaanites. "For Yahweh detests . . . and hates what they have done for their gods, even burning their sons and daughters in the fire" (Deut. 12:29–32). Two thousand years later, other prophets' repeated warnings of calamities, such as the Assyrian and Babylonian conquests, should the Israelites fail to observe God's commandments, had been burned into the consciousness of religious Jews.

Sixty-five years after the crushing by the Romans of the Bar Kokhbar revolt in 135 C.E., the Mishnah was completed. Now dispersed through much of the known world, the Jews had a road map for living without state, temple, or priests. For those who remained Jews, the rewards were still attractive. The ancient promise of sacred space was seen as having been broken not by God but by the failure of the people themselves to live up to their covenant. The Jews would be returned to their holy land should they return to God. Following the road map of Torah and Talmud would lead someday back to Jerusalem. In the meantime, the honor and respect promised in Psalm 112 would come to those who observed God's commandments

Following the road map meant becoming a new kind of husband and father. Of all the prophets from Moses on, Hosea (in Israel, approximately 750 B.C.E.) provides the most singular example of how far the Jews had departed from the typical Mesopotamian idea of patriarchy in their emphasis on the absolute importance of every child having a father. What makes the Hosea prophecy such a powerful expression of the importance he and other like-minded Israelites placed on fatherhood is that he forgave his wife for adultery.

Hosea married a whore, who bore him three sons. She was unfaithful to him, but Yahweh instructed him to take her back. The message of Hosea is clear: Although the people of Israel played the fool, fathered bastards, trampled on justice, and offered sacrifices to the *ba'alim*, Yahweh, like a father, loved the people even in their wickedness. Even though he destroyed their kingdom for their infidelity, God, the father, was ready to forgive them for the sake of the children. Moved by

Yahweh's promises of tenderness, love, and faithfulness to the people of Israel despite their wickedness, Hosea took his wife back. Her children once again had a father, as he promised to love the one named "Unloved" and to say to the son named "No-People-of-Mine," "You are my people." The metaphorical lesson was extraordinary for the ancient Near East: There is nothing more important for a follower of Yahweh than to be a father to his children, especially sons, even if that means, as in this case, forgiving an adulterous wife (Hos. 2:19–22).

Jews took Hosea, the other prophets, and the entire Bible with them to the communities to which they dispersed following the destruction of the Second Temple. More than ever before, the synagogues became the focus of Jewish religious life, institutions in which Jewish males were expected to participate through prayer and study. Although synagogues had definitely appeared as early as the third century B.C.E., now they existed throughout Judea, Babylonia, Persia, Greece, Rome, and wherever Jews settled. There, Jews engaged in a new form of male bonding and competition, centering on the study and practice of Torah. Here was no contest at sports, gaming, womanizing, hunting, fighting, or storytelling. Instead, adult males vied with each other for reputations as Torah scholars, givers of charity, and husbands and fathers modeled after Yahweh; they disparaged other forms of male bonding and competition found in non-Jewish cultures.

It was quintessential patriarchal bonding nonetheless. Only males could be counted in the minyan, the group of ten necessary for religious services three times a day. Only they were obliged to carry out all time-bound commandments. Only males felt the weight of responsibility for guarding the sacred knowledge of God and teaching it to their sons. Only they could decide on disputed points of Jewish law and custom. Synagogue male bonding assigned to males an importance for the continued life of their people in the diaspora, comparable to the importance that the rabbis said biology had given to their wives. It was a system that conferred status, power, and privilege on males, but at the same time they studied law, prophecy, wisdom literature, and later the Talmud, which, under the prodding of rabbis, pushed them to become faithful and loving husbands.

In the diaspora, synagogues, previously houses of assembly, became houses of prayer, study, and charity as well, where most activities of mutual aid were performed; they also became Houses of Judgment, where rabbinical law prevailed after the lengthy and complicated Talmud became available. Whereas priests had gained their position through inheritance, the status of rabbi (teacher) could be achieved by any learned man. The wisest of them won recognition far and wide. With the spread of rabbinic law through the Talmud there developed a hierarchical system of interpretation through the *Gaonim* (Excellencies), who were rectors of the religious academies from the end of the sixth century to the first half of the eleventh century. Men of culture and intellectual attainment, their judgments on matters of law tended to unify the exiled Jewish community from Persia to Spain (partly by making the Babylonian Talmud supreme) and to strengthen further those characteristics that set Jewish husbands and fathers apart from most Christians and Muslims in their ideal of manliness.

Jews probably would not have survived as a people without their synagogue-based system of male bonding to enforce the study of Torah. By the Middle Ages they had long since lost control of the sacred space promised to them. They were buffeted about from country to country, often brutally persecuted and sometimes expelled for their distinctive ways. Some apostatized. Others were murdered in the Crusades, the Inquisition, and pogroms. Yet the promises, the incentives, of Yahweh retained a powerful hold on the consciousness of enough synagogue worshipers to sustain the continuity of the Jews as a people and, indeed, as a civilization that made significant contributions to the dominant cultures in which they lived. Repairing to the synagogue three times a day for religious services, on Shabbat each week, and for many special holidays throughout the year, they read commandments, prophecies, homilies, stories, and metaphors that, among other things, provided the model of an ideal Jewish father and husband.

From talmudic times on to the late Middle Ages, the taming of Jewish males was reinforced by the role explicitly assigned to them for the study of Torah and the worship of its source. It was not enough for the pious man to observe and enforce the commandments within his own house. Study of Torah itself became a way of life, and learning became the hallmark of the most pious men. The Jewish hero became not just an observer of law but a master of learning. As was written by the biographer of Akiba ben Joseph, a giant among giant scholars in the talmudic period who was martyred by the Romans: "The Talmud was 'their hobby, their pastime, their sport, their theater, their concert house, their cinema, their newspaper, their radio, their life . . . the study of the Talmud did not lead to Paradise; it was Paradise."[7]

The male bonding system of Torah study, including the Talmud, provided an extraordinary mechanism for reinforcing the Torah's prescriptions for the ideal husband and father. Since women could not be substituted for men in the minyan, it was difficult for males to escape attendance. Over the past two thousand years, Christian churches frequently have been crowded by women, often praying for their absent husbands and sons, while Jewish synagogues were crowded with adult males, reminding themselves and each other of God's commandments, including those that prescribed a certain kind of father and husband. Jewish fathers were to be deeply involved in the teaching of their sons, as discussed in chapter 7. To make that possible, it was necessary, according to this particular road map, for Jewish men to sanctify lust in monogamous marriages and ban it everywhere else, a phase of the story told in the next chapter.

CHAPTER 5

THE SANCTIFICATION OF LUST

N ONE OF ISAAC BASHEVIS SINGER'S BEST KNOWN SHORT STORIES, "THE SPINOZA OF MARKET STREET," DR. NAHUM FISCHELSON, A SHORT, hunchbacked older man, proposes marriage to a woman called Black Dobbe. Dobbe, a neighbor who took care of Fischelson when he was sick, has a broken nose, a moustache, and a tall, stringy body, and she speaks with the hoarse voice of a man. As might be expected in such a match, a series of minor calamities bedevils the wedding ceremony. Fischelson has a difficult time locating Dobbe's ring finger when he tries to put the wedding ring on it; and when it comes to the smashing of the glass, he kicks the goblet several times without breaking it. But that night in the marriage bed, kissing, touching, and speaking love, the aches and pains leave Fischelson as he presses Dobbe's body against his and in the words of Singer, becomes "again a man as in his youth."[1]

Most talmudic rabbis probably would have approved, since they believed that pleasure in sex with one's wife, with the proper attitude is holy. They also believed that sex, for men as well as women, must remain in the marriage bed. The Jewish answer to the question, how can we keep lust from destroying families, was to sanctify it in marriage. Writing in the first century C.E., the Jewish historian Flavius Josephus explained to his Gentile readership that Jewish husbands could have intercourse only with their wives and that Jewish women must never be taken by violence or persuaded by deceit or guile.[2]

In all other major patriarchal civilizations, from Babylon in 1700 B.C.E. to the Incas in 1500 C.E., it was the norm for the most powerful males to have large numbers of sexual outlets outside marriage. Anthropologist Laura Betzig found that in 104 politically autonomous societies, power predicted the size of a man's harem. Where monogamy was prescribed—only 16 percent of 853 cultures surveyed by Helen Fisher—it was normal for high status, powerful men to have multiple sexual partners. Marriage, whether monogamous or polygynous, enabled a man to pass on status and property to his heirs, as Roman nobles did, even as they kept female slaves. In medieval Christian countries, monogamous marriage, assuring patriarchal fathering for heirs, and polygynous mating, assuring sexual outlets for their fathers, coexisted comfortably.[3]

Long before Josephus wrote about monogamy as the norm for Jews, male ancestors of the Jews behaved, as already seen, in sexually predatory ways, using sex both as an instrument and as a benefit of power. We learn from the Bible that they offered wives to powerful men as a form of hospitality and as an expression of deference and that fathers gave daughters to powerful strangers. Daughters and wives were virtually owned by male patriarchs, and males engaged in warrior competitions to determine the most powerful of them. Saul the king, anointed by the prophet Samuel and by Yahweh, had a substantial harem. His successor, David, arguably the most popular figure in Jewish history, built an even larger harem. He also satisfied his lust for Bathsheba by arranging her husband's death in war; and King David's son Amnon, tormented with lust for his virginal half-sister, Tamar, raped her despite the distraught girl's cry that "such a thing is not done in Israel" (2 Sam. 13:12–15). David's son Solomon established a harem that was much larger than that of his father.

The rabbis of the Talmud repudiated those ancient ways. Other cultures continued to makes males into responsible fathers, in part by giving them opportunities for sexual activity outside the primary marriage relationship through prostitutes, courtesans, concubines, or plural wives; but the Jews adopted an ideal of monogamous sex as holy and joyous, as illuminated in Prov. 5:19: "Find joy with the wife you married in your youth, fair as a hind, graceful as a fawn. . . . Let hers be the company you keep, hers the breasts that ever fill you with delight, hers the love that ever holds you captive." Marriage made bride and groom holy in a mix of fleshly and spiritual love. There was only one term—*ahavah*—for both kinds of love, a verb used when calling Jews to love their God, their neighbors, or their spouses (the term for sexual desire is *ta'avah*). By contrast, the Greeks spoke of two kinds of love: eros, or carnal love, and agape, or spiritual love.

Having proclaimed the passion that creates life to be good, the Jews also recognized that this particular passion could cause a great deal of trouble. To prevent trouble, the rabbis of the talmudic era became strict constructionists of the Seventh Commandment, teaching that Jews must channel sexual passion entirely into marriage so that they would fulfill their ancient commandment to be fruitful and multiply and also create stable families within which to nourish, instruct, and discipline children. They taught that by focusing sexual passion in marriage, spouses would be interested in and faithful to each other. Husbands and wives would not marry just to combine family lines and merge family interests, as was true in the great extended family systems of the Far East, but also to develop close, loving companionship based in part on sexual affection. To oversimplify: sex outside marriage would be minimized if men and women enjoyed it more within. In striking departure from the view and experience of others, talmudic sages often emphasized that marriage was for pleasure and companionship in addition to having children.[4]

Polygyny could still be found in the first thousand years of the Common Era in some Jewish communities in Asia and North Africa; but even in societies where it was the rule, Jewish marriage contracts often specified that the bride would not be subject to polygyny. In central and western Europe it became increasingly rare, virtually extinct; until finally, in the year 1000, a decree attributed to Rabbenu Gershon (960–1040) was issued against Jewish men having plural wives in Germany and Provence. Henceforth, polygyny would be prohibited in the marriage contract even if the wife was willing to consent to it, in contrast to the highly polygynous societies of the Far East. When Jewish men were tempted with lustful thoughts, they were told by the rabbis to take a cold bath in Torah, not to take a concubine even if they could afford one. But the issue of sex outside the primary marriage relationship did not die entirely and was debated into the twelfth and thirteenth centuries by the rabbis, most notably by Maimonides (Rabbi Moses ben Maimon, 1134–1204) and Nahmanides (Rabbi Moses ben Nahman, 1194–1270).

The question at that time revolved around the *pilegesh*, the concubine, who did not have a marriage contract but whose children were fully legitimate and had equal standing with the children of regular marriages. Here was the last legal concession to the pattern found commonly in other cultures of men insisting on more than one sexual partner. The *pilegesh* was not comparable to a mistress in ancient Roman or Greek societies or later in Christian nations; a mistress had no legal standing in relationship to her married lover. Since the *pilegesh* relationship was so rare, it may seem surprising that the rabbis paid as much attention to the issue as they did, but it was the way of rabbis to have weighty arguments over matters that may have affected only a few persons. Maimonides saw the practice as a dangerous concession to male lust, one that threatened the stability of Jewish families, and he became the first rabbi to deliver a significant ruling against it.

Decades later Nahmanides disagreed on the legal issue even though he agreed with Maimonides that concubinage should not be encouraged. Nahmanides saw no legal prohibition against it as long as the *pilegesh* belonged to one man who acknowledged his responsibility as the father of her children. Then a *pilegesh* could be a barrier against casual liaisons. But he lost the argument, and provisions against concubinage were placed in marriage contracts and in local community ordinances with increasing frequency in the Middle Ages.

Maimonides and Nahmanides actually were in substantial agreement, compared to the prevailing views on sexuality and marriage in the Islamic and Christian societies in which they lived. In the Muslim world a man could marry up to four wives if he could afford them and if he performed his conjugal responsibilities as prescribed by the Koran. Unlike the Christians, the Muslims did not idealize asceticism. Christian departure from the Jewish position probably began with Paul's view in 1 Cor. 7:6 that the husband and wife should render each other what is due "by way of concession, not commandment," meaning, as later church fathers asserted, concession to sin. Eventually, celibacy became the ideal of Christian philosophers and theologians. All of the major Christian writers on the subject—Augustine, Jerome, Tertullian, and St. Thomas Aquinas—carried forward the basic doctrine of marriage as a concession to sin. Eventually, the Protestant Reformation repudiated celibacy, but Luther only reluctantly endorsed marriage as necessary medicine, a cure for the sexual impulses that drive every man. "No matter what praise is given to marriage," he said, "I will not concede to nature that it is no sin."[5]

In contrast, because of the Jewish ideal of the sexual act as holy and joyous within the marriage relationship, many rabbis encouraged Jews to cultivate and appreciate it. To give proper advice on sexual matters, medieval rabbis, including Maimonides and Nahmanides, relied on two sets of biblical and talmudic requirements: the laws of marital obligation and the laws of family purity (more about the laws of family purity later). The laws of marital obligation (*onah*), addressed to married men, are based on Exod. 21:10, where they are specified as "food, clothing, and sexual rights," later spelled out in considerable detail in the Talmud, which actually asserted that a prenuptial agreement by a woman to forgo her claim to sexual rights is not to be recognized, even though an agreement omitting rights to food and clothing might be.

A comparable restriction required that a husband who wished to change his occupation to one that might demand longer absences from home must first obtain his wife's approval.[6] In detail not found in any sex manual today, the oral law provided a basic timetable for men in different trades to follow in meeting their wives' sexual needs. Thus, a camel driver was required to perform the duty of *onah* once a month, sailors only once every six months. A man of independent means was expected to make sexual love more frequently, and students of Talmud once a week, preferably on the night of Shabbat. Special consideration was shown to what the rabbis thought were the needs of wives by encouraging a husband to initiate sex with his wife before he went away on a journey, near her menstrual period, and throughout pregnancy.[7] As Maurice Lamm has pointed out, it is only recently in the West that the idea of sex as a man's right and as a woman's duty has been widely repudiated.[8]

With so much instruction from the Talmud, there still were points of uncertainty requiring commentary and decisions by rabbis. For example, Abraham ben David of Posquie`res (Rabad, ca. 1120–1198) composed a well known guide for the pious life, in which he gave an entire chapter to the subject of sexuality and marital conduct, arguing that if a husband sees a wife hinting at her desire for sexual relations, he is commanded to please her.[9] Such a ruling rested on the injunction in the Deuteronomic code in which husbands were commanded not just to be faithful to their wives but to make them happy. "If a man is newly married, he shall not join the army, nor is he to be pestered at home; he shall be left at home free of all obligations for one year to bring joy to the wife he has taken" (Deut. 24:5).

The sexual advice given by medieval rabbis/philosophers was less concerned with the frequency of sex than with the intention of it. Sexual pleasure, including foreplay, was sanctioned by them but only when in the service of God. The author of the *Iggeret Ha-Kodesh* (Letter of Holiness), who may have been Nahmanides, observed that sexual intercourse is "an elevated and great thing when it is proper."[10] "Therefore engage her first in conversation that puts her heart and mind at ease, and gladden her . . . speak words that arouse her to passion, union, love, desire and eros . . . never may you force her . . . win her over with words of graciousness and seduction . . . do not hasten to arouse passion until her mood is ready; enter with love and willingness so that she 'seminates' [has an orgasm] first."[11] The *Iggeret* also reminded husbands that wives should not be taken against their will or when they are asleep.[12]

The importance of wives achieving orgasm was emphasized by other rabbis. Judah the Hasid (?1660–1700) linked his prescription for lovemaking that satisfies wives to the conception of male children, reminding his male audience that they should delay their orgasms until the wives had theirs first. Another wrote that the husband "should arouse her with caresses and with all manner of embracing in order to fulfill his desire and hers so that he does not think of another, but rather only of her."[13] Rashi, the extremely influential eleventh-century rabbi, interpreted a text from Rabbi Hisda (c. 217–309) as advice to his daughters to prolong foreplay. "When your husband caresses you to arouse a desire for intercourse and holds the breast with one hand and 'that place' with the other, give the breast to increase his passion and do not give him the place of intercourse too soon, unless his passion increases and he is in pain with desire."[14]

Rabbinic advice encouraging sensuality as an expression of holiness rested on a biblical foundation, most remarkably in the love poetry of the Bible's sensual Song of Songs, in which lovers repeatedly describe each others's sexual attractions in anticipation of sexual joy. The Song of Songs clearly recognizes and honors the sexual agency of women as they frankly describe the sexual attraction of their beloved husbands or grooms-to-be:

> His lips are lilies,
> His lips are lilies,
> distilling pure myrrh.
> His hands are golden, rounded,
> set with jewels of Tarshish.
> His belly a block of ivory
> covered with sapphires.
> His legs are alabaster columns
> set in sockets of pure gold.
> His appearance is that of Lebanon,
> unrivaled as the cedars.
> His conversation is sweetness itself,
> he is altogether lovable.
> Such is my Beloved, such is my friend,
> O daughters of Jerusalem.
>
> SONG OF SONGS 5:13–16

There are other examples of romantic love in the Bible. The term used for Isaac's sexual relationship with his wife is "rejoicing." In describing Jacob's wooing of Rachel, it is recorded that "he kissed Rachel and wept aloud" (Gen. 29:11).[15] Even without the romance of the Song of Songs, Jews could not avoid the idea that women are also sexual beings, as they read the Pentateuch. Many Jewish heroines took sexual initiatives outside the marriage relationship for good purposes. Esther saved the Jewish people through her sexual attractiveness (Esther 2:15–17). Tamar seduced her father-in-law, Judah, forcing him to live up to his obligations as a father and to allow her to be a mother, for which she ultimately won Judah's praise (Gen. 38:15–19). Ruth, upon the advice of her mother-in-law, Naomi, seduced her kinsman Boaz, leading him to marriage and securing the male line of her dead husband and giving birth to the grandfather of King David. The women who attended the birth told Naomi that her daughter-in-law "is more to you than seven sons" (Ruth 3:6–18, 4:13–16). Judith became a great heroine by using her sexuality and good looks to get invited to the tent of Holofernes to slay him and prevent the destruction of the Jewish army by the Assyrians (Jth. 10:1–5, 11:20–21, 13:6–10).[16]

Female sexuality for a holy purpose—saving the Jewish people, having Jewish children, providing loving, joyous companionship to one's husband—was honored by the rabbis of the talmudic era. Sensuality for the right purpose in the right way was good. It was a position often carried forward through Jewish poetry during the golden age of philosophy and poetry of Spanish Jewry from the middle of the eleventh century to the end of the fifteenth. The poet Judah ben Samuel Halevi, a talmudic scholar and physician, wrote of brides disporting themselves "in the garden of love" and of young men whose "glory shall rise" on their wedding nights as they "gather the fruit thy joy shall bear."[17]

The *Zohar*, the important mystical commentary that first appeared in Spain in the thirteenth century and remained a revered work in all classes of Jews for hundreds of years, emphasized that the pleasures of sex in marriage also gave joy to the Divine Presence. The *Zohar* offered Jewish men who were far from home a way to channel erotic energy into mystical religious feelings while remaining true to God and to their wives. The Jewish concept of *shekhinah*, the felt presence of God, giving off a special kind of radiance, was cast into the role of a celestial female accompanying a traveling peddler or student away from his wife.

The Zohar prescribed that before an extended journey, a traveling man should pray with his wife for God to send *shekhinah* to him when he was away. Wifely assistance in bringing *shekhinah* was acknowledged by obliging the husband to have intercourse with his wife when he returned home. Emphasizing that *shekhinah* is no purer or holier than human intercourse, the *Zohar* stated that the *shekhinah* is present during conjugal union. Here was a religious sanction for the emotional enjoyment of married sexuality, an extraordinary way of reinforcing the marriage bond.

The *Zohar*, like all of kabbalah, the great mystical writings of the medieval period, was studied only by males. But like much of the wisdom literature of the Jews, it probably had the effect of reinforcing the paradigm of a Jewish husband and father modeled after Yahweh in relationship to the people of Israel. The kabbalists conducted Sabbath rituals that included hymns to welcome the Sabbath bride, with the mystics playing the role of bridegroom. In one manual of the period, "it is written: 'Behold the Torah, she is the wife God has given . . . and the other wife is of flesh and blood . . . the King, blessed be he, commanded us to love her (too), but the real love should be for the former.'"[18] Later, the Baal Shem Tov (d. 1760), the founder of Hasidism, told his followers that "every *mitzvah* or act of holiness starts with thoughts of physical pleasure" and "it is proper for a man to have physical desires, and out of them he will come to desire the Torah and the worship of God."[19] The idea was not to suppress desire but to elevate and transform it to achieve spiritual transcendence in marriage while refraining even from contact with women outside it. Rabbi Eleazer of Worms (1165–1230) summed up the dual approach: "One should avoid looking at other women and have sex with one's wife with the greatest of passion, because she guards him from sin."[20]

Not all of the rabbis were so welcoming to the passions of sex, even in marriage. As David Biale has shown, there was constant tension between a positive view of sensuality in marriage, as a way of nourishing devotion to God and the marriage, and a more repressive, so-called purity tradition, emphasizing the dangers of sexual passion even within marriage. In the centuries leading up to the talmudic era, the priests of Jerusalem issued many rules for keeping men and women apart. They were not to sit together at a festive table nor drink a cup of wine together at a social gathering. Some talmudic rabbis ridiculed these restrictions, recalling that in biblical days Hebrew men and women tended flocks together and met at watering troughs, where romances blossomed.[21] They pointed out that in ancient days, women gathered the sheaves behind the reapers and sat alongside the men at mealtime, shared with men in the building of the sanctuary, and joined them for worship in the observance of festivities there. Women participated in public celebrations as dancers and singers. They hailed military heroes, sat on governing councils and even fought alongside men in unusual circumstances.[22]

But in the Second Commonwealth, before the Talmud was written, sex began sometimes to be called "the evil impulse," a precursor to what would become official Christian doctrine later.[23] Yes, sex in marriage was good and even could be holy, but it was an impulse that had to be kept in check. It could, as the rabbis said, build a family and a home, but it also could destroy them. Modesty would, it was reasoned, lead to purity. Maimonides was one of the medieval rabbis who emphasized an ascetic view, urging modesty, temperance, and respect. He and others believed that if males became too sexually aroused, they would be led away from a purely spiritual life.[24]

The purity tradition was based in part on the laws of *niddah* (a menstruating woman). These began in Leviticus and include the prohibition against approaching and uncovering the nakedness of a woman during her monthly period (Lev. 18:19). Later regulations interpreted that proscription to eliminate sex for married couples for up to fourteen days every month, including days before and after the wife's period. Husbands and wives had to avoid physical contact and discover bonds other than sex to sustain their intimacy before the wives immersed themselves in the *mikvah*, the ritual bath, to symbolize their return to sexuality and fertility. But even the laws of *niddah* have been joined to the sensuality tradition by some rabbis, from the talmudic era to the present, who emphasized that abstinence during that period would heighten the desire for sex and its pleasure during the time when they were permitted.[25]

The two traditions—sensuality in marriage and modesty in marriage—can been seen as complementing each other, but they often have been in tension and competition, with the modesty tradition gaining in the late Middle Ages. Both were incorporated in the extremely important *Shulkhan Arukh* (The Set Table), written by Joseph Karo (1488–1575), which became the definitive code of Jewish law in the sixteenth and seventeenth centuries. Karo wrote the *Shulkhan Arukh* to provide a relatively short summary of the vast existing material that had come from rabbinic commentaries in one readable, self-contained code for ordinary synagogue-goers who had been expelled from Spain and Portugal and were dispersed in Turkey, the Netherlands, Asia Minor, Palestine, and other areas. He agreed that it was acceptable for women to enjoy sexual pleasure and that males were obligated to provide it; but he emphasized the danger of males' becoming too sexually aroused, because it would lead them away from the purely spiritual life.[26] On the side of sensuality, he urged husbands to be responsive to wives who indicated a desire for sex, particularly at certain times, such as when a wife was nursing or before a husband went away on a trip.[27]

Drawing on other rabbinic sources, Karo prescribed a loving honeymoon of eleven days, during which time husbands were to abstain from work, neither buying nor selling in the marketplace. Karo also encouraged sexual relations during the last six months of pregnancy, on the ground that it would be good for the health of the embryo and that delivery would be quick. Karo repudiated the laws of *onah* regarding the frequency of sexual obligation for husbands, including the injunction that sex was required for learned men each Sabbath eve; and his overall emphasis, while acknowledging that sex could partake of the divine presence, was to emphasize sex for men as an obligation rather than as a joy.

Missing from the *Shulkhan Arukh* was the sensuality of the kabbalistic *Zohar*. Asceticism was occasionally incorporated into kabbalah, too, but Karo's work, in Blu Greenberg's words, "emanated a certain prudishness going beyond either the modesty tradition or a mystical ascetic point of view."[28] The code warned against sexual indulgence, even in marriage, as injurious to health. Intercourse in the spirit of levity was forbidden. Sex in marketplaces, public squares, gardens, or orchards was prohibited. A husband was told that he should not glance at his wife's genitals ("that place") or, even worse, kiss them, a position that had not even been taken by the relatively ascetic Maimonides. And the *Shulkhan Arukh* found in the modesty tradition a prescription for darkness for the sexual act and, of course, that husbands should think of Torah or other holy subjects while performing it.

Both the sensuality and the modesty traditions were advanced on the ground that they would strengthen the marriage bond. That meant bolstering the continuing commitment of fathers, not just to study Torah but to teach it to their sons. Given the overarching mitzvah to preserve life, it became possible to lean on one or the other or both traditions with regard to premarital sexual intercourse. Some of the rabbis of the Middle Ages prescribed strong discipline for those who violated rules against premarital chastity. Other rabbis accepted the premarital sexuality of those who were long betrothed. Some even allowed for a private association between bride and groom prior to nuptials, despite general public opinion and specific prohibitions against it. In Rumania there was a tendency to follow the old Judean practice of allowing private intimacies between the betrothed before the marriage ceremony, and in Sicily and southern Italy many Jewish brides actually came to the marriage canopy already pregnant.[29]

As late as the sixteenth century, rabbis in Prague fought against the fairly common practice of permitting engaged couples to sit together and indulge publicly in displays of affection, with the approval of parents and other members of the family. The general tendency throughout the late Middle Ages and into the eighteenth and nineteenth centuries, partly because of the influence of the *Shulkhan Arukh*, was to narrow the possibility of physical contacts between men and women who were not already married to each other. One way to do that was to marry early; the *Shulkhan Arukh* stipulated that a man should marry in his eighteenth year and argued that it was even more laudable to marry earlier, although no one should marry before thirteen.

These issues were among those that preoccupied rabbis from talmudic days through the nineteenth century. They inherited two great traditions and were obliged to face inconsistencies, contradictions, and complexities between and within them. Yet both traditions probably strengthened the commitment of Jewish husbands to remain married to the wives of their youth and, as fathers, to emulate the model presented by Yahweh and become teachers and disciplinarians to their children.

In a striking departure from the generic patriarchal paradigm described in part I, the Jewish model asked patriarchs not only to be faithful to their wives but to acknowledge their wives' sexual rights. It did not mean the end of misogyny, nor did it mean that Jewish women became the equals of men with respect to family law, economics, politics, or religion. Indeed, patriarchy was firmly entrenched. But it did mean that Jewish fathers were bound to family responsibilities by their fidelity to the wives of their youth.

CHAPTER 6

PATRIARCHS WHO

DEPEND ON WIVES

ROBABLY NO OTHER PEOPLE HAS MADE SUCH
A FUSS OVER A MAN BECOMING A HUSBAND
AS HAVE THE JEWS, SINCE FOR JEWISH MEN
marriage became an indispensable gateway to knowledge of God. On
the morning of Shabbat before the traditional Jewish wedding, the
groom was (and still is) honored by being called up to the reading of
the Torah in the synagogue. After the final blessings were recited, candy
and raisins were thrown at him as a symbol of the sweet life to follow.
In the Middle Ages, many a groom would return to the synagogue on
the Sabbath following the wedding, surrounded by happy friends singing gleeful Hebrew songs.

Marriage was so important that the Talmud warned: "And whoever
lives without a wife lives without well-being, without blessing, without a
home, without Torah, without a protective wall, without peace."[1] From
infancy on, marriage was idealized for Jewish boys as the route to a significant and fulfilling life. At the tender age of eight days, when a Jewish
male is circumcised, the celebrants in the traditional ceremony still chant
on his behalf: "As he is entered into the covenant, so may he be permitted to enter into the study of Torah, under the *chuppah* [the marriage
canopy] and into the performance of good deeds." The howling infant
boy does not know it, but he is being told that to lead a Jewish life he
must marry, a mandate that must have made life extremely difficult for
countless homosexual men from talmudic times to the present.

The contrast between the Jewish approach to marriage for males and that of other cultures is stark. When in *Zorba the Greek*, the novel by Nikos Kazantzakis, the scholarly young man asks Zorba if he is married, the answer comes back swiftly: "Aren't I a man? I mean, blind. Like everyone else before me, I fell headlong into the ditch. I married. I took the road. I took the road downhill. I became head of a family, I built a house, I had children—trouble."[2] Despite such cynicism, Christian marriage ceremonies have been joyous throughout the ages, but they did not emphasize the absolute dependence of males on marriage for their completion as persons. To the contrary, celibacy was the Christian ideal for those who wished to be close to God. To marry was to give in to a lesser ambition at best, and perhaps—from a theological point of view—to weakness and sin.

Muslims, borrowing from the Jews, did not idealize celibacy; but the marriage ceremony itself, in contrast to that of Jews who lived among them, focused on the necessity of joining the frequently hostile worlds of males and females to continue clan and family relationships. As one scholar wrote of Islamic weddings in the Middle Ages: "The opposition of the world of males and the world of females seems to have had central importance in the Muslim ceremony in contrast to that of the Jews."[3] In both Muslim and Christian lands, there was nothing comparable to the Jewish seventh blessing said under the wedding canopy and repeated after the feasts and dancing were over, which reminded all that God "hath created joy and gladness, bridegroom and bride, mirth, exaltation, pleasure and delight, love, peace, and friendship" with the hope that there "may soon be heard in the streets of Jerusalem and everywhere in the world the voice of joy and the voice of gladness, the voice of the bridegroom and the voice of the bride."

Marriage often was idealized even when a couple had no children, as more than one Midrashic story told.[4] But the main purpose of marriage was to have children who would themselves follow the laws of Torah and influence future generations to observe them. For this, a Jewish man needed a wife who would bring peace in the home (*shalom bayit*) while he continued to study and teach Torah. The Talmud repeatedly reminded Jewish husbands that "whatever blessing dwells in the house comes from her [the wife]." Since there is "a substitute for everything except the wife of one's youth" and since "a wife is the joy of a man's heart," then it follows that a husband, as the Talmud instructs, "should be careful not to irritate his wife and make her weep" and that she should not be vexed, "for God notes her tears."

How to avoid vexing a wife? The Talmud warns that a man should not quarrel with his wife to please his parents; that if she is tiny, he should bend down and listen for her counsel; and that "while a man should not eat and drink less than he can afford to," he "should lavish more on his wife." The end result: "He who loves his wife as himself, who honors her more than himself; who rears his children in the right path . . . it is written, And thou wilt know that thy tent is at peace."[5] A peaceful home was vital to the study of Torah; therefore, Proverbs warned, "It is better to live in a desert land than with a contentious and fretful woman" (Prov. 21:19, 25:24). Since a pious husband had a great stake in avoiding strife in the home, his wife theoretically held unusual power if she threatened to disrupt family peace. Undoubtedly, there were many tyrannical husbands and probably some abuse of wives, the extent of which is unknown; but from Talmudic days on through the Middle Ages, a Jewish husband who was known to strike his wife, contentious or not, risked ostracism by his peers, a reversal of what was and still is true in many cultures. A Jew who abused his wife physically in the Middle Ages was regarded as a monstrosity, and rabbis punished such a man severely. One rabbi in northern France said of a wife beater: "We must excommunicate him, scourge him, chastise him with all kinds of punishment."[6]

While God's blessings might come to a man through a good woman, there was little one could do when married to a difficult one. The metaphor of the author of Proverbs, "a wife's quarreling is a continual drip of rain" (19:13), indicated little control on the part of the husband. Many husbands probably lived in fear of the power that women had to bring or destroy peace in the home. In one talmudic story a pious couple without children decided to divorce. The man then married a bad woman who influenced him in negative ways. The first wife remarried a bad man, but she, being pious, made him good. "So," the story concluded, "all depends upon the woman." The dependence of husbands on good wives was a theme repeated throughout the Middle Ages in Jewish literature, including the *Zohar*, which insisted that the *shekhinah* could rest only on a married man, because one who was not married was only half a man.[7]

Who was this woman whom Jewish husbands were urged to treat with kindness, praise, and even deference? A remarkable archetype is presented in Proverbs, chapter 31, a poem that probably dates from before the fifth century B.C.E. and has been read for many hundreds of years by Jewish men around the family table every Shabbat evening following their wives' blessing of the candles. She is not, of course, a Torah scholar, but she is a resourceful, assertive manager of the family's economic life who has economic rights of her own. She not only works hard in managing the household—"she gets up while it is still dark, giving her household their food"—but she also makes decisions for the family: "She sets her mind on a field, then she buys it; with what her hands have earned she plants a vineyard." In addition, "she weaves linen sheets and sells them, she supplies the merchant with sashes." She practices *tzedakah* (justice and charity): "she holds out her hand to the poor, she opens her arms to the needy," and she is wise: "when she opens her mouth, she does so wisely; on her tongue is kindly instruction."

She is entitled to praise for her own valuable qualities, not because of who her husband is. In fact, the poem says of such a woman: "Her sons stand up and proclaim her blessed, her husband, too, sings her praises." It is because of her that "her husband is respected at the city gates, taking his seat among the elders of the land." The poem concludes that "the woman who is wise is the one to praise" and that "her works [not her husband's] tell her praises at the city gates."

A husband preoccupied with Torah study might well value a wife who "keeps good watch on the conduct of her household" and for whom there is "no bread of idleness"; but the recognition that she is an independent economic force, to be given "her share in what her hands have worked for," and of her decision-making power is extraordinary for the ancient Near East or for the Christian and Islamic civilizations that developed subsequently. The contrast between the ideal type of

Jewish wife presented in Proverbs, chapter 31, and the ideal type in other great civilizations emphasizes her power to make economic decisions and her economic rights.

In contrast, the model Confucianist wife was described by a woman writer, Pan Chao, in the classic *Seven Precepts for Women.* The *Precepts,* which go back to at least 106 C.E. and were part of a popular manual of instruction for women, stressed that an ideal wife would be yielding, humble, adaptable, and subservient. As long as she possessed these attributes, it did not matter if she was not brilliant or "skilled and ingenious beyond that of others": "To be pure and reverential; to have leisure as of moonlight through an open door; to be true and constant; to be quiet, retiring; to treasure chastity and control habit until it is regular as a field of grain; to recognize that light conduct may cause the ears to redden with shame; that energetic action and calm behavior have each their law; such is described as the moral excellence of women." Such an ideal wife was expected to work hard, but unlike the wife in Proverbs, chapter 31, her portion depended entirely on the generosity of her in-laws and husband.[8]

The woman praised in Proverbs, chapter 31, is an energetic, decisive and wise, like many of the women of the Pentateuch. These women were not goddesses, like their counterparts in the Roman and Greek cosmology; queens, as in Egypt; or empresses, as in China. It was as ordinary human beings who did extraordinary things that they became familiar to Jewish men, who read about them repeatedly in the synagogue. The stories of Sarah, Rebecca, Leah, Rachel, Naomi, Miriam, Deborah, Hannah, Abigail, Judith, Esther, and others showed them to be "assertive, resourceful, good strategists."[9]

Their stories tend to follow a pattern: The women size up a situation and act decisively, often at considerable risk, to do something or oblige men to do something to protect the Jewish people and their destiny. Sarah knows that Abraham needs an heir, so she tells him to take Hagar as a concubine. Later, after the birth of her own son Isaac, who will now become Abraham's heir, she tells him to banish Hagar and her son, Ishmael, who is now a threat to family stability. In both instances, Abraham listens (Gen. 16:1–5, 21:8–15). As one contemporary Orthodox commentator says, Sarah is "a woman of power and confidence, a voice to whom women, men, and angels listened."[10]

Rebecca is not as straightforward as her mother-in-law, Sarah. When she decides that Esau, the oldest son born to her and Isaac, could not and should not be the progenitor of the Jewish people, she tricks her nearly blind husband into giving the younger son, Jacob, a deathbed blessing. By directing Jacob and taking upon her own head the curse that might be provoked by the deception of Isaac, Rebecca assured the ascendancy of her second son, who becomes the father of the twelve tribes of the Israelites. Earlier, it was Rebecca's intervention with Isaac that led to Jacob's being sent to choose a wife from among the daughters of Laban, Rebecca's brother, rather than to marry a Canaanite woman, as Esau had done twice, to the displeasure of his parents (Gen. 27:1–46, 28:1–5). Wise and assertive wives did what had to be done to ensure the continuity of the people who would become Jews.

We saw in the previous chapter how unmarried women such as Tamar, Ruth, Esther, and Judith used their sexuality assertively on behalf of the Jewish people. The main point of their stories is not that they used their sexuality to effect a desirable result but that they had the ability to size up a difficult situation and to take action in a commanding way—although in Ruth's case it is her mother-in-law, Naomi, who seizes the initiative to continue the family line by persuading Ruth to seduce Boaz, who then took Ruth as his wife (Ruth 3:1–5). In the Judith story, sex is a minor theme. Following the return of the Jews from exile in Babylon and the rebuilding of the Temple, Holofernes came from the north demanding that the Israelites worship his god. When they were under siege, with only five days left to hold out, Judith, the pious widow of three years, crossed enemy lines, engaged her enemy in conversation, got him drunk and asleep, and beheaded him with his sword, thus breaking the morale of his army (Jth.: 10–15). Sarah, Rebecca, Naomi, Esther, and Judith fit Sylvia Barack Fishman's description of heroines in the Bible as "those who analyze the situation, plot, plan, and direct others in order to bring about the desired future."[11]

Deborah, the judge, prophetess, and military strategist, is another such woman. It was she who told Barak, the military commander, when he should charge down from Mount Tabor with ten thousand men to attack Sisera, the Canaanite commander. The minor heroine Jael killed Sisera when he was asleep by driving a peg into his temple with a workman's mallet. Jael is remembered in the song of Deborah and Barak; but Deborah is celebrated for her wise leadership (Judg. 4:4–22, 5:1–31), as are Huldah, the prophetess (2 Kings 22:11–20), and Miriam, the sister of Moses, who helped him lead the Israelites in the desert and also had the audacity to speak out against her brother (Num. 12:1–16).

Although there are ordinary women of great initiative, decisiveness, and judgment in the Bible, they live in a patriarchal world of clans. Each tribe is repeatedly referred to as a patriarchal "house." Only men are registered in the census. Men dominate public positions and continue to do so up through the destruction of the Second Temple and the dispersion of the Jews (Queen Shulamit, who reigned extremely effectively during the Second Commonwealth, is the only major exception). But the rabbis of the Talmud, making selective use of Torah, interpreted it to reinforce and extend the sexual, reproductive, and economic rights of women. Rabbi Hillel, teaching around 40 C.E., led in interpreting the oral law in new ways that gave women protection. For example, prevailing against the opinion of his antagonist Rabbi Shammai, Hillel ruled that a girl could exercise the right to refuse marriage at any age, even during her girlhood, whether or not she was betrothed and regardless of whether it was her father or some other male relative who arranged the match.[12] Hillel's influence and that of other rabbis led to the success of Jewish women in initiating divorce against husbands when they had valid grounds for divorce. One rabbi, Ami (third century C.E.) decided than when a husband and wife charged each other with infertility, the presumption should always be in favor of the woman.[13]

The talmudic rabbis also allowed for birth control and abortion. The Talmud gave permission to use a *mokh* (a fine, soft cotton to block the cervix and absorb semen) under three conditions: a woman who was a minor; one who was nursing; or one who was pregnant. Later, some medieval rabbis interpreted the right to birth control more liberally. Solomon Luria (?1510–1574 C.E.), whose rulings were accepted by many of his contemporaries, defended birth control as possibly necessary for the physical and moral welfare of children already alive, in addition to avoiding danger or extreme pain for the mother. But many rabbis held more strictly to the initial talmudic exceptions.[14] The Talmud also gave permission for abortion to save the life of the mother, with the underlying justification that the fetus is not a living person and has no independent status because it is a part of the mother's body.

Despite these talmudic changes and subsequent interpretations, women generally were disqualified witnesses in religious courts (there were some exceptions). An oath or a vow made by a wife or a daughter still could usually be annulled by her husband or father (Num. 30:14). Although both men and women were obligated to pray, only men could form a minyan in which the Torah was read publicly. Women were obliged to follow three ritual commandments—observe the laws of family purity, light the Shabbat candles, and bless the challah (Shabbat bread) on Shabbat to symbolize the Temple tithe—but all other ritual observances in the home still were the obligations (privileges) of men.

To explain the imbalance of power between men and women, some rabbis in the Middle Ages deprecated the intellectual power of women, as when Maimonides explained why wives could not be permitted to make vows separately from their husbands. "Women," he said, "are easily provoked to anger, owing to their greater excitability and the weakness of their minds." To permit vows to be "entirely under their control would cause great grief, quarrel and disorder in the family."[15] Following Maimonides, Joseph Karo in the *Shulkhan Arukh*, while acknowledging that women might study Torah, recommended against it because, he said, they were likely to have a limited understanding and would misinterpret and misconstrue its teachings.[16] A few talmudic rabbis had been misogynistic as well, even criticizing Deborah, the judge, and Huldah, the prophetess, for their haughtiness toward men,[17] but statements of praise and respect for women, as already shown, were abundant in the Talmud, including "God has endowed woman with a special sense of wisdom which man lacks."[18]

Going beyond biblical law in acknowledging the rights of women, the Talmud gave young women the legal right to refuse any suitor, no matter what their parents said, although it is impossible to know how many exercised that right. According to the Talmud, daughters could inherit property from their mothers, and a woman's right to retain separate property that she owned prior to marriage was protected. Dowry money, for example, was to be held in escrow, along with other property brought into the marriage. These rights, some of which were already observed during the Second Temple period, were guaranteed by the *ketubah*, the marriage contract, probably put into widespread practice in the first century of the Common Era. The Talmud also provided that a wife could keep her earnings and waive all or part of her husband's support if she wanted to, and it stipulated that her children—sons and daughters—not her husband, would inherit her property. So strong was the protection of women in the matter of the dowry that a rabbinic ruling insisted that the wife receive all of it, even if she wanted to give a portion of it to her husband (perhaps under coercion or influence). She could not waive her dower rights, as was permitted later under Islamic law, which stipulated that it was no crime if the husband and wife agreed between themselves to have the woman voluntarily remit a portion of her dowry to the man.[19]

The rabbinic laws on divorce also extended rights to wives, although the balance of power remained markedly in favor of husbands. The basic talmudic premise was that "he who divorces his wife is hated by God." The Talmud stipulates that a man cannot divorce a wife who has become mentally ill and cannot take care of herself or one who had been taken captive. In divorcing a wife, a husband had to present a *get* that is handwritten, making it clear that he releases his wife to marry any man that she wishes. It also recognized a woman's right to initiate a divorce if her husband failed to fulfill basic conjugal obligations, abused her, led a dissolute life, or was impotent, although in any circumstance he would have to consent to the divorce before a rabbinic court would set her free. When he balked, there was little the court could do about it; and the wife could be chained to a husband, making her an *agunah*, who could not remarry even when their union had been destroyed in all but name. The problem of the *agunah*—a woman who has either been deserted or whose husband is insane, missing, or presumed dead without the death being verified by two witnesses—continues to this day, although the testimony of a widow has often been taken in rabbinic courts as adequate proof of her husband's death, reversing the requirement that two male witnesses were necessary.[20]

The most important inhibition on a husband seeking an excuse for a divorce was the *ketubah*, which made him liable for three types of payment in the event of a divorce and possibly a fourth: the assets his wife brought with her to the marriage (the dowry), with an addition of no less than half that amount; the additional sum specified in the *ketubah* as a divorce settlement; and occasionally additional funds agreed to by the parties to the divorce. Since the *ketubah* belonged to the wife, not her father, it was she who received the payments, a fundamental departure from the old clan system. Even a woman who refused to have sexual relations with her husband could retain her dowry property if she could show that her husband was repulsive to her; although in this, as in other cases, a rabbinic court could not force but only persuade a husband to grant a divorce.

Sometimes the talmudic rabbis increased the amount to be paid a divorced woman beyond that specified in the *ketubah*. In one case, the great rabbi Akiba (?50–132 C.E.) insisted that a man pay his wife double what had been provided, even though it constituted all of his remaining estate. In cases where the husband refused to pay his wife the amount specified, she could appeal to the courts, which might attach his lands and goods in order to satisfy her claim. In any case, he was obliged to support her until the dowry was paid.[21] Divorce law clearly favored males, and rabbinic authorities were always male. Yet the rights of Jewish women regarding arbitrary divorce and the possibilities for Jewish women to initiate and gain divorce made their situation relatively protected, compared to that of Muslim women (a Muslim husband could leave his wife as a matter of his decision only) and Christian women, who had no power to initiate divorce until the modern era. The protections of Talmud against a coercive marriage, the right to initiate divorce and not to be divorced arbitrarily, along with the recognition of the importance of birth control and even abortion in protecting the life and health of a mother became the norm.

It is impossible to know the extent to which the norms set forth by the Talmud were manifest in reality.[22] How many cases of disagreement on such intimate matters as alleged conjugal rape actually reached the rabbis for decision is impossible to know. Historical information on the economic agency and rights of Jewish women is much more abundant, going back almost a thousand years before the closing of the Talmud. Fifteen-hundred-year-old papyrus scrolls of a Jewish community discovered in Egypt tell about a Jewish woman named Mibtahiah, who arranged her own marriage contract to safeguard her right to divorce. Mibtahiah, who was born in 476 C.E., owned property and loaned money in her own name, even after her marriage.[23] Jewish documents found in the ancient town of Fostat, not far from modern-day Cairo, covering a period from 900 to 1200 C.E., when Egypt was a center and crossroads of Jewish life, tell of many successors to Mibtahiah. They report Jewish women involved in making business arrangements, fixing dowries for prospective brides, and paying ransom money for captives taken during the Crusader wars. Letters written by Jewish women in Iraq, Tunisia, Palestine, and Libya show that they often worked outside the home.

Women were doctors, midwives, textile merchants, scribes, and undertakers, among other occupations. Jewish women appeared in court regularly and sometimes made their own wills, dedicated Torah scrolls, and contributed money to charity.[24] A businesswoman-broker-banker appeared in Jewish court in 1098, notwithstanding the talmudic proscription against women being witnesses in a court of law. In her will she left her husband nothing but insisted on a proper Jewish upbringing for their only son, stating just which rabbi should teach him and how much he should be paid. An eleventh-century woman, living about forty miles from where ancient Carthage had been located, was the authoritative head of a large extended family.[25]

Jewish women in Europe also worked for pay in the Middle Ages. In fourteenth-century Navarre, in Spain, they worked in the building trades. In sixteenth-century Holland, wives turned the grindstones in the home-bound diamond cutting and polishing industry. Jewish business women in medieval France and Germany sometimes were money-lenders to nobles and peasants, and women were appointed as trustees of communal funds. At different times in Europe, Jewish women worked as copyists and translators and later as typesetters and publishers, even as ritual slaughterers. Strictly speaking, Jewish women in sixteenth- and seventeenth-century Poland did not have authority to accept credit in business without their husbands' approval, but in fact women minded stores, traded, borrowed and lent money, repaid debts, and accepted payments on their own, acting as agents for their husbands. In practice, a husband who refused to pay his wife's debts would be ostracized in the marketplace.[26]

Among those women who left records of economic activity, the best known is Glückel of Hameln (1646–1724), who wrote seven books of memoirs in Yiddish. God-fearing, pious, and knowledgeable in Torah, she was married before she was fourteen and was pregnant within a year, after having been taken from her well-to-do father's house in the big town of Hamburg to the dull, shabby village of Hameln. Her husband was a successful trader, but it was study, not business, that brought him joy, according to Glückel. She writes lovingly of his devotion to Torah. Not once did he miss learning the appointed Talmud lesson for the day. When he died prematurely, after having fathered thirteen children, she raised them, married off twelve of them by herself, and carried on her husband's business affairs successfully. Her narrative, free of resentment and complaint, is often filled with joy.[27] Undoubtedly, Glückel was not typical of seventeenth-century Jewish wives. Even the poem that described the perfect wife in Proverbs, chapter 31, begins: "A perfect wife—who can find her?"

During more than fifteen hundred years, until the late Middle Ages, the Jews evolved a complex, highly nuanced form of patriarchy in which mothers as well as fathers played roles in bringing sons into the male bonding system that, among other things, socialized them to be unusually faithful husbands and committed fathers, the kind of man whom Glückel married. Historian Israel Abrahams has written that passages of endearment written by husbands to their wives "are too numerous to quote," although he provides several.[28] According to Abrahams, Jewish men in the early Middle Ages were remarkably domesticated. A Jewish man frequently shopped on Thursdays and Fridays for food for Shabbat and on Friday would help in the cleaning of crockery and saucepans. This was a home-loving patriarch, the kind who often addressed his wife in terms of respect and endearment.[29]

For all of the praise that Jews gave to women such as Glückel, the boy child was special because he would one day become a father in a religious culture that was still patriarchal. For girls, there was no equivalent to the *bris*, or the ceremony called the *pidyon ha-ben* (redemption of the son), when the firstborn male infant in a Jewish family was redeemed for service to the community (in ancient days, dedicated to service in the Temple), or the bar mitzvah (son of the commandment). Girls did not put on tefillin and begin each day with a morning prayer; women did not visit the synagogue each evening at sundown, read from Torah there each Saturday, say kaddish for the dead or, despite the precedent of Rashi's daughters, put on the *tallit* over their shoulders. These things were vouchsafed to males only. Only a boy was taken at the age of three to a small-children's school with his father, who distributed cakes and candies to the boy's schoolmates to help him associate learning with pleasure. From that time until he had to learn a trade, he was expected to study.

Nearly all males understood that what little there was in their family in the way of Torah study and instruction belonged to them, not to women. Whatever a husband might do to earn a living, as a trader, tailor, cobbler, silversmith, carpenter, or moneylender, Torah was his responsibility. Compared to men, few women were known for scholarship before the modern era. Beruryah (wife of Rabbi Meir, second century C.E.), who put on tefillin every morning and studied three hundred laws each day, was a major exception. Known for his devotion to his wife, Rabbi Meir was quoted in one of many talmudic stories in honor of women as praising her for exercising keener moral judgment than his. Incensed by the evil behavior of certain persons, he prayed for their destruction, only to have his wife correct him, saying that he should pray for the end of error, not for the death of the evildoers, since the wicked will be no more when error ceases.[30]

Yet it was Rabbi Meir who inserted in the Jewish prayer book the prayer in which men thank God that they were not born as women. His explanation of that prayer was that, although women are clearly the moral equivalent of men (since Torah categorically states that both were created out of God's divinity), males should express a special appreciation of having so many Torah commandments assigned to them. Women, the rabbis insisted, had to be excused from the obligations of men. Only they give birth and care for infants in a way that is impossible for men; and they have important responsibilities in bringing peace to the home.

It was precisely the assigning of commandments to males, enforced by an exclusive male bonding system, that constituted the basis for their status and privilege. Beruryah is the only woman mentioned in the Talmud as a respected scholar, teacher, and debater of Jewish law.[31] Some women in the Middle Ages engaged in the public performance of ritual, and Rashi's daughters actually put on tefillin. They were exempt from positive commandments that had to be performed at specific times, such as wearing the *tallit* or putting on tefillin, but they chose to do it.[32] These were aberrations. Indeed, the separation of women from men in the temple may have occurred in talmudic or pretalmudic times, on the ground that it was necessary to prevent an atmosphere of frivolity; and the Talmud specified that wives could not substitute for husbands in saying the blessings.[33] The study of Torah was kept from the vast majority of Jewish wives, the very women on whom their husbands depended so much. Yet the Talmud did command and cajole their husbands to accord greater respect and affection to them than were normally given in any of the Christian, Muslim, Hindu, or other societies in which they lived.

If women wanted to observe the positive commandments, it could happen; but evidently it helped to be the wife of a famous rabbi, as in Beruryah's case, or the daughter of one, as was true of Rashi's three daughters. A twelfth-century rabbi, Samuel ben Ali, taught his daughter Bible and Talmud, and she is said to have lectured students at the Baghdad Academy from behind a screen or an adjoining room. Perhaps the most noted woman scholar of all was Miriam Shapira, the wife of Rabbi Solomon Luria, already mentioned for his liberal interpretations of Talmud. She lectured in rabbinics and Talmud in Italy in the thirteenth century. But neither she nor Dulcie of Worms (who held public discussions on the Sabbath and who was killed by Crusaders in 1213) was ever called to read from the Torah in the synagogue or included in the minyan.[34]

Giving males nearly exclusive guardianship of the Torah shut Jewish girls and women off from the very thing that gave a Jew the highest esteem in the community of Jews. Yet it was that set of obligations imposed on men that made for a greater dependency on their wives, who often made important economic decisions on behalf of the family and who were accorded significant specific protections in matters of marriage and divorce. Presumably, husbands showed greater regard for their sexuality, too, and an appreciation of their capabilities as decision makers and persons of wisdom in matters of family, economics, and charity than could be found in other major civilizations until the eighteenth century. Such a sweeping generalization is justified by what is known about the normative prescriptions of the Jewish patriarchal paradigm and what is confirmed by the historical record regarding family matters, as thin as that record is with regard to intimate matters between husband and wife.

The Israelites first appeared in the land of Canaan about 1250 B.C.E. It took more than a thousand years to develop the patriarchal paradigm that made Jewish husbands and fathers so distinctive. Although the patriarchy established by the Jews was as explicit as any of the others, it resulted in a new kind of husband. A letter from a woman in Prague in the seventeenth century, written in Yiddish to her sister and brother-in-law, describes such a model. Henele writes: "I have also been told how your dear husband stayed with you and did not move from you [she had been seriously ill]; he has behaved not like a husband but like a father," writing also of her own father as her teacher.[35] It would be a mistake, given the paucity of historical evidence, to sentimentalize the behavior of the man in this particular anecdote or to assume that it was typical. But it did fit the distinctive model of loving and involved husbands and fathers set forth in Torah and explicated in Talmud, one that had a powerful hold on the behavior of many Jewish men for well over a thousand years.

CHAPTER 7

TO TEACH THE

CHILDREN DILIGENTLY

THE JEWISH PATRIARCHAL MODEL TOOK AWAY FROM MALES THE NEAR-ABSOLUTE POWER OVER FEMALES THAT OFTEN HAS CHARACTER-ized patriarchy. It also deepened their role as guardians of the religious culture of the Jews by repeatedly reminding fathers of their responsibility to teach Torah to their children, especially their sons. Biological fathers, not priests or shamans or even rabbis, bore the responsibility for the transmission of Jewish culture. It was the father's job to renew the living covenant with God through his children, especially his sons. A story in the Midrash tells that the Holy One would not accept the patriarchs' guarantee that they would guard the Torah but was pleased when they asserted that their children would be guarantors.

The guaranteeing of Torah by the children mandated that their fathers instruct them in its ways. Abraham was chosen, said Yahweh, "that he may charge his children and his household after him to keep the way of the Lord by doing righteousness and justice" (Gen. 18:19). When Moses finished speaking to the people of Israel prior to blessing them, he urged: "And these words which I command thee this day shall be upon thy hearts: And thou shalt teach them diligently unto thy children" (Deut. 6:4–9), a commandment that was later incorporated into the Jewish liturgy and that follows the most important of Jewish prayers: "Hear, O Israel, the Lord our God, the Lord is one." After the diaspora, Jewish fathers knew that it was up to them to teach their children, "whether resting in the house, walking by the way, or rising up or lying down." When they read Psalm 78, they knew it was to them that Yahweh gave "strict orders to teach it [Torah] to their children" and even "the children still to be born." Teach, teach, teach—relentlessly—was the message.

This key patriarchal mandate for Jews did not lead to the normal accoutrements of power—territory, women, slaves, or other forms of wealth. "Better gain wisdom than gold, choose discernment rather than silver" (Prov. 16:16). The cynic might say they did not have many choices. In any case, the teaching of Torah became the guarantee of a father's immortality. The Book of Proverbs instructs that "The good man bequeaths his heritage to his children's children" (Prov. 13:22). Talmud makes the link to immortality even more explicit: "he who teaches his son is as if he had taught his son, his son's son, and so on to the end of all generations."[1]

It was particularly important to teach sons their special obligations under the law, for three reasons. Daughters could be expected to learn how to be Jewish wives and mothers from close observation of their own mothers. It was assumed, as it is universally, that mothers are programmed biologically to nurture their infants and children. It was also assumed that male children were more rebellious than females and, being more difficult to socialize, required instruction and discipline by adult males. The Jewish answer to ensuring adult male intervention in the socialization of children was to oblige only males to obey the time-bound commandments of Torah, such as having to pray for a parent for eleven months after his or her death and on its anniversary each year following.

By late talmudic times, the obligation of males to learn Torah meant that boys at the age of five were expected to study scriptures. They were supposed to take on the Mishnah at ten, to fulfill the commandments at thirteen, and to begin the more detailed study of the Talmud itself at fifteen.[2] Later, the *Zohar* would instruct: "Who teaches his son to study Torah and takes him twice daily to school is as if he observed the Torah twice daily."[3]

The Talmud imposed on a father five obligations to his son: He must circumcise him, redeem him (in the case of the first male child), teach him a craft, take a wife for him, and, by far the most important of all, teach him Torah.(There is also a reference to his obligation to teach him to swim.) The act of circumcision represents the covenant between the Jewish people and God and is a symbol of Jewish identity. The redemption of the first male child (*pidyon ha-ben*) is a ritual performed thirty days after birth that represents his redemption from the plague in Egypt. In that way, the first son is introduced to the memory of Egypt long before his intelligence permits him to understand it. As one contemporary commentator points out, "in traditional Jewish terms, memory is the very essence of manhood," for the Hebrew word for male, *zachar*, comes directly from the word for memory, *zachor*.[4] In daily service, Jewish men recited the *Amidah*, praising "the God of our fathers, God of Abraham, God of Isaac, and God of Jacob," taking on the weight of the obligation to repeat the "teachings of our sages." One chapter in the Midrash, on the teaching of ethics, called *Avot* (The Fathers), was incorporated into the Jewish prayer book, to be read every week between the Shabbat after Passover and the Shabbat before the Jewish New Year. There were many opportunities to teach besides the Shabbat, including births, bar mitzvahs, and sixteen major holidays and festivals. On these occasions, fathers had specific responsibilities for teaching their meaning.

Discipline was a handmaiden of instruction. Discipline, including physical punishment, was necessary for children to grow into healthy adults. "The rod and reproof give wisdom, but a child left to himself brings shame to his mother" (Prov. 29:15); "Discipline your son while there is hope; do not set your heart on his destruction" (Prov. 19:18); "Do not withhold discipline from a child; if you beat him with a rod, he will not die" (Prov. 23:13). The renowned teacher Jesus ben Sirach (200 B.C.E.) pointed out in *Ecclesiasticus* that a father should not overlook mischievous acts, lest the child ultimately hurt himself. The wise father will apply the rod to his son so that the child will grow to adulthood in health and happiness (Prov. 30:10).

The Book of Proverbs and the Talmud provide enough advice on the subject of discipline of children to constitute a fairly detailed child care manual. The talmudic rabbis tended to soften the emphasis on physical discipline found in the Book of Proverbs. "If thou must strike a child, strike it with the string of a shoe."[5] Other sensible rabbinic advice admonished the father not to threaten a child. "Either punish or forgive him."[6] This preoccupation with the proper methods of discipline continued through the Middle Ages. One widely read seventeenth-century book advised Jewish parents not to use physical punishment as a method of disciplining children. A popular edition of the *Shulkhan Arukh*, published in 1864, warned fathers against losing control of their feelings when disciplining children. It was permissible to pretend anger in order to let children know when you believe they have done something wrong, but, the reasoning went, real anger is dangerous and not effective.[7]

The Book of Proverbs presents constant reminders of the importance of fathers teaching their sons on behalf of both mothers and fathers. "Hear, my son, your father's instruction, and reject not your mother's teaching (Prov. 1:8–9). "My son, keep your father's commandments and forsake not your mother's teaching" (Prov. 6:20). The son is reminded repeatedly that, if he listens to his father and mother, he will lead a peaceful, happy, and prosperous life; if he mocks a father or scorns to obey a mother, calamities will follow (Prov. 30:17). The son who leads a life of righteousness, a life in Torah, will make his father *and* mother glad; such a life will enable "her who bore you [to] rejoice" (Prov. 23:25).

The instructions in the Book of Proverbs and in the Talmud that the teachings of mothers as well as fathers must be observed was an expression of males' understanding that both husbands and wives had parts to play in raising children in the right path. The overriding obligation of this partnership was the responsibility for the children. In return, Jewish children were supposed to honor and respect their mothers and fathers and to perpetuate their memory after they died. In this giving of filial love, generations were to be linked by a reciprocity of obligation. In the Midrash, young men read: "Great is the honoring of father and mother, yes, the holy one, blessed be He, even gave it precedence over the honor due Him."[8]

There could be no greater calamity than for children not to give respect (*derekh eretz*) to their parents. *Derekh eretz* was, as the Talmud said, something that was owed to parents because they, like God, had a share in the making of the child. The child honored his parents by living in ways of Torah. "The father of a virtuous man will rejoice indeed; he who fathers a wise man will have joy of it. May you be the joy of your father, the gladness of her who bore you!" (Prov. 23:22–25). Or "a wise son is his father's joy, a foolish son his mother's grief" (Prov. 10:1).

The constant repetition on listening to and honoring mothers as well as fathers in the Book of Proverbs—"Keep your father's principle, my son, do not spurn your mother's teaching" (Prov. 6:20–22)—probably stems from the original instruction in Levi. 19:3, where Yahweh commands that "every person shall revere his mother and father." The talmudic rabbis later pointed out that in the Ten Commandments (*Deut.* 5:16) the father was put first, but in the commandment from Leviticus it is the mother who comes first: One reveres the mother and father and respects the father and mother, a difference that led to considerable talmudic discussion. One rabbinic homily actually states that if a man is in captivity with his father, his life comes before the father's, but "his mother comes before them all."[9] Whatever the reason—and one explanation might be that mothers are more valuable to the life of the child—the Torah paradigm made the case that mothers are due unconditional love from their children and evolved various strategies for encouraging it.

Not to bless one's mother is, in the words of Proverbs, to be unrighteous, a destroyer. Such a one, Deuteronomy and Proverbs warn, would come to the worst of fates. But with the evolution of ethical monotheism and the talmudic paradigm, Jews did not speak of ravens of the valley plucking out the eyes of a child who did not obey his mother. That was the language of their ancestors in prehistory, long before Talmud. But children versed in Torah knew how God despised the rebellious son (Isa. 1:2–3, Exod. 4:22–23, Hos. 11:1–9, Jer. 3:19). The emphasis on respect for fathers, mothers, and other elders is not uncommon in other cultures. For the Chinese, filiopiety was even more central to their culture than for the Jews. But the Jews gave much greater emphasis to married couples being active partners in raising their children.

Jewish fathers were urged to nurture as well as teach and discipline their children. By embodying the ideal of fathers as nurturers, those who comfort and forgive children, Jewish males were encouraged to acquire attributes commonly thought of as feminine. Such characteristics were acceptable for Jewish fathers, who, according to the Jewish paradigm, were to be modeled in relationship with their own children after God in relation to the children of Israel, as expressed in Hosea: "When Israel was a child, I loved him . . . yet they have not yet understood that I was the one looking after them. I led them with reins of kindness, with leading-strings of love. I was like someone who lifts an infant close against his cheek; stooping down to him, I gave him food" (11:1–4). Much later, one finds in the Talmud the eighty-year-old Rabbi Hanina extolling the importance of frequent warm baths for infants and the feeding of eggs and milk to small children. He even offers psychological advice, explaining that small children must be given things to break, such as imperfect earthenware, presumably to express aggressive feelings.[10]

Ivan Marcus's examination of rituals of Jewish childhood shows how fathers in the Middle Ages took care that their children at five or six associated education with sweetness and love. Their approach was vastly different from that described by Philip Ariès in his history of childhood from the Middle Ages until modern times in France, where parents, unlike the Jews, did not relate to children according to their stage of development.[11] Marcus tells how a Jewish boy living in medieval Germany or France would be taken by his father at the age of five of six to a teacher to learn letters. After encouraging the boy to repeat each sequence, the teacher would spread honey over the letters for the child to lick off. Cakes on which biblical verses had been written would be brought in. Shelled hard-boiled eggs followed, with more verses on them. After some additional instruction, the child would get to eat fruit, nuts, and other delicacies. Maimonides wrote about motivating youngsters to study Torah through the rewards of sweets. It was not possible to motivate a small boy to study, he thought, "since he does not know its value." Hence, it was important to reward him with "a nut or a piece of candy."[12]

According to Marcus, the practice of associating initial learning with rewards and sweetness was widespread and persisted over time. Midrashic and Gaonic sources encouraged a father to begin teaching his son when the infant began talking or at age three. The father, with the assistance of teachers at later times, had the full responsibility and authority to teach a child after age six.[13] A fourteenth-century German-Jewish prayer book showed a picture of a father carrying a child wrapped in a cloak. One of the child's hands caresses the father's cheek and the other holds a round cake.[14] Variations existed in Jewish child rearing between Muslim and Christian countries, but the association of sweetness with learning Torah remained a constant, as did the responsibility of fathers for introducing their sons (and in some cases daughters) to both.

Soft words, ones that would be considered motherly in most societies in most times, came easily from the lips of many Jewish fathers. In the Middle Ages fathers spoke of "my son, the joy of my eye" and "the dearest to me of all mankind." A twelfth-century physician in Provence, Judah ibn Tibbon, wrote: "Thou knowest, my son, how I swaddled thee and brought thee up . . . I fed and clothed thee. . . . My son! Devote thy mind to thy children, as I did to thee; be tender to them as I was tender; instruct as I instructed."[15] In the words of one eighteenth-century rabbi in Lithuania, even discipline should be "tender and caressing."[16] In Arab countries, Jews called sons *muhja* (life blood), or the blossoming rose. Their most common word of endearment for a son was *chamud* (delight).[17] The emphasis on nurturing went beyond the classic pair bonding responsibilities of males to protect and provide for and even to teach their offspring. Historian Schlomo Dov Goitein has written of Jewish fathers in Mediterranean countries that being a father "formed a prominent, central and, so to say, public component in a man's life to a far higher degree than is customary in our own society."[18]

The obligation of fathers to teach their children diligently led in the Middle Ages to a distinctive Jewish genre, the ethical will, in which Jewish fathers give practical and ethical advice to their children. The tradition goes back to the biblical Jacob, who gathers his children around his bed to tell them how they should live after he is gone. Another model for those wills appeared in the apocryphal Book of Tobit, probably written between the fourth and fifth centuries B.C.E. Before his death, Tobit tells his son Tobias to honor his mother, give charity, avoid prostitutes, treat laborers justly, and deal honestly with others (Tob. 4:1–23).

There are examples of ethical wills in the Talmud that also provide a basis for the plethora of them written in the Middle Ages. One of the first of these was written by Eleazar ben Isaac of Worms in the middle of the eleventh century.[19] Eleazar, who begins almost every paragraph with "My son," provides a litany of behaviors to follow even after he, Eleazar, is dead. Infants are not to be left alone in their cradles in the house by day or night. His son must never create an atmosphere of fear in the household, "for this is the cause of many evils." He should listen to the cries of the poor and never treat them with harsh words. Charity should be given in secret, the sick and the mourning visited frequently. He should approach his wife with kind words, treating her gently.[20] Eleazar's fatherly advice about infants was not unusual, and it persisted through the Middle Ages. More than seven hundred years after Eleazar, one man wrote precise instructions about nursing and keeping an infant from sleeping facedown in its crib or having a pillow fall on its face.[21]

Although some of the ethical wills were addressed to daughters, most of them spoke to sons, who often were instructed on the proper treatment of their wives as well as their mothers. Nahmanides wrote to his sons from Palestine in the eighth decade of his life, quoting from Proverbs: "Hear, my son, the instruction of thy father, and forsake not the teaching of thy mother," and went on to tell his sons that they must honor their wives "for they are your honor."[22] Judah ibn Tibbon wrote: "My son! I command thee to honor thy wife to thine utmost capacity. She is intelligent and modest, . . . Thou [art] bound to treat her with consideration and respect . . . if thou wouldst acquire my love, honor her with all thy might."[23] Rabbi Asher of Germany, writing from Spain in the early fourteenth century, instructed his son never to be angry with his wife. "If thou put her off from thee with thy left hand, delay not to draw her to thee again with thy right hand!"[24]

By emphasizing the importance of loving and honoring wives, the authors of ethical wills probably expressed their understanding of the fragility of marriage in nuclear families. One eighteenth-century poet and rabbi from northern Italy reminded his sons that if they show honor to their wives, the women will reciprocate by doing "full honor to their husbands."[25] To be a good Jewish father, it was important to keep a marriage intact by being a loving husband. Divorce was always possible, but children would be likely to suffer.

One did not have to be a biological father to be a loving father. The Talmud reminded Jewish men and women that "he who brings up the child is to be called its father, not he who gave him birth."[26] One often-quoted ethical will was written in the mid-seventeenth century by Nathaniel, son of Benjamin, who, having no son, wrote instead to a young disciple: "Ye know that from your boyhood I have reared you and that my love has never failed. As a nursing father carries the suckling child, I have borne you. I have shown you the road to wisdom. I have guided you in paths of righteousness. . . . Ye were the object of my unceasing thought."[27]

Sometimes the ethical wills seem to have been written almost to reassure their authors that they had done a good job as fathers. Judah Asheri, who succeeded his father as the rabbi of Toledo, wrote before he died in 1349: "What have I left undone for you that a father could do for his children?" adding that his every thought was directed toward his children.[28] Daughters were taught as well as sons, although their obligations to learn were not nearly as extensive; and it was acceptable, even approved, for fathers to express deep affection for their daughters. But the main point of the male bonding system was to lock Jewish fathers into a powerful commitment to teach, discipline, and even nurture their sons while at the same time honoring their wives in law and in practice more than in any other great patriarchal civilization.

It was the combination of these developments that constituted a radical reform in the generic patriarchal paradigm, changes that resonate with calls for a new kind of father in our own time. From a religious point of view, fathers in the Jewish paradigm were to behave so that

God's laws would be followed by successive generations, something many Christians, Muslims, and Jews believe today. Whether one believes that or not, the model promoted behavior by Jewish males—the honoring of wives in monogamous marriages and the teaching, disciplining, and nurturing of children—enhanced the survival prospects of those children.

PART III

THE JEWS AND
MODERN PATRIARCHY

The Jewish patriarchal paradigm was distinctly different from that found elsewhere until the eighteenth century, when major economic, religious, and social changes resulted in the rise of middle-class capitalism and the ideals of the Enlightenment in Europe. A modern secular patriarchy emerged that undermined the religious-based authority of fathers. The roles of fathers and other family members were altered swiftly and radically in the United States especially, as Jewish men competed in new male bonding systems in business and the professions. Then, in the last four decades of the twentieth century, major changes in the technology of work and reproduction, combined with an increasing acceptance of the ideology of equal rights, led many women and men to call for the end of patriarchy altogether.

CHAPTER 8

CONTINUITY AND CHANGE

IN EUROPE

B Y THE TIME OF THE CLOSING OF THE TALMUD, THE JEWS LED LIVES THAT WERE LARGELY INSULATED FROM OUTSIDE FORCES, ESPE-cially in the Christian world. Segregated communities afforded Jews the best opportunity for enforcing dietary laws, building a *mikvah*, and attending synagogue three times a day. The hostility of the Christian world reinforced segregated living and thinking among the Jews. Christians, all of whom were Jews at the time when Jesus lived and shortly thereafter, began to think of themselves as a new church in possession of a truth that non-Christian Jews stubbornly refused to acknowledge, especially after the defeat of the self-proclaimed competitor Messiah Bar Kokhbar by the Romans in 175 C.E. Christian ostracism of Jews began with the decision of the Council of Elvira in Spain in 305 C.E. forbidding Catholics to socialize with them.

According to historian Judah Goldin, the church in the fourth and fifth centuries did what it could to make Jews outcasts and to pauperize them, except during the eighteen-month rule of the Emperor Julian (361–363).[1] Yet persecution of the Jews tended to be relatively mild in the first thousand years of the Common Era, compared to the organized mob violence that began with the first Crusade in 1096. Then, under the church in France and Germany in the eleventh century, forced conversions and expulsions became common, fueled perhaps by resentment against the Jews, who had become successful in trade in most of the major towns of western Europe. In the twelfth century, wagonloads of Talmuds were burned publicly in the streets of Paris, a precursor to the time four centuries later when the papacy itself endorsed burning them.

Christian laws such as the one issued by the Synod of Breslau in 1266, which commanded that Jews dwelling in the province "shall not live among Christians," tended to insulate Jews from exposure to outside cultural forces.[1] Yet Jews were blamed for every sort of calamity afflicting the Christian world. Following the bubonic plague in the fourteenth century, for which Jews were blamed (the commandment to wash their hands before eating probably accounted for their relatively good health), 60 large Jewish communities and 150 smaller ones were destroyed. By the fifteenth century many ghettos had been created by ecclesiastical synods and other church councils, and with the establishment of the Roman ghetto by Pope Paul IV in 1556, Jews were forced to live in them throughout the Christian world. Much later, Israel Zangwill, the apostle of the great American melting pot, described Gentiles from the point of view of many ghetto Jews: "They mock our God and our Torah, they rob us and spit on us, they slaughter us more cruelly than the *shochet* [ritual slaughterer] our cattle. Go not outside the ghetto."[2]

By the sixteenth century, Jews had been expelled from England and Wales, France and Provence, Sicily and Sardinia, almost all of Spain and Portugal, and most cities of Germany. Leaving the West, they settled for the most part in Italy, Poland, other areas of eastern Europe, and the Ottoman Empire, including Jerusalem. Those from Spain and Portugal, the Sephardim, joined many already established Jewish communities in southern Italy, Greece, North Africa, Turkey, Bulgaria, the Balkans, and Islamic Iran—Arab lands, where for most of the time persecution was less severe than in Christian countries. Those who came from Germany and central Europe, the Ashkenazim, went to Poland, Ukraine, Russia, Austria-Hungary, Lithuania, and other places in the East.

In their wide dispersion, the Sephardim and Ashkenazim remained faithful to the same Torah, celebrated the same festivals, and observed the same fundamental rules of family life. Despite cultural variations and differences in language, the Jewish patriarchal paradigm shaped by the Talmud remained largely intact. The Hebrew spoken by Sephardim was influenced by their having lived in Spain and other European Mediterranean countries and in Arab lands, whereas Ashkenazic Hebrew was shaped by German and, to a much lesser extent, other languages of middle and eastern Europe. But through the seventeenth century, Jews everywhere in Europe and even in Sephardic countries, regardless of language and other cultural variations, would recognize each other's family lives as distinctively Jewish. Through Torah there was, as Jacob Katz has written, "a strengthening of the bonds between the various widely separated sections of the Jewish people."[4]

The synagogue became a meeting place for Jewish strangers from all over the world. The officers of the synagogue played critical roles in managing the functions of Jewish community life. The Jewish tribunal, the *beth din*, issued sentences that were executed by the *shamas*, the beadle. In some instances, synagogues were bound by a kind of governing federation, such as the Council of the Four Lands in Poland. Often synagogue leaders were responsible for paying taxes to the outside ruling powers, including the tax permitting Jews to live in a ghetto.[5] Every community had its cemetery, often called the "house of life." All had public baths and ritual bathhouses and a communal bake house and slaughtering place. Schools were usually housed in the synagogue: an elementary school, or *cheder*, and sometimes a yeshiva for older boys. There usually was a board of guardians to care of the poor and perform other charitable work.

The movement to Poland at first brought some relief from persecution for the Jews who settled there. While some engaged in farming or trade in small villages, many Jews in towns became intermediaries between the nobles and the peasantry. The Council of the Four Lands appointed rabbis, passed laws for the Jews, and imposed taxes.

A Ukrainian officer named Bogdan Chmielnicki launched a series of pogroms in 1648 that destroyed three hundred communities and at least ten thousand to twenty thousand Jewish lives, with more made homeless. Some Jews believed that the end of days was near and waited expectantly for the Messiah. In the eighteenth century, many Jews were swept up by the new Hasidic movement, which called for Jews to come closer to God in joyous and ecstatic prayer, song, and dance. Others became more wedded than ever to formal talmudic study and disputation. Whatever the reaction to the destruction wrought by Chmielnicki, the ideal of a husband-father type modeled after Yahweh in relation to the people of Israel remained the basis of the Jewish patriarchal paradigm. Wherever Jews lived, whether in Christian eastern or western Europe or in the lands of the Ottoman Empire under Turkish rule, the essential elements of Jewish patriarchy persisted into the eighteenth century: a male bonding system dedicated to the study of Torah that perpetuated the privileges that went with male obligations; fathers who were devoted to teaching the main precepts of Torah to their children, especially their sons; husbands who were dependent on wives for peace in the home and often for bread on the table; early marriages (usually arranged) that were monogamous and long-lasting; and wives whose normative sexual and economic rights were greater than those in non-Jewish communities.

Although there were unifying similarities based on Torah between the lives of Jews in the West and in the East as they related to family life, by the end of the eighteenth century those who lived in the West had been increasingly exposed to the new ideas of the Enlightenment. Those ideas—human rights, freedom, tolerance—led to a relaxation of some of the restrictions on Jews. No single event, not even the French Revolution, marked the beginning of the modern age. But civil rights were acquired by Jews in several European countries. The Jews of Holland gained civil equality in 1796, and emancipations took place in Belgium in 1815, in Denmark in 1849, and in Norway in 1851.

In the wake of Napoleon's successful campaigns in 1799 and 1804, the Jews were emancipated by his decree in areas under his control, including much of western Europe and northeastern Italy. Later, in 1808, he signed another decree imposing restrictions on Jewish moneylenders and on the movement of Jews within France, but the ideas that the Napoleonic movement had unleashed earlier changed western Europe dramatically for the Jews. There some Jews professed Enlightenment ideas of their own in a movement called the *haskalah*, urging their coreligionists to adopt the languages and customs of the countries in which they lived that were not inconsistent with their religious beliefs. In the West, Jews could now become, at least to some extent, a part of the outside world. In western European countries during the first half of the nineteenth century, Jews became increasingly integrated into the economic and even, in some cases, the political life of the nations in which they lived, although social anti-Semitism and even restrictions on the civil life of Jews persisted.

Seventy-five percent of the world's Jews lived in eastern Europe throughout most of the nineteenth century, with four million of them restricted to the Russian Pale in shtetlach of usually between one hundred and one thousand persons in villages and middle-sized towns. There the new ideas of the Enlightenment had much less currency than in the West, where religious reform within Judaism began in Germany. In Reform synagogues women could sit with men and share in what heretofore had been exclusively male Jewish religious activity. Even in the East, spokesmen for the Russian *haskalah*, the *maskilim*, or "enlightened ones," believed that it should be possible to be a Jew and also a citizen of Greater Russia, speaking Russian, not Yiddish, and participating in Russian culture. Although the vast majority of Jews in the restricted area of settlement, the Pale, spoke Yiddish right up until the twentieth century, there was considerable movement from shtetlach to the larger cities of Odessa, Kiev, Warsaw, Lvov, and Krakow. The sons of shoemakers, tailors, and carpenters came to the bigger cities to make a living. Some even came to study, not Talmud but secular subjects. By the end of the century, a sprinkling of middle-class Jewish daughters in those cities had piano teachers and dancing masters.

Powerful new ideas came to Jews, even in the shtetlach, that undermined their religious patriarchy. By the middle and especially at the end of the nineteenth century, a growing number of young Jews (the population had recently expanded) began to challenge the old patriarchal system.[6] One of the big new ideas was socialism. Young Jewish socialists spoke of two kinds of emancipation: the first from traditional religious patriarchal power and what they viewed as the parochial, ritual-bound medieval Jewish life in which they had been raised; the second, from the oppressive tsars, who were brutal to all poor people, not just the Jews. The socialists often spoke of a new world of equality in which women participated alongside men in the construction of a just society. Another big idea, secular Zionism, was based on the belief that Jews should not wait for the Messiah to restore Israel as a nation among nations. Only by creating a new Zion could Jews have a truly healthy and happy existence. This idea too was often associated with the abandonment of religious patriarchal controls, especially among the socialists who were Zionists. Implicit in all of these ideas was a fundamental challenge to the core of Jewish patriarchy—the exclusive right of males to be the sole makers of major decisions and guardians of a religious civilization.

Many changes resulted from the attacks by the *maskilim* on some of the old ways. Young Jews rebelled against being pushed to marry at thirteen or fourteen, and many of their elders agreed that such practices were wrong in the modern age.[7] Secular life was attractive to a growing number of Jewish women, who felt confined by the male-dominated religious culture of the Jews, compared to the possibilities they saw outside its limits. Some went so far as to convert to Christianity. More of them joined the Jewish Labor Union in Russia and Poland, the Bund, in which they participated as organizers of workers and fundraisers. Some combined their feminism with Zionism. Others resented having to work to support husbands, arguing that it was unfair for women to work outside the home.[8]

Women continued to play an economically active role in Jewish communities right up through the nineteenth century, but it was not always one that they preferred.[9] Many of the *maskilim* were critical of the Jewish tradition in which women worked outside the home to support their scholar husbands. They also opposed the old system of young scholar-husbands, often still in their teens, living during the early years of marriage in the homes and under the thumbs of in-laws. Although quite puritanical about sex, many *maskilim* called for marriages based on romantic love, in which wives ceased working for money after marriage, following the pattern of non-Jews in the European middle classes. In emancipated homes, seen in Germany particularly, husbands would maintain disproportionate legal power, but their main role would be as providers for the family, striving to be successful in the world of work outside the home.[10] A modern patriarchal system was emerging in an increasingly capitalistic economy. Modern alpha males were the best economic competitors, the ones best able to provide for their families, even to give their wives luxuries.

Yiddish fiction writers provide a wealth of information about the struggle between tradition and modernity in Jewish families in eastern Europe. According to them, the Jewish ideal, whether among the *maskilim*, the *hasidim*, or the traditional rabbis, was that sex was still to be sanctified only through marriage. For most shtetl dwellers, the modesty tradition of the *Shulkhan Arukh* had long since triumphed over the sensuality tradition embodied in the Song of Songs and the *Iggeret*. Some writers tell of the wedding night as being traumatic, since young boys, knowing it was their duty to have sex, were ignorant of the arts of wooing.[11] I. L. Peretz and Isaac Bashevis Singer wrote of young women who were filled with shame the morning after their wedding night.[12] A pious wife in the shtetl did not talk to her husband about sex. A pious husband made certain that he said a blessing before making love to his wife, that the room was dark, and that the children were fast asleep.[13] Some women in the shtetl abhorred sex altogether. Although Hasidic Jews (a large minority in Poland) were likely to believe in the mystical view taken from the Hosea story that sexual union is a symbol of a spiritual binding with God, David Biale writes that much of their erotic energy was turned toward God in ecstatic worship.[14]

More than any other Yiddish writer, I. B. Singer, who wrote in the twentieth century, was preoccupied with how Jews did or did not confine lust to the marriage bed. In his stories, sexual passion must be transcended by love in marriage; if it is not, the consequences will be dire. In "The Destruction of Kreshev," Lise, an adulteress, never repents her infidelity and is tormented until she hangs herself.[15] In Singer's panoramic novel of Jews in Poland, *The Manor*, Clara commits adultery with her son's tutor, is abandoned by her husband, discovers that her lover is married in New York, and dies a miserable woman.[16] In another novel, one of Singer's characters, Miriam Liba, combs her hair on the Sabbath, reads romantic novels in Polish and French, and complains that women should not wear wigs after they marry. Eloping with the man of her fantasy, she is miserable ever after.[17]

Singer remained loyal to the ideal of marriage as sanctifying sexual desire in his great novel *The Slave*, clinging to the belief that lust can be transformed by love of God through the commitment that its hero, Jacob, makes to Torah and to the well-being of Wanda, a Gentile daughter of a Polish farmer, for whom he lusts and whom he eventually marries. That Singer and others wrote often of extramarital sex in Jewish families indicates that all was not well with the ideal set forth in the Talmud. In a story about that ideal, Singer wrote of a childless wife who was urged repeatedly by neighbors to divorce her husband but who refused because of her love for him. He in turn tells her tenderly that "Were I sure I could sire the twelve tribes of Israel with another, I still would not leave you. I cannot even imagine myself with another woman. You are the jewel of my crown."[18]

To judge from biblical warnings against contentious wives, strife in Jewish marriages was an issue long before the Talmud. Men in Yiddish fiction often are portrayed as accepting marriage without enthusiasm, as something desired by God. While many shtetl husbands must have been petty tyrants, others lived in fear of the power that wives had to destroy peace in the home. The eighteenth century philosopher Solomon Maimon of Poland, who abandoned his wife and children, wrote that he was not only under the slipper of his wife, but also under the lash of his mother-in-law.[19] Some of the power of Jewish women in eighteenth- and nineteenth-century shtetlach is reflected in Yiddish sayings: "If the wife wears the fur cap, her husband wears the house slippers" and "If the wife wears the pants, her husband must rock the cradle."[20] One young husband pleaded for peace in a Yiddish folk song, "Why, Why Do You Pout and Frown?" begging his wife not to be angry. "Speak to me, my dear young wife, what have I done wrong?" Concluding his plea, he asks that she sit beside him, eat, and "let me kiss you, dear."[21]

The ideal wife honored in the book of Proverbs, the woman of energy, force, and entrepreneurial and managerial skills, often was a reality in eastern Europe. As two anthropologists of the shtetl, Mark Zborowski and Elizabeth Herzog, put it: "The economic area is more nearly an extension of the woman's domain than of the man's. To bustle about in search for livelihood is merely another form of bustling about managing a home."[22] Jewish women talked often about how busy they were and of how much was expected of them. "Everything lies on my head!" But Zborowski and Herzog write that it would be wrong to infer that they were asking to have tasks taken from them. Rather, such a statement was a kind of a boast: "See all I can do—and secondarily, don't I deserve great credit for it?"[23] Three Yiddish words described the bustling, highly competent married woman of the shtetl: *balbatisheh* (a woman of responsibility and consequence), *berrieh* (a woman of tremendous competence, who gets things done well), and *baleboosteh* (an excellent household manager).

They did dozens of things, almost at once it seemed, these miracle women. They washed clothes and children, ironed, gardened, shopped, suckled and rocked infants, baked, cooked, and kept stalls in the marketplace; and they worried about pogroms and their children's health. In some families, the wives, not surprisingly, made important decisions for the family as a whole. Sholom Aleichem wrote a fictional account of a woman who picked out husbands for her daughters, arranged their marriages, and examined her sons-in-law for knowledge of Torah.[24] Young and robust when they married, the women of the shtetl often were haggard before they were forty. When the burdens of poverty were too great, some of them were driven to defy even pious husbands. I. B. Singer wrote of such a woman, who calls her husband, Reb Moses, "a murderer," because he would not compromise his piety in order to earn more money,[25] a theme that would recur with greater frequency in the immigrant generation in the United States. There were other ways a wife made her anger known: not eating, not sleeping with her husband, or—the opposite of nagging and the greatest punishment of all—withdrawing into hostile silence.

While Jewish wives had enormous responsibilities and influence in the household, their formal status was subordinate to that of their spouses. Although they may have been competent in business and in the language of the marketplace, hardly ever were they significant figures in the Jewish community. The husbands, at least, were called "Reb," while wives might be referred to by men at the synagogue as "Samuel's Rebekah" or "Isaac's wife." According to Sol Gittleman, who has written of the late-nineteenth-century Yiddish writers as presenting the Jewish family in crisis, "The woman worked alongside the male, frequently bitter at her state, cursing her life if she became depressed enough, often venting her anger and frustration on her husband."[26]

Sholom Aleichem wrote about conflict between husband and wife often, as in "The Purim Feast," in which the central theme is a dominating wife who tells her husband: "If God saw fit to put more brains into my little toe than your whole head, I'm not to blame."[27] Golde, the wife in Aleichem's Tevye stories (the basis of the popular *Fiddler on the Roof*) was also a complainer, particularly about the poverty that afflicted her life with Tevye and their children. It was only after Tevye put thirty-seven rubles on the table and told Golde that he had been given a milk cow that she felt she had become the wife of someone who could justifiably be called "Reb" Tevye. Yet an early-seventeenth-century ethical work called "A Good Heart," written in Yiddish, which was read widely in Poland and in Germanic and Slavonic lands and went through at least nineteen editions in less than one hundred years, urged wives never to be contrary to their husbands but to "do everything he tells you" in order to win his everlasting love and have him "serve you with joy."[28]

Conflicts between husbands and wives about finances often were exacerbated by tension between parents and children. Although Tevye adores each of his five daughters, three of whom are brought into conflict with him by the new ideas that penetrated many shtetlach in the 1870s. As Gittleman writes of Tevye: "All of his Jewish education and values have not prepared him to deal with his daughters' increasing awareness of the outside world."[29] One daughter does not want to accept an arranged marriage. Another, who can write in both Yiddish and Russian, falls in love with a Jewish socialist and announces her betrothal without prior approval from her father; later she moves to be with her beloved in exile in Siberia. A third daughter falls in love with a Gentile intellectual. The shtetl had a Yiddish proverb for the afflictions felt by Tevye: "Small children won't let you sleep, big children won't let you live,"[30] a variation of the Yiddish proverb "Small children, small problems; big children, big problems."

By the time of the beginning of the great eastern European Jewish migrations to the United States in the 1880s, many shtetl marriages probably were based on romantic love, although that was not yet the norm. The old system of arrangements through a matchmaker had come under heavy attack from the writers of the *haskalah*.[31] Historian ChaeRan Y. Freeze, taking advantage of recently released government records in the former Soviet Union, has shown that the divorce rate among Jews in Imperial Russia, especially in the 1860s and 1870s, was much higher than had previously been thought.[32] From her study of the records on divorce and her examination of rabbinic *responsa* literature, it is clear that the family cohesion for which Jews had been known for more than fifteen hundred years had begun to erode. A major factor in its decline was that traditional religious learning no longer had nearly universal prestige, which eroded the religious basis for Jewish patriarchy.[33] There occurred a gradual undermining of Jewish communal leaders, including the Jewish courts, which had held formidable judicial power over civil and criminal suits and were usually headed by the rabbi, courts that had been asked to make decisions on everything from whether a chicken with a broken bone was kosher to whether a woman whose husband was missing could have permission to remarry.[34]

The decline of strict religious controls meant greater freedom for women at the very time that secular opportunities were opening for them. There was an expansion of women's secondary schools in the second half of the nineteenth century, and many Jewish women, coming from a culture that valued education highly, took advantage of secular education, some of them even running away to gain it.[35] In St. Petersburg, Jewish auditors in the women's medical courses comprised more than 20 percent of the admissions, quite disproportionate to their numbers in the population as a whole. One woman who sought a degree in dentistry was accused by her husband of being capricious. She argued back with what sounds like the language of the 1960s in the United

States: "My striving for development and self reliance met with desperate opposition from my husband, and I decided to study dentistry in order to [satisfy] my thirst for knowledge and to be able to support myself and my children in the event of a divorce."[36]

Many Jewish women took advantage of a law passed in 1864 that made secular judges more accessible to them. The following year, in Odessa, 149 Jewish divorces were recorded in state courts.[37] The records of those courts in the 1860s and 1870s reveal that petitioners in divorce cases had disputes over monetary matters, adultery, childlessness, relations with in-laws, insanity, religious conversion, and psychological and even physical abuse.[38] Physical abuse of wives was still an ugly, reprehensible transgression at a time when it was taken for granted by many Poles, Ukrainians, and Russians, but it is impossible to know how many wives suffered from it without bringing charges.

There was trouble with the Jewish family model. The protections of the *ketubah* did not always work in cases of divorce, as when a divorcing woman found that her husband had already squandered her dowry or had actually fled. Moses Leib Lilienblum, born in 1843 in Lithuania, told how his laborer father divorced his first wife without providing the usually required settlement because she had stayed at the house of a Gentile without a chaperon. Moses was a good example of the intellectual, emotional, and spiritual uncertainty that afflicted a growing number of Jews in the mid- and late nineteenth century. He abandoned the Talmud taught to him with devotion by his grandfather, sought answers in the rationalism of the *haskalah*, and, after repudiating that, turned socialist and then Zionist. In his autobiography, Lilienblum projects his own confusion onto the younger generation: "All the younger generation is fleeing [from Judaism], but they do not know where to."[40]

Pauline Wengeroff, whose father had been deeply immersed in Talmud, wrote with anxiety about the new ideas and their impact on family life. Her husband, a businessman, no longer spent time studying with the rebbe. After they moved to St. Petersburg, she took off her wig and even gave up her kosher kitchen. In Minsk she felt that modern schools estranged her children from Judaism. Jewish children distanced themselves from their parents: "in their eagerness to knock down everything old, assert their individuality, and test everything present, the younger generation no longer had any boundaries."[41] Lilienblum and Wengeroff were not historians; they made broad, sweeping generalizations about the rebelliousness of youth, based in large measure on their personal experiences. But court records provide documentation of intergenerational strife in Jewish families: a son who was accused of tricking his illiterate father into signing a contract concerning the use of the father's land in 1853, another son who sued his father in 1849, and others.[42]

Marital discord and intergenerational strife almost certainly were not the norm for a large majority of Jewish families living in the shtetlach. According to Zborowski and Herzog, who interviewed 128 Jews and read 50 life histories of Jews who had grown up in shtetlach, the stories of these Jews were overwhelmingly positive about family life. They may have exaggerated good memories and downplayed bad ones, but their recollections represent at least a portion of the reality of Jewish family life in the shtetlach. Nearly all remembered Shabbat as a time of happiness. Frequently recollected was "father in a silken caftan and velvet skull cap, mother in black silk and pearls, the glow of candles, the waves of peace and joy, the glad sense that it is good to be a Jew."[43] The father at the Shabbat meal and during the evening and the next day must have been an impressive and respected figure in many Jewish families. He led in the blessings on Friday night and went with friends to the synagogue afterward and again on Saturday morning. On Shabbat afternoon, after a nap and a glass of tea, he often examined his sons to see how they were progressing as students.

The Shabbat was also the time of the wife, who was the center of an enormous amount of activity and preparation for the most joyous day of the week. If friends or relatives dropped by on a Saturday afternoon, she probably had cookies or cakes ready for them. Her role in lighting the candles on Friday night could acquire something of the ministering qualities of a priestess of the home. "Honor the Lord with light," urged the prophet Isaiah (Isa. 24:15). Perhaps the Pharisees, who are credited with making mandatory the kindling of the Shabbat lights, wanted to emphasize the importance of women in family life by assigning this special mitzvah to them. Probably no single religious act has had as powerful a hold on the imagination of Jews in emphasizing the importance of family as the lighting of the candles by women each Shabbat eve. In drawing the holiness that rises from the flames, the shtetl wife represented the entire family. Immediately following her prayer, her husband usually sang or spoke the traditional poem of praise of Jewish wives from Proverbs, chapter 31.

Although most Jews may have remembered the Shabbat as a time of dignity and peace, that peace was often was tested during the rest of the week. As Freeze points out, many quarrels arose over financial matters. Some women, like Golde, resented their husbands for not being able to make a living. Not to have a new cap for the child, a pot for the chicken, or a chicken for the pot was a hard price to pay for a husband's piety and scholarship or, as in Tevye's case, pseudoscholarship. Many Jewish women and their families lived in a single room with a few chairs, a couch, a table, some beds, and improvised racks for dishes. The homes of the poor often had no floors, and some even lacked chimneys, the smoke escaping through a hole in the roof. These poor Jewish women did not need their husbands' permission under Jewish law, as did the enlightened, wealthy non-Jewish women of western Europe, to set up their own bank accounts; but even though they usually administered what little money the family had, the amounts were so small that there were no bank accounts.

Whether or not they worked for income outside the home, the vast majority of shtetl women undoubtedly thought that their first responsibility was to their children and husbands and to the laws that governed *kashruth*, the Shabbat and the festivals. Many wives, according to stories about the shtetl, strove to excel in cooking and household management because they knew that nothing would please their husbands as much or add more luster to their own reputations. Some took pleasure in helping their husbands deepen their commitment to Torah. Peretz wrote of a woman whose greatest joy was to observe her husband at prayer in the synagogue or to watch him with a charity box in one hand and a brass-knobbed stick in the other, asking the villagers to contribute to some good cause.[44] Even some wives who were described as shrews looked to the creature comforts of their husbands. Did he have the largest portion, the best piece of meat (if there was meat), and the only remaining bed? After cursing her husband and throwing boots at him, one wife set a lovely table and brought out her husband's favorite food and a bottle of wine. Peretz described a woman who kept cursing her husband for his mistakes until the moment he appeared to be ill. Then she threatened to faint and screamed "My husband! My treasure!"[45]

The accounts of men and women who grew up in the shtetl, like the representations of wives and husbands in Yiddish fiction and the records from divorce cases, can give only snapshots of what life was really like. Perhaps some Jewish men, even in talmudic times, acted as though they had done their wives a favor by marrying them, giving praise on Friday night by rote without conviction. Probably many Jewish husbands in the shtetl took little interest in the thoughts and opinions of their wives and took their hard work for granted.[46] As the century wore on, a growing number of women appeared to resent their subordination and what Mary Antin would later call "the pious burden of wifehood."[47] Like others among a growing number of young women in eastern Europe in the late nineteenth century, she felt there was something fundamentally wrong with assigning the intellectual world, so highly esteemed in Jewish culture, only to males.

Boys could begin to read the sixty-three tractates of the Talmud even before their bar mitzvah. Girls often received a year or two of instruction in reading and writing Yiddish. They may have learned to recite but not usually to translate Hebrew prayers and to read only a Yiddish version of the Pentateuch. Peretz wrote about one such woman, who refused to bake challah in preparation for a festival and ran away to live among Gentiles. Later she came back to tell her brother: "You locked away the beauty, the love, the high, terribly high and noble things in your lives! You kept that for your men-folk only! From us who wanted life, who struggled, with all our youth, with our flesh and blood to experience life, you asked only cakes, golden *challah*, baked with saffron."[48]

Like Peretz and Sholom Aleichem, I. B. Singer wrote of women who resented being shut off from the very thing that gave a Jew the highest esteem in a Jewish community. In Singer's story about Yentl, Reb To-dros, bedridden for many years, studied Torah with his daughter, an only child, as if she were a son. He told Yentl to lock the doors and drape the windows while they read Pentateuch, Mishnah, Gemara, and the Midrash. Yentl was brilliant. She had, the father said, "the soul of a man." So she grew up like a man, pretended she was one, and, as might be expected in a Singer story, came to a horrible end because the natural order of things had been defied.[49]

Yiddish was in its nature a revolutionary language, a language of the plain people, women and men; but it was especially a women's language, since women were not expected to learn Hebrew. Women who later wrote in Yiddish frequently spoke of their struggle to find a voice that was equal to that of men. In Yiddish short stories written by women from 1927 to 1986, mostly in the United States, the feminist perspective prevails. In some stories there are women who are miserable at the prospect of marrying and having sexual relations with men they do not know. In others a young woman's helplessness against parental authority is the theme.[50] Perhaps these writers imposed an American view on a world that most of them did not experience firsthand. Even Mary Antin wrote in the United States, where she experienced most of her young womanhood. But she remembered well how in her hometown of Polotzk her father hated her poetry. "A Jewish daughter must not make rhymes," he said.[51] After he burned her poetry one morning, the little girl frightened her father into an apology by saying that she wanted to die. Although he was filled with remorse, she decided to leave for America. She knew that there was no future for her intellectual ambitions in their village of Polotzk, and her mother, who believed in her talent, encouraged her to leave.

Assigned to an intellectually inferior role, it is likely that thousands of Jewish women felt disparaged. Did many women secretly wish to be men or at least to be able to study Torah as they did? Did some of them feel demeaned because there was no female equivalent for the *bris* or bar mitzvah as there would be later in the United States? Did any of them feel stigmatized during the days of menstruation, when their husbands were not allowed to touch them or certain objects that they had touched? Did women resent not having the opportunity to attend the yeshiva? Did they envy their husbands, who each morning in the process of dressing, just before putting on the phylacteries and the *tallit*, recited the ancient prayer of the Orthodox prayer book written by Rabbi Meir, "Blessed art thou, O Lord, our God, king of the universe, who hast not made me a woman!"

It is impossible to know the answers to the questions, since we have no reliable historical record of how most women felt on these matters through the eighteenth century. Mary Antin described going to the *mikvah* in matter-of-fact terms. In her town it was a social activity for the women, as well as a place where rituals were performed. The young girls who visited the *mikvah*, according to Mary, were treated "like heroes returned from victory" when they came home to extra pieces of cake to eat with their tea. The young bride who went to the *mikvah* the night before the wedding was accompanied by her sisters and other women, who admired and caressed her hair before shaving it and covering her head with a satin handkerchief. They said prayers to let the sun shine in her life and, at the very least, to bring her children, preferably a son.[52] That was the main point of life still—to raise children in Torah. Some women may have thought that the *mikvah* was a sign of their inferiority, and some may have rebelled against it, perhaps thinking it to be a ritualistic nuisance that could not be defended rationally.

Mary was not the only daughter of Polotzk to rebel against the old ways. The beautiful daughter of a rabbi showed her magnificent black curls like a maiden, even after marriage, and without censure from her father or mother. Another woman defied one of the rules of modesty. Although she kept kosher, visited the *mikvah*, and otherwise tried to keep many of the rituals of the Orthodox, she often was seen shaking hands with men and looking them straight in the eye. She spoke Russian, as Mary put it, "like a gentile" and even kept a dog. Some middle-class young women carved out positions of public leadership in the Jewish community, notwithstanding the widespread prejudice against it. Puah Rakowski, a Zionist leader who was born in Bialystock in 1865, read modern Hebrew literature at fifteen and even studied Gemara. She married at seventeen but after five years left her husband, taking her two small children; she completed her education and became teacher-principal of a girls' Hebrew school in Warsaw. The school, known as "Puah Rakowski's First Hebrew School," had a large enrollment of mainly middle-class girls, who learned from Puah about Zionism. Rakowski, who died in Haifa in 1955, also recruited a group of active women to create a separate women's committee of the Jewish National Fund. "It was high time, I told them, for us to stop being errand girls for our male comrades."[54]

The achievements of Rakowski and others were possible only because of the vast changes sweeping Jewish life in the major cities of the east. In the shtetlach, most husbands and wives did not think much about Zionism. Their overriding obligation was to care for the children. It was a task that they were supposed to undertake as a team. The child's moral and religious training was up to them, not to the school, the grandparents, or the neighbors. It was a calamity for children not to give respect to their parents. Zborowski and Herzog tell of a man recalling his childhood, saying, "No sooner did we see the adults than we would stop fighting, because no matter how angry you are, you still retain *derekh eretz* for an adult." Often the children spoke of mother and father as if they were one person. A neighbor might scold a child who had done something wrong, saying: "Your Mammeh-Tatteh will be upset," or give praise to a child who deserved it: "How proud will be your Mammeh-Tatteh!" It was common for children in the shtetlach who wanted to play house to exclaim: "Come, let us play Mammeh-Tatteh!"[55] According to Maurice Samuel, some children also lied, skipped passages in prayers, and did not obey their parents, at least not always. But Samuel also observes that the children saw their poor fathers at home taking time from the struggle to earn a living to read a little Talmud or to rehearse the week's portion of the Pentateuch. As Samuel writes, "Boys were learning in *cheder* what their fathers knew and cherished."[56]

CHAPTER 9

IMMIGRANTS AND THEIR

CHILDREN, 1880–1920

THE ASSAULT OF MODERNITY ON TRADITION WITHIN JEWISH FAMILIES CONTINUED AT AN ACCELERATED PACE FOR IMMIGRANT JEWS to the United States at the turn of the century. It was in America—a vast, relatively open land of abundant natural resources seeking human capital—that the idea of individual freedom found deep, rich, nourishing soil. The Declaration of Independence spoke of God-given rights for all. Abigail Adams reminded her husband, John, that women had rights, too. He had better not forget "the ladies" because, she told him, all men would be tyrants if not checked.

It would take another two hundred years for women's rights to become firmly established in the American constitutional system; but by the time the Constitution was written, American young women had more freedom than their counterparts anywhere else in the world. Unchaperoned dates, freedom to travel, marriage based on free choice, and freedom to speak one's mind were becoming the norm for young women in what the Europeans were beginning to call "a woman's country." It was a large exaggeration. New male bonding systems based on competition and camaraderie in business, the professions, and politics virtually excluded women. Men controlled property, politics, and the law, even in matters of divorce and child custody, despite Mrs. Adams's admonition.

Yet the idea of freedom in the American environment was irrepressible.

It led to Thomas Jefferson's extravagant assertion that each generation should consider itself "as a distinct nation, with a right, by the will of its majority, to bind themselves, but none to bind the succeeding generation." Jefferson's repudiation of prescriptive authority would have shocked the Puritan governors of New England and the plantation cavaliers of his own Virginia 150 years earlier, but even then strong forces were pushing children to defy parental authority. In 1657 the Reverend Ezekial Rogers wrote that he found "greatest trouble and grief about the rising generation. Young people . . . strengthen one another in evil by example and by counsel." Then, in a lament familiar to parents of each succeeding generation, he complained: "Much ado have I with my own family." By the early eighteenth century many parents complained of difficulty in controlling children. The influential preacher Jonathan Edwards observed in his home city of Northampton, Massachusetts, that parents were permitting their children amusements, visiting, and late hours on the grounds that children of others were permitted excesses. Children began to challenge the privileges of older siblings, and open warfare between them became commonplace. Judge Samuel Sewell complained in his diary in 1692 that his son threw a brass knob and hit his sister on the forehead so as to make it bleed and swell.

Seventeenth- and eighteenth-century parents wondered what they could do about the younger generation. A seventeenth-century plaint went: "What little hope of a happy generation after us, when many among us scarcely know how to keep their children managed!" By the early nineteenth century at least three dozen foreign visitors had made comments comparable to the remarks of one who said that it was not to be wondered at that "boys assume the air of full-grown cockscombs . . . when most parents make it a principle never to check [them]." With horror he observed boys from well-to-do families shouting and swearing in the public streets. Visitors usually found parental indulgence to be responsible for the unkempt behavior of children. They were shocked to see even young girls convulsed in anger at their parents without being reproved. Faces went dirty and hair uncombed.[1]

Of colonial and family history the nearly two million Jews who came to the United States between 1880 and 1920 knew little. But they also wanted freedom—freedom from poverty and pogroms—and America was their best chance. Many had already broken with the Orthodoxy of their forebears. Constrained by anti-Semitic restrictions limiting their admission even to high schools, most simply wanted a better life in a country where they would be free to practice their religion and to make a living, too. When violent mobs attacked Jews in twenty-two cities and towns in 1881 and 1882, they began to talk incessantly of emigration. The news from America came to them in a steady stream. Letters told of mirrors that reached from floor to ceiling, buttons and switches on a wall that lit up a room at a touch, and water that came out of a pipe with a handle that was attached to the wall itself. In America—this was hardest to believe of all—there were Jewish policemen. Businessmen talked of it over their accounts; market women discussed it from their stalls; tailors, seamstresses, milkmen and bakers saved for the journey; and even children played at emigrating. On they came, mostly between 1899 and 1914, when nearly 1.5 million arrived from Latvia, Lithuania, Poland, the Austro-Hungarian Empire, Ukraine, and Russia.

Almost a quarter of a million Jews were living in the United States in 1880, of Sephardic, Polish, Dutch, English, Hungarian, and especially German ancestry. The Germans often had begun as peddlers in cities and rural areas and even on the frontier earlier in the century, and many of their children and grandchildren had become highly successful merchants in the western states and territories and in the South, as well as in the East. By 1880 they were known for strong, cohesive families and for philanthropy.[2] Although German Jews were subject to widespread social prejudice and economic discrimination in the United States, they lived in safety and, for the most part, in relative prosperity. These American-born Jews, already established in Philadelphia, Cincinnati, New York, Baltimore, Charleston, San Francisco, and other cities, watched with a mixture of sympathy and anxiety as the new immigrants—those overwhelmingly poor newcomers from eastern Europe, many of the men with long beards and side curls, and wives who were virtually illiterate—now shaped the image most Americans held of Jews.

The nation to which the immigrants came had evolved a modern middle-class system of patriarchy. The earliest seventeenth- and eighteenth-century European immigrants to America found a sparsely settled land that in a short period of time encouraged even third and fourth sons to believe they could own some of that land and make it pay, especially when helped by wives and children. By the early nineteenth century, the big man, the American mensch, especially in growing towns and cities, was the high achiever and the good provider, the man who made money and spent it on his family. Unmarried women were, as already mentioned, much more independent than young women in Europe; but once married, wives were economically dependent on their husbands, whose preoccupation with succeeding at work outside the home led to the doctrine of the two spheres in which wives took major responsibility for the moral training of their children.

Although the American dream applied to both sexes, the roles of men and women in pursuing it were different. Whereas men were expected to compete with other men in making a living and spending their rewards generously on their wives and children when they could afford to, women were to realize it by marrying such men and by excelling at what historians later called "the cult of domesticity." But as historians Nancy Cott, Carl Degler, and others have pointed out, the American situation was different from that in Europe. In the United States, women gained new recognition and power within the home and, to a considerable extent, modified the patriarchal power of men in family affairs. There were exceptions in relations between husbands and wives to the modern patriarchal paradigm, and there were elements of it that could be found in Europe in the nineteenth century, but it prevailed among American middle-class families as nowhere else.[3]

The idea that men could achieve status and wealth beyond that of their fathers captivated the young among the poor and especially, perhaps, the immigrant poor, who were taught it by their peers and by American schools, newspapers, books, and magazines. Never before had immigrants, including Jews, lived in a country that so highly valued personal achievement and the money that it brought. Exceptions to the general rule could be found, particularly among religious communities such as the Hutterites, Old Order Amish, Mormons, and other more traditional Christians. But when looked at from a cross-cultural perspective—Latin Catholic, Hindu, Chinese, Muslim, Buddhist, eastern European, or even northern European—Americans had developed a secular patriarchy in which males controlled its politics, economics, and property, while rewarding wives with material comfort to the best of their ability and praising them as the moral guardians of family life.

Because so many of the Jewish immigrant fathers at the turn of the twentieth century were extremely poor, they became preoccupied with making a living. Anti-Semitism did not keep Jewish immigrants from seeing that there were possibilities for their sons in a nation where Jews could own land, vote, sometimes attend the most prestigious colleges and universities, and even be elected to public office. The way out of the dark, gray, four-, five-, or six-story buildings in which their families lived, described by one resident in a Yiddish story as "unfriendly as a prison," was to earn money.[4] There was reason enough to want get out. The tenements of New York, Buffalo, Chicago, Philadelphia, Detroit, Baltimore, and Boston were not healthy places for children. The rays of the sun and the circulation of air were blocked by outside walls pressed against each other. Inside, the hallways and rooms were stifling hot in summer and biting cold in winter. The smell was a special tenement house odor, a mixture of infant and children smells, garlic, fruits and vegetables, fish, tobacco, and chicken. Not infrequently, four apartments on a floor would house five or six families and several additional male and female boarders, all perhaps sharing a bathroom down the hall. They lived in small, boxlike rooms with faded wallpaper whose grease stains did not show in the semidarkness.

Outside was the street, which the writer Michael Gold said never slept, a street where women screamed, dogs barked, babies cried, and people pushed. Above was "a tenement canyon hung with fire escapes, bed clothing and faces. Always these faces at the tenement windows." The sound of the street, he said, was like the blast of a great carnival.[5] Probably no one has depicted the seamier side of poverty in New York's Jewish East Side more vividly than Gold. Food riots, evictions, men suddenly thrown out of work, pimps, gamblers, and prostitutes cross his pages, along with devoted Jewish mothers, pious fathers, and ambitious sons. A high-minded Yankee observer, William Dean Howells, said that his first impression of the tenements was "of their loathsome-ness." Tenement life, he thought, was a kind of squalor that "could not be possible to outrival anywhere in the life one commonly calls civil-ized." But Howells was amazed to find that the Jewish children to whom he spoke not only seemed intelligent, but most of them could speak English, while their elders knew only Yiddish. It was indecent, he thought, that whole families lived together in one room, but it was astounding that the death rate among them was one of the lowest in the city.[6]

Poverty took its toll—tuberculosis, diphtheria, and hungry children were common—but poverty did not destroy the hopes of most Jewish immigrants for a better life for their children and grandchildren, any more than it does for most poor immigrants today. The carnival of street noise that Gold described was mostly the sound of people strug-gling, working, and planning to beat poverty, move to a better apart-ment, or save a few pennies for the theater, a book, or lessons for their children. There were signs of the possibility of change. Abraham Cahan, socialist editor of the popular Yiddish newspaper *The Daily For-ward*, wrote in his autobiographical novel, *The Rise of David Levinsky*, that on his first day in America David saw poor men wearing stiff col-lars and neckties and women wearing hats or bonnets. He sensed the possibilities of change for the better, even as he watched a mother and her two little boys being evicted from their apartment while their furni-ture was being taken out of the house. In his European village, the chairs and the couch he saw on the sidewalk would have been a sign of prosperity.[7]

Change was an imperative in the United States in a way that it had never been in Europe. Although the Talmud-based ideal of a patriarchal mensch had undergone considerable change for many Jews in Europe, poverty itself did not keep a serious Torah scholar from being thought of as a mensch by the community in which he lived. In the United States, poverty was a curse, not just because desperately poor children might die of tuberculosis, as awful as that was, but because fathers who were terribly poor could easily be disregarded as failures. The Torah ideal called on eastern European fathers to study and to teach, nurture, and discipline their children, although, as seen earlier, the ideal was often far from reality; the American ideal called for fathers to make money to provide their wives and children with ever increasing comfort.

The search for upward mobility did not mean the elimination of the Jewish patriarchal paradigm altogether. Great paradigms, like great heresies, do not disappear entirely, even in several generations. German-American and Sephardic-American Jews had been writing ethical wills for generations before the great eastern European migrations, and continued to do so, wills that emphasized the typical themes of reverence for mothers, respect for wives, modesty, and compassion toward all in need.[8] But these American Jewish fathers, already largely successful in American terms, made many concessions to modern American culture. Most men had long since shaved their beards, and most American Jewish families prior to the emigration of the eastern European Jews did not even observe Shabbat. In Reform synagogues, women and men sat together, and organ music was played.

Harry Golden and others have written that on the Lower East Side many new immigrant families tried to retain religious practices in the face of enormous pressures to abandon them.[9] Hutchins Hapgood reported that Orthodox boys were still taken to the *cheder* by their fathers and that the old custom of a father giving his boy a taste of honey before he began to learn the first letter of the alphabet was commonplace.[10] In many immigrant households no one sat down to the dinner table until the father came home from work, and no one would say anything until he did. Many fathers were still strict, some of them to the point of psychological abuse, and, according to Golden, "[m]any a boy said he would rather submit to a whipping than suffer 'The Look' from his father."[11]

Some American Jewish writers told much later of fathers who commanded patriarchal respect. When father Herzog of Saul Bellow's novel *Herzog* is beaten up by hoodlums and the children in the kitchen see that he is hurt, Herzog says that it was more than he could bear that anyone should lay violent hands on him—"a father, a sacred being, a king."[12] Such feelings probably were unusual, but in the fictional (semiautobiographical) *The Island Within*, Ludwig Lewisohn writes of Arthur Levy as having a special kind of reverence for his father that would not allow him to feel "kindly, tolerant and amused," as his Gentile wife did toward her father.[13] Herbert Gold also described his father as a towering presence in Gold's autobiographical *Fathers*. When Gold's father, who had long since abandoned Torah study, took his boys to the Russian baths on the Lower East Side, in another form of male bonding, the eleven-year-old felt exalted. "What a joy to exclude women . . . from the naked and spreading world of the baths . . . I was my father's son, his eldest."[14]

Mary Antin, who resented her father's unwillingness to countenance her literary aspirations, wrote with some admiration of how he took her and her siblings to school on their first day. "He would not have delegated that mission to the President of the United States," she said. She and her siblings stood around the teacher's desk while their father, "in his impossible English, gave us over in her charge, with some broken word of his hopes for us that his swelling heart could no longer contain."[15] Mary Antin's father faced the typical patriarchal dilemma in America. He had come to the country so that his children could lead better lives. Then he turned them over to the authority of the school, the settlement house, and the streets, in what were their first encounters with America's powerful marketplace culture.

At the other extreme from Herzog's father were those who, having failed in American terms, completely lost the respect of their children. Reb Smolinsky, in Anzia Yerzierska's renowned autobiographical novel *The Bread Givers*, is one such father. He remains devoted to the study of Torah but earns no money and provides nothing for his family. Losing their respect, he becomes frantically insistent on his position as a patriarch, saying to his wife at one point: "Woman! Stay in your place! You're smart enough to bargain with the fish peddler. But I'm the head of the family."[16] Although he was a Torah scholar, his children would not support him as he aged. "Has a father no rights? . . . Why should children think only of themselves? Here I give my whole life . . . to spread the light of the holy Torah. Don't my children owe me at least a living?"[17] The man who aspired to become his son-in-law warned him that in America everyone has to earn his own living. "You got two hands and two feet. Why don't you go to work?"[18] Reb Smolinsky's inability to provide for his second wife in a way that she expected led her to cry: "All I ask of you is to be a man like other men. Pay the rent. Give me bread. Buy me a decent dress. I married to better myself."[19]

Henry Roth wrote about another embittered father in his brilliant autobiographical novel *Call It Sleep*. The Austrian-born Albert Schearl, who was probably a near-sociopath before he came to the United States, feeling that he was an utter failure within it—neither a Torah scholar nor a success on American terms—becomes brutal toward his wife and son.[20] Roth later wrote of his own father as going "completely berserk . . . he would beat the hell out of me."[21] The failure to succeed on American terms often undermined what authority a father might have had in the old country as an observant and pious Jew. An extreme case is depicted in Bud Schulberg's *What Makes Sammy Run?* When Sammy Glick, a youngster who loves to make money and hates Hebrew school, angers his father by handling money on Shabbat, the boy screams at him: "You big dope!" The father begins to pray and looks as if he had a stroke.[22]

The vast majority of Jewish fathers, whether they studied and practiced Torah or not, must have been much warmer, kinder, and more thoughtful than Smolinsky and Schearl and their sons more respectful than Sammy. But those who sought to observe Torah ran the risk of failing as American husbands and fathers under the new patriarchal system. How crazy it was, explained a man at the synagogue, that he could not offer David Levinsky, a Torah scholar, a night's rest, even though the Talmud says that hospitality is one of the greatest joys. His wife, he explained, kept insisting that he, the old man, "must make a living here." In Russia he had studied Torah all day while his wife had a nice little business selling feed for horses, happy to be married to a man of learning. In America women did not support men who sat and read books. Now, he could no longer slip into a synagogue on an afternoon to read a page or two for fear of being caught. "She has become a different woman here. Alas! America is a topsy-turvy country."[23] "For it was the wrong time," wrote Harry Roskolenko in one of the many autobiographical explorations of the East Side ghetto, "for a man of half skills who preferred God to the making of money to be in the United States of America."[24]

It was difficult to balance a life of piety with success in business, both requiring a considerable amount of attention and time. One religious scholar, Isaac Jacobson, did not want to become a peddler in the streets, as thousands of others were doing during the depression of 1893; nor would he let his wife open a store as she wished, something he might have encouraged her to do in the old country. Jacobson's daughter Miriam later wrote that he was too proud to do work that he might have found and too timid to find out what he would have liked. So he taught Hebrew in his home on East Fourth Street, never leaving its protective environment to test himself in the great American competition for success. It was Jacobson's good fortune that his wife understood his humiliation and insisted that the four working children give their household contributions to their father rather than to her, as they probably would have done in the shtetl.[25]

According to historian Jonathan Sarna, no work better depicts Orthodox Jewish life among early eastern European immigrants to New York or lays out the contours of the struggle between tradition and change from the traditionalists' point of view than Moses Weinberger's *Jews and Judaism in New York* (1888). Weinberger, who arrived from Hungary in 1880 at the age of twenty-six, remained a staunchly Orthodox rabbi who praised Jews for resisting Americanization. For him, progress meant founding a haven for Talmud study and the strengthening of ritual observance. He warned religious Jews in Europe to stay home. America was no place for the truly pious. Democracy and the separation of church and state and especially American individualism undermined religious authority at every turn. Preoccupied with the strength of synagogues, Jewish charitable institutions, Jewish education, religious functionaries, and Jewish bookstores, Weinberger says nothing about women or children in family relationships. His list of charitable organizations includes the Hebrew Orphan Asylum, the Ladies' Lying-In Relief Society, the Deborah Nursery, and the Gates of Hope Ladies' Benevolent Association; but there is no discussion of women at all, let alone as wives and mothers.[26]

Many immigrant fathers felt tremendous pressure to get ahead, at least to escape from poverty, and that might mean abandoning Shabbat and other aspects of Torah. To maintain love for Torah at the expense of becoming a good provider might mean becoming a failure in the eyes of one's wife, children, or more Americanized coreligionists. Jacobson did not let his wife open a store in America because that would have been a *shanda* (disgrace), letting one's wife support him. Later, in 1903, the Educational Alliance, established by German-American Jews in 1889 to help the newcomers adapt to American ways, issued a Yiddish-language guidebook that told them that Americans treated women with respect by not burdening them with work outside the home. It warned that if Russian Jewish husbands were idle while their wives worked for pay, American courts could compel the men to find jobs. Husbands had a "duty" to support their families.[27] The pressure was on men to make money. Never had there been such possibilities for its use. It could bring a brother, sister, or even more distant relative from the old country. Money squirreled away in mattresses provided insurance against illness and other calamities, such as factory accidents and fires. In America, money made money, which of course was a ticket to status in the gentile world. A Jewish dollar, an Irish dollar, and even a Yankee dollar were equal when Jews paid their dues to Tammany Hall or when a Jewish landlord bribed a building inspector or paid tuition for his son at Columbia University. It was the American way.

The pursuit of money was an important factor in the breakdown of the old patriarchal system. In a Charles Angoff semiautobiographical novel of Jewish immigrant life in Boston, one of the main characters, Moshe Polansky, observes that once a Jew works on the holy Sabbath, he becomes more tolerant of other practices not sanctioned by Torah, including shaving. After trimming his beard, he cursed Columbus for discovering America.[28] David Levinsky first puts aside his phylacteries, then shaves his beard, and finally abandons the Shabbat. Why not? The terrors that his mother and teachers had told him would take place if he became a disbeliever did not materialize. Besides, hard work sometimes paid off handsomely in America, as it did in David's case. But men often came home exhausted, with little energy left for Torah or family.

The presser of cloaks, standing on varicose veins, pushed a ten-pound pressing iron, sweating and coughing. Hapgood wrote that there were "few more pathetic sights" than to see an old man who might have been a Talmud scholar in the old country "carrying or pressing piles of coats in the melancholy sweat shop or standing for sixteen hours a day by his pushcart in one of the dozen crowded streets of the ghetto."[29] Thousands of tailors, with fingers stiffened from working in poorly heated buildings in winter, went from factory to factory looking for piecework.

As historian Thomas Kessner has written, tailors dominated the occupational landscape among Jewish skilled workers, three quarters of whom made garments produced by the clothing trades, New York's principal industry.[30] Many tailors aspired to become manufacturers and investors in real estate. Some succeeded, and by 1905 a growing white-collar class among the immigrant Jews included insurance salesmen, real estate agents, and salesclerks.[31] Through hard work and with the income from unmarried children and sometimes wives, families were able to climb out of the meanest kind of poverty.[32] Of the one thousand Jews who had applied for help in 1894 from the United Hebrew Charities in New York, only sixty-seven required assistance five years later and only twenty-three in 1904.[33]

Although the goal of most immigrant Jewish men was to adapt to the American way of not having wives work, many of them, unlike Jacobson, accepted their dependance on income earned by their wives. But they preferred that the women do their work at home. Some wives became peddlers, as they did in the old country, but more did piecework at home and/or took in boarders. Immigrants, as historian Susan Glenn says, came to think of wives working outside the home "as a source of embarrassment, just as Americans did."[34]

Because the burden of earning a living in America fell overwhelmingly on men and because their authority as patriarchal Torah scholars often eroded quickly, most immigrant mothers took on increasing authority within the home, even more than was the case in Europe. It was common in America for Jewish husbands to turn over their wages to their wives, who became cashiers, taking the money once a week, giving back a fixed sum to the husband, and managing the rest by paying the rent and the insurance in addition to buying food and clothing and giving the children allowances for carfare and lunches.[35] According to the compiler of one short book of memoirs based on interviews with the children of turn-of-the-century Jewish immigrants, they said repeatedly: "My mother ran the family."[36]

Charles Angoff wrote of his grandmother, "alte Bobbe," who "was the great encourager and comforter, the one who never failed anybody."[37] Even in immigrant families that did not keep Shabbat, the Friday night meal was anticipated by a frenzy of cleaning, washing of clothes, and cooking by the mother. In almost every home, even the irreligious ones, there would appear on Friday night the traditional gefilte fish on lettuce leaves, red horseradish, sour pickles, chopped liver, and challah fresh from the bakery or the kitchen oven.

From the kitchen, mothers provided a steady stream of advice to husbands as well as children, issuing warnings, perhaps threats, and even commands. Alfred Kazin wrote in his autobiography, *A Walker in the City*, that "the kitchen was the great machine that set our lives running; it whirred down a little only on Saturdays and holy days. From my mother's kitchen, I gained my first picture of life as a . . . starkly lit workshop redolent with Jewish cooking, crowded with women in housedresses, strewn with fashion magazines, patterns, dress material, spools of thread."[38] What mattered most to the family was in the kitchen—pots and pans, the samovar for tea around which the family sometimes talked late into the evening, the candles for Shabbat, perhaps a huge stove with a water boiler over it, a tub to be used for washing clothes and for the weekly bath before Shabbat if the family did not attend the public baths, and a sewing machine. The kitchen probably also held most of the *pushkes*, the little tin boxes with openings for nickels and pennies, kept for charity, now more likely to be opened by the mother than by the father.

That women should be in charge of dispensing family charity was consistent with the subtle shift that took place in the acculturation of Jews to American life. In the United States, women were the principal guardians of religion and good works. The German Jewish press in the middle of the nineteenth century often expressed the idea of women's importance in maintaining Jewish religion and culture. As historian Paula Hyman has written, many Jewish women leaders accepted the American idea of "true womanhood," which assumed that women were naturally more spiritual than men. As Hyman writes, it became the duty of women "to realize the potential of the home as a sacred sphere for the transmission of Judaism."[39] The synagogue could be left to the men, but in many homes the women assumed the largest share of responsibility for promoting a religious life and transmitting Jewish cultural values, including the celebration of Jewish holidays. Jewish men would compete in the world of commerce and civic affairs and take leadership positions in the synagogue, but Jewish knowledge and identity was to be communicated mostly by mothers.[40] It also was usually the mothers who talked to teachers and librarians and settlement workers. They organized their children to earn what pennies and nickels they could selling papers, delivering rolls, or doing piecework. When illness came, women took command, since men were considered to be relatively helpless about such things.

Most immigrant women probably assumed that child rearing and home management were their most important responsibilities, and many undoubtedly took pleasure when they were complimented for performing them well. But some young women rebelled against the roles assigned to married women by the American patriarchal system, just as they did against the Torah's patriarchal paradigm. The *Jewish Ladies' Home Journal* printed an article that called for an end to patriarchy.[41] Cries for change also appeared from time to time in women's letters to Abraham Cahan, the editor of the *Jewish Daily Forward*, seeking his comments in the "Bintel Brief" (Package of Letters) column, inaugurated in 1906. One woman wrote that she took care of her children and her husband, but she was young and wanted to go to school two nights a week. Although her husband claimed to be a socialist and to believe in the emancipation of women, he was furious at her for wanting to attend school.[42] In his reply, Cahan advised that it was her absolute right to attend school and scolded the man for wanting to keep his wife enslaved; but Cahan's views, like this woman's, were exceptional.[43] He was sympathetic to such women and put a women's page into the paper that included a considerable amount of information on politics, the labor movement, and the international women's movement.[44]

How many Jewish immigrant mothers read about politics or were active in some aspect of it is impossible to say. Most mothers focused on helping their families break out of poverty and in some cases, keeping their families together. As had been true in eastern Europe, poverty was probably the major cause of stress between husbands and wives. There probably never had been a time in Jewish history when there was as large a flight from fatherhood as in immigrant families in the first decade of the twentieth century. In the early editions of the *Forward* there were numerous letters of complaint from women who were not being supported by their husbands or—the greatest horror of all—who had been deserted by them.

The deserted wife had been a rarity in Jewish history until the nineteenth century in Europe. Now, in America, it was common enough that the *Forward* ran a regular feature seeking husbands who had deserted their wives, and the Jewish Information Agency of New York set up a bureau to find them. Historians of eastern European immigrant life in Baltimore and Buffalo have written of women left alone, unable to support their children.[45] One deserted wife wrote to the editor of the *Forward* in 1908 to plead with her husband, Max. Writing that she had been loyal and loving, she wondered: "Have you ever asked yourself why you left us? Max, where is your conscience. . . . You lived with me for six years, during which time I bore you four children. . . . Who will bring them up? Who will support us? Have you no pity for your own flesh and blood? Consider what you are doing. My tears choke me and I cannot write any more."[46]

An abandoned wife often meant abandoned children, who were at risk for getting into all kinds of trouble. For a short time on the Lower East Side and in other cities, the Jewish experience confirmed what Irish, black, and other families already knew: the combination of poverty and fatherless homes breeds trouble for children. Prostitution flourished for a short period of time on the Bowery and especially on Allen Street. For every girl who got into trouble, many more boys did.

Some of them became well-known gangsters with colorful names such as "Greasy Thumb" Guzik and "Sammy Purple" Cohen.[49] Much later, Larry King, the popular TV talk show host in the 1990s, said that in his group the gangster Lepke Buchalter (eventually executed at Sing Sing in 1944) had been a hero.[48]

The Jews, assisted to a considerable extent by those of German descent who were in a position to help the newcomers, set up a panoply of charitable organizations—homes for the aged, hospitals for the ill, orphan asylums, free loan associations, and even homes for young prostitutes. They established settlement houses for young boys and girls to get them off the streets, including the aforementioned Educational Alliance in New York, the so-called Palace of Immigrants, which became an after-school school for youngsters, a social hall, a library, a religious center, a bath house, and an athletic facility. In the Educational Alliance, youngsters could take classes in virtually every academic subject, play a variety of sports, and put on theater productions.[49]

It is impossible to calculate just how important such institutions were in preventing serious delinquency, but it was in the Educational Alliance that Benny Leonard, Ruby Goldstein, and Barney Ross learned to box, and Leonard Baskin, Chaim Gross, and Ben Shahn learned to paint. There were a half dozen settlement houses in New York and several in other major cities, utilizing volunteers, sometimes poets, artists, and writers, to help the children of immigrants become socialized and acculturated to American ways.[50] There were debating, ethical, and literary clubs, and for those who could afford to continue their education and were qualified, there was the miracle of City College, with its free tuition, and New York University and Columbia University, with scholarships for the bright and needy.

As important as these institutions were in the education of youngsters, they had tremendous competition from peer group gangs and clubs that spawned on the Lower East Side and other areas of immigrant settlement. These clubs and gangs were introductions to American-style male bonding systems: camaraderie and competition in an all-male world of sports, taunting, and fighting, from which most would eventually graduate to other male bonding systems at work. Daniel Bell, one of the most influential American intellectuals of the mid-twentieth century, has described the turf wars of his street gang on the Lower East Side. Jews, Italians, Ukrainians, and Poles—each group had its own neighborhood, but whenever they went roller skating, they risked being attacked by a rival gang and having their skates taken away. Even those boys who did not belong to gangs sometimes competed in unsavory activities. Another outstanding sociologist, Irving Louis Horowitz, has told of how he and his buddy Eddie Jefferson set off fire alarms so that they could sneak into the movies or how he would steal a dime from his father to pay his way in.[51]

Girls could be found in the streets, too—small groups of them, running errands, gossiping, bringing books back from the library, or playing at jacks or skipping rope. But they usually did not venture far from Mother's watchful eye. They were needed to set tables, wash vegetables, and help with laundry. They had more freedom in America than their female ancestors ever had, but they usually dared not do the wild, crazy things done by their brothers, such as walking around the edges of roofs, diving into the East River, or hitching onto streetcars. Bella Spewak, who later became a highly successful journalist, screen writer, and coauthor (with her husband) of the books for several musical comedies, tells in her memoir, *Streets*, of joining a group of girls on Columbia Street who were called "toughs" when she was in fourth grade (1908–1909). The toughs were girls who played with the boys, filched money from their mothers' handkerchief knots, and went for walks on the Williamsburg Bridge.[52]

It was extremely difficult for parents to keep an eye on such children, a job that fell overwhelmingly to mothers or older children, as the Bella Spewak memoir, among others, describes. It was particularly difficult for non-English-speaking parents to maintain their authority, especially in the case of the Jews, where the old system of patriarchy fell so far when it collided with the new one. Young boys and girls gained power within the family by being able to make money selling rolls or newspapers or even dancing in the streets. Sometimes an adolescent son earned more money than his Papa and, as in Sammy Glick's home, asserted his right to speak down to his father.[53] Another major factor that often undermined the authority of the father was that he looked and talked like an immigrant Jew. Even if his beard had been taken off, he spoke with an accent and gestured with Jewish mannerisms and probably had a Jewish-looking face. Clearly, he was not an American in a cultural sense. Only the children had a chance to become Americans that way.

Parents often depended on children to interpret America for them. Such dependence meant, as Mary Antin wrote, that she began "to make my father and mother, as truly as they had ever made me." In America, she asked, "Did I not become the parent and they the children, in those relations of teacher and learner?" A new Yiddish proverb emerged on the East Side: "In America the children bring up the parents."[54] It was not that the children were more precocious than they were in the Old Country, where a seven-year-old sister might act almost as a mother to a baby brother, or a boy at four or five might have begun to study scriptures. But in the shtetlach, aggressive, irreverent behavior was not usually permitted. Now parents often felt obliged to make one concession after another to their children. What if the children flew kites or rode on roller skates? Would it kill them? Did it make them bad? So what if Sammy plays a little cards. Gambling, I'm sure he doesn't. Running around with bad boys? He wouldn't do that.

As closely as immigrant mothers tried to watch their children, they were deceiving themselves if they thought they knew everything that was going on. Kate Simon writes that she and her brother kept dozens of little secrets from their parents. Mothers lived in hope for *nachas* and told exaggerated stories of good sons and dutiful daughters with high grades and other achievements. But in America, the obedience of one's children could not be counted on nearly as much as in the shtetl because, among other reasons, fathers could not be counted on to discipline them. In America, according to Simon, "We children rarely connected with the men, the voices that filled our world were those of women, the Mothers."[55]

There are many accounts of immigrant fathers made despondent by their impotence in dealing with American children. Irving Howe wrote about the poignant and anguished chasm between the generations, citing Lincoln Steffens's observation on passing a synagogue of several boys sitting on the steps outside smoking cigarettes while their fathers "with high hats, uncut beards, and temple curls [were] going into the synagogue, tearing their hair and rending their garments." One son of an immigrant, Howe tells us, reported what thousands of them must have felt—a disturbing, even miserable feeling "that our folks were just nobodys."[56] One of Jerome Weidman's stories tells about an immigrant father who sat alone in the dark, staring straight ahead of him, not quarreling or remonstrating, but simply staring, silently.[57]

In trying to fill the authority gap, as American mothers often have, these immigrant mothers set the guidelines, made decisions, and implored their children to be good. Perhaps their authority was more credible because it did not depend so much on a position of status or power outside the family as it did for their husbands. Irving Louis Horowitz writes of his father, for whom he had little respect, that "he unloaded all of his frustration, sorrow, and inability to make good in the New World onto me."[58] But even mothers lost authority because they were old fashioned in a world of constant change. "I had other ideas about her happiness," said Dora about her daughter in *The Rise of David Levinsky*, "but I am only a mother and was not even born in this country. So what does my opinion amount to?"[59]

In Meyer Levin's novel of Jewish life in Chicago, *The Old Bunch*, Mrs. Greenstein complains that she slaves night and day to make silk dresses for her daughter. After twenty-two years in America, life was still strange to Mrs. Greenstein. No longer frightened of pogroms, she was afraid of the very thing that America offered its young—freedom. When her daughter Estelle cut her hair in the 1920s fashion, it was seen as an omen of worse things to come. Now, God forbid, she might marry a goy or become a whore. How could Mrs. Greenstein talk to her daughter rationally about her fears without seeming to be a neurotic, possessive, old-fashioned woman? To speak of sex was out of the question. She couldn't even think of the English words, "while in Yiddish you always felt you were talking up, not down to your children."[60]

Parents spoke of their children with great pride as *gantze Yenkis* (100 percent Americans) when they won prizes in school or were praised by the local policeman. But what parents wanted was that their children should be 100 percent Americans and proud of being Jewish, too. That was more likely to happen in a smaller community or town outside the big cities, as in Savannah, Georgia, or Burlington, Vermont. But even in Savannah, where mothers kept kosher homes, most Jewish business-men opened their shops on Shabbat because they felt they could not af-ford to close them.[61] In Burlington there was a cohesive Jewish immi-grant community where families also commonly observed kosher rules. But even in that Yiddish-speaking community, compromises were made, and after synagogue worship on a Saturday morning children might be given a few coins to go to the movies.

Parents wanted their children to be happy and to have some free-dom. But freedom often led to disobedience and even trouble. One un-happy man wrote to the *Forward* that he ran a small stationery store that he had to watch all the time. His two little girls, ages ten and thir-teen, were running around the streets with small boys who gave them candy, chocolate, and peanuts. They were even seen to sneak into hall-ways, where they laughed coarsely and were overheard agreeing to meet with the boys in the evening at Hester Street Park. Pleading for advice, he wrote, "I cannot keep them in the house; and so I can find no way out. . . . What is to be done, Dear Editor?"[62]

Such unsupervised children were an American phenomenon. One of them, Leo Dugovka, appears in *Call It Sleep*. He lives with his single mother without any parental supervision. It was nothing for him to roller-skate to Greenwich Village to play with a gang of tough Irish boys. For such boys, the streets became their first home. Some immi-grant parents spoke of them as "Amerikane kinder, Amerikane kinder"!—as if nothing could be done to redeem them. "A curse on them!" muttered Rabbi Yidel Pankower, the Hebrew teacher of eight-year-old David Shearle in *Call It Sleep*. He hated these children, the "sidewalk and gutter generation." He knew them for what they were, he thought, "[b]razen, selfish, unbridled." Where, he wanted to know, "was piety in observance? Where was learning, adoration of parents, deference to the old?"[63]

Except for a diminishing number of Orthodox boys, the old inter-generational male bonding system of Torah study was passing. The bar mitzvah, which used to signal the formal entrance into advanced talmudic learning, often became a major social affair for the benefit of parents as much as for their sons. Even Orthodox bar mitzvah boys might stop studying and refuse to put on the tefillin (phylacteries) for daily prayers following the bar mitzvah. One boy told his teacher irreverently that since his four brothers did not put straps on their heads and arms, he was not about to do so either.[64]

The new systems of male bonding were American, suitable for a culture in which manhood is not accepted at the age of thirteen by a commitment to perform Commandments but by graduating from high school and getting a full-time job that produces a paycheck. Immigrant parents knew that success would be likely for children who did well in school. The pressure to achieve began in elementary school. America offered a free education. What could be better? Education, wrote Mary Antin, "was the one thing that [my father] was able to promise us—surer, safer than bread or shelter."[65]

But Alfred Kazin did not associate elementary schoolwork with learning, only with the necessity to succeed, "to get ahead of the others in the daily struggle to make a good impression on our teachers." He tells of the endless series of tests—"surprise tests, daily tests, weekly tests, formal mid-term tests, final tests."[66] Parents could not provide much help in preparing the homework or in getting ready for tests, but the rewards for getting through were magnificent. It meant solid preparation for attending high school and perhaps going to college. In *The Adventures of Augie March* by Saul Bellow, Augie is reared by "Grandma" Lausch (actually a boarder in his home), who teaches him to be clean and mannerly but, above all, to go to college to become successful. "Just so you want!" she tells him. "Heaven and earth will be moved."[67] Immigrant mother Dora speaks proudly of her son Danny in *The Rise of David Levinsky*, exclaiming that he was always first or second in his college class and one of the best players on the football team, too.[68] Immigrant parents said, "Achieve, achieve."

When the philosopher Morris Raphael Cohen returned home to tell his mother that he had passed the entrance examination for college, tears flooded her eyes. She had promised her relatives that she would be a washerwoman and scrub floors if necessary so that her Morris could have a college education.[69] Jacob Riis, the journalist, wrote that "the poorest Hebrew knows . . . that knowledge is power, and power is the means for getting on in this world that has spurned him so long."[70] College meant at least an entry point into the male bonding systems of work, in which Jews would compete perhaps more successfully than any other immigrant group. By 1916 they constituted 13 percent of the enrollment at Columbia University, 21 percent at Fordham (a Catholic-sponsored school), 44 percent at Hunter (the free city college for women), and 73 percent at City College (Hunter's counterpart for males). The Industrial Commission found that the poorest of Jews, like Morris Cohen's mother, would make all kinds of sacrifices to keep their children in school.[71]

In some ways, many of these immigrant parents were giving their children up to America, as many of the Orthodox who remained in Europe feared would happen. But the point of the migration was that their children should succeed in America. "My father and mother worked in a rage to put us above their level," wrote Alfred Kazin. "We were the only conceivable end to all their striving; we were their America."[72] The teachers from whom parents expected so much and to whom children were urged to give the utmost respect, the Miss Reilys and Mr. Smiths who dominated the lives of the children through most of the day, probably edged them away from their parents' authority without always meaning to. Teachers seduced a particularly able Jewish child into the excitement of secular culture and literature. Norman Podhoretz told of his Protestant English teacher, who saw in his beautiful mind something apart from what the teacher perceived as his vulgar Jewish ways. How could the Hebrew instructor—who might be an egg salesman or barber or worker in a cigar store, teaching Hebrew on the side to earn a few dollars a month—or even the father compete against the all-American Mr. Smith or the beautiful Miss Reily?

When little David Shearle in *Call It Sleep* thought of his Hebrew teacher, he mused: "Tobacco reek. Sweat. Matted nostrils under red, speck-stripled nose. Moist drab gums of false teeth. Revolting." Jewish boys were not likely to draw back from the comely-looking, well-endowed blonde young ladies of twenty-six who taught poetry or civ-ics.[73] Besides, the teachers were the ones who would lead the children to success in American life. They, not the immigrant parents, knew what was best for their youngsters. As one male immigrant said in 1908, "The teachers were looked up to as if they were God, and the fact that they were not Jewish had nothing to do with it."[74]

The hardworking, aspiring young Jewish boys and girls found sym-pathetic teachers to encourage them. Imbued with a powerful intellec-tual tradition previously focused on Torah study for boys, a large num-ber of Jewish girls and boys brought that tradition to bear on their opportunity for secular education. Cahan remembered how pleased he was when the Gentile children and teacher in his class were surprised that he read well.[75] Morris Hillquit, who became a leading socialist pol-itician and labor leader, recalled that he liked the friendly atmosphere of the school and appreciated the sympathetic interest that teachers took in his progress.[76] But deeply pious parents sometimes regretted that they even had let their children go to a public high school. As one Or-thodox immigrant woman recalled: "Whatever we in the house said did not count. The teachers in the high school stole my girl's heart from me. The friends did the rest. We were ignorants, foreigners. She knew everything better."[77] But most parents felt that they had no choice. It was important to help their children become good Americans, to re-spect the teachers and librarians. They were proud when a story in the *New York Evening Post* of October 3, 1903, told of the admiration of Jewish children for the friendly librarians at the Chatham Square Branch of the Public Library. The girls gave them presents, wrote them letters of admiration, and ran errands for them in a gush of gratitude.[78]

The attraction of becoming an American for these youngsters was much deeper than the friendliness of this or that librarian or teacher. Despite anti-Semitism, the central aspects of the culture were easily ac-cessible to most of these immigrant children and even more so to their children and grandchildren: political freedom, economic opportunity, and the mass popular culture.[79] But in most immigrant homes the rush to Americanize did not break down Torah observance altogether. Many young children experienced firsthand some of the rituals and ceremonies that had sustained Jewish families for centuries: the *yahrzeit*, the observing of the anniversary of the death of one's parents; the chanting of the kaddish, a prayer for the dead spoken every day by males for eleven months following the death of a close relative; and the sitting of shivah, when survivors stayed at home for seven days after the death of a close relative and received neighbors, distant relatives, and friends who brought food and talked of the deceased and the tasks ahead.

With the romantic, benign nostalgia that often characterizes aging adults who do not want their children to repudiate the past altogether, American-born children of immigrants, who are now grandparents and great-grandparents, still speak of the Shabbat meal, challah and candles, and of their generous parents who sacrificed so much to help their children succeed. Typical is the comment in the memoir written by comedian Sam Levinson:

> As long as Papa was at the head of the table, we were made aware of the unity of body and soul . . . Friday night's dinner was a testimonial banquet to Papa. For that hour at least, he was no longer the oppressed victim of the sweatshops, the harassed, frightened and unsuccessful breadwinner, but the master to whom all heads bowed and upon whom all honor was bestowed. He was our father, our teacher, our wise man, our elder statesman, our tribal leader.[50]

Although many boys loved the Shabbat meal, it was difficult for them to see the attraction of the old adult male bonding system. Why, after his bar mitzvah, would an American boy of thirteen or fourteen want to go to the synagogue to pray with old, bearded men? What did that, or the shaven heads of women, have to do with God anyway, wondered Harry Roskolenko. "Why all this stupid separation? We were in America, free, with jobs. . . . I believed in myself—young, indestructible, combative, verging on atheism, suspecting all the appeals of Judaism."[81] Those boys who grew up in America sensed the inconsistency of their parents. They were told to study Torah but also to become Americans. They sensed the vulnerability of their parents in trying to have it both ways, parents who often seemed helpless in the face of the gargantuan power of American culture. Alfred Kazin wrote of his parents always discounting themselves, hoping for "a few condescending words of official praise from the principal at assembly" for their children, the very same principal who might invoke the word "Americanism" as an accusation of everything the immigrants culturally were not.[82] Harry Golden tells of the awe in which principals and teachers were held in the Jewish community. "How frightened our parents were when a teacher summoned them to school!"[83]

There were many ways to retreat or break from the traditional Jewish patriarchal paradigm for young men and women passing to adulthood in the first two decades of the century. Just as they had in the cities of Europe earlier, some became socialists or labor Zionists. But most of them embraced an idea of the good life that was more typically American. They worked hard, married young, and sought security in the American dollar—the passport to an apartment in the Bronx or Brooklyn (or its equivalent in a dozen other cities) and to venetian blinds, an automobile, summer camps for the children, fake fireplaces, and wall-to-wall carpeting.[84]

The parents realized that America was more than a thief. It was a whirring, pulsating factory of rewards for those who were bright, who hustled, and who knew its language and ways. They understood that there was a future for their children and for those who would come after them. Working, saving, planning became a way of life that they preached to their children. Whether a boy was paid for rolling empty milk cans, mixing soda at the drugstore, or peddling newspapers, his mother (less likely his father) would see that at least a portion of his income was saved. If they worked hard and saved, the children were told they could live somewhere better, perhaps even near a park with trees and flowers. A college education was out of the reach of most of the children of immigrants, but they could move up in other ways. New industries emerged to meet the incessant demands of American consumers for ready-to-wear clothes, furs, furniture, and hardware for home and automobile maintenance. In Hollywood and Tin Pan Alley, even more glamorous industries attracted entrepreneurial Jews whose Torah obligations were now largely ignored.

Most Jewish boys born in the United States whose parents had immigrated between 1880 and 1920 focused their adult energies on making a living in order to achieve clear objectives. They would escape the foreign, meager circumstances of their parents and marry an American type of girl who would cook Jewish food well and keep a fine, more or less Jewish home. Together they would give their children the college education that most of them had missed. The men would strive to be good providers who could also afford to participate in social, professional, and civic activities, where they could win status among other men and their wives. Most of the high achievers would compete in business and, in smaller numbers, the professions. The old patriarchal paradigm going back to talmudic times, already frayed in Europe in the eighteenth and nineteenth centuries, was being replaced by a new one in America in which most Jewish fathers would no longer teach Torah to their sons.

CHAPTER 10

THE AMERICANIZATION OF

FATHERS: 1920–1960

MOST OF THE AMERICAN-BORN CHILDREN OF JEWISH IMMIGRANTS EMBRACED THE DOMINANT VALUES AND BEHAVIORS OF the American middle class. They abandoned the patriarchy of most of their grandparents for the patriarchy of modern America. In the Jewish patriarchal paradigm, there was basically one male bonding system that mattered, and it was rigidly exclusive. In America there were many male bonding systems at work, war, sports, and politics—but they were not always exclusive, certainly not by the period 1920–1960. There were women doctors and lawyers in the United States, for example, although they were rare. Women could testify in court, serve on juries, and even be judges. They did not need a dowry to marry, they moved about and spoke freely, and they arranged their own marriages.

Most daughters born to immigrants in the United States embraced the relative freedom of American women. They also accepted the middle-class ideal that good providers make the best husbands. "Herschel has a good business," a prospective bride's mother might say. "He's quite a catch." A new husband-father ideal type emerged. Of course, a Jewish husband should not beat his wife, chase after other women, drink too much, or gamble. But it was not expected that he would be much of a Torah scholar, and it was often forgiven if he neglected the children because he was so busy making a living. The main thing, much more than ever before, was to be a good provider. There was honor in being a good provider, and it made one feel like a good American, too, a taxpayer, and someone who was capable of purchasing an American middle-class lifestyle for one's family. There was also the reward of success in whatever it was that one did—salesman, fur broker, accountant, or doctor. From success one gained recognition and approbation from one's colleagues even if it meant neglecting one's family. A doctor who practiced actively in the 1920s and early 1930s reported, probably with some exaggeration: "I wasn't a very good father because I was busy practicing medicine." He would rush to the hospital to deliver a baby regardless of the hour. "How can you pay attention to your family when you get up at 3:00 AM one day, then 5:00 AM the next, then 8:00 AM, and you are busy all day with *tsurris* [trouble]? You can't be a good father. Either you are a good doctor or a good father. You can't be both."[1]

Many Jewish businessmen felt the same way about the conflict between work and family, and it was to business that most sons of immigrants turned to make a living. Often excluded from major industries and commercial institutions, Jews could be found, in Henry L. Feingold's words, "as shoestring capitalists practicing free enterprise in the riskiest areas of the economy," as in the new film industry.[2] Many Jews working for others in the 1920s and 1930s looked for a chance to start a business on their own. Often unable to obtain credit at major banks, Jewish men borrowed from free loan societies, some of which were affiliated with religious congregations. Over a period of thirty years the Hebrew Free Loan Society (not religiously connected) provided about $15 million to 400,000 shoestring entrepreneurs or those seeking further education.[3] By 1937, still deep in the Depression, two thirds of the 34,000 factories and 104,000 wholesale and retail businesses in New York City (most of them quite small) were owned by Jews, far out of proportion to their numbers in the population.[4]

While most of the children of immigrants could not afford to complete college, the emphasis on education pushed Jews to enroll in colleges at rates unprecedented for new immigrant groups, as mentioned in chapter 9, and even in graduate and professional schools. The number of Jews who became doctors, dentists, lawyers, pharmacists, accountants, social workers, teachers, and civil servants rose during the 1920s and 1930s. In Cleveland in 1938, Jews, who were 8 percent of the city's population, were 21 percent of the physicians, 18 percent of the dentists, and 23 percent of the lawyers. By 1941 the proportion of Jews in the professions in the United States was double that for the population as a whole.[5] Of those who could manage to get through graduate or professional education, an increasing number were becoming lawyers rather than doctors because law school was much less expensive and discrimination was much more restrictive in medical schools. Having passed the bar, a Jewish man might eke out a bare living as a lawyer during the Depression, but at least his parents could speak of "my son, the attorney." The tremendous emphasis that Jewish parents still placed on education—now secular rather than religious—persisted in the face of continuing anti-Semitic discrimination in colleges and universities.

Parents did not give the same encouragement to daughters as to sons. Unmarried younger sisters often would be pressured to contribute to their older brothers' education, something that was commonly true among Gentiles, too. A trick was played on many of these American-born women. They all entered elementary school on an equal basis with boys for the first time in Jewish history, and most of them probably outperformed their brothers during their elementary and high school years. But after high school the education of girls usually ended abruptly, as if a signal had been given to cease all intellectual activity of the kind that might actually keep one from making a good match. (There were exceptions, girls who became significant scholars who also married.)

Most Jewish girls were encouraged to believe that what most Jewish boys wanted in a wife was a good homemaker and mother, talents not to be learned at Hunter College, the free city college of New York for women. Even the director of the Educational Alliance, which had been so eager to educate young girls, told the *New York Tribune* in August of 1903 that the attendance of Jewish girls at the Alliance (most of its 3,200 students were girls) did not signify disagreement with the view that the most important functions performed by women were in the home. Most young women who, when unmarried in the early 1920s, enjoyed unchaperoned public life at amusement parks and dance halls, knew, once married, that their main responsibility as American mothers aspiring to middle-class values and privileges would be almost entirely in the domestic sphere.

Coming from a culture that valued education so highly, many unmarried Jewish women flocked to night school and even sought university education. In 1910, when Jews made up approximately 19 percent of the population in New York City, 40 percent of the women enrolled in night school were Jewish. In 1925, Jewish women in Philadelphia constituted 70 percent of the night school students. By 1934, more than 50 percent of the female college students in New York were Jewish, although Jews were less than one third of the population.[6] Some women continued as teachers or social workers even after marriage. A few remained in important leadership positions in the trade union movement. But the vast majority of women left such positions after marriage. One daughter of immigrants, who had been in charge of girdles at a department store where she supervised eight people, remembered that she loved the responsibility. Her income enabled her to pay for her own vacation. After marriage and a baby, she had to stay home and take care of the child and the house, and she hated it.[7] The Herschels they married—the good catches—usually did not believe that proper middle-class women should work outside the home.[8] Jewish men wanted women who would be good homemakers and also moral custodians of Jewish family life. As asserted in one Jewish magazine in 1924, mothers were the only ones who "could plant in the child a deep and true love of his people."[9]

The good catches sought by desirable young females were not usually Torah scholars, unless they were Orthodox (less than 10 percent of the Jewish population). They were handsome, well-built young men with prospects. Such a man looked for a young woman who was physically attractive and whose parents might be able to help them get started as a couple. Most young women realized that flirtation was a part of the dating game, but they knew from their parents' icy stares and pronouncements that premarital sex was wrong for Jewish girls. From the same parents, usually the mother, they also heard how important it was to get married. Women over twenty-five became particularly desperate, hoping to be introduced to a friend of a friend, and in the 1930s departed for singles weekends at Jewish hotels in the Catskills "to meet a fella." Since the old Jewish fence rules dividing men from women had little meaning in the United States, they learned how to be independent American girls, the good girl–bad girl of American theater, the carefree, casual girl who knew how to play but also how to hold onto the prize of virginity. Later, the Kinsey reports would show low rates of premarital sexual intercourse and more sexual intercourse in marriage for American-born Jewish men and women, compared to that of Gentiles from the same socioeconomic backgrounds, possibly a link to the Torah's insistence that sex in marriage sanctifies desire.[10]

A newly married American-born wife and her husband wanted to set up their own home, usually in a rented apartment, just as quickly as possible. That was part of the American way, too. Then a husband who succeeded at work could buy his wife and children the accoutrements of success. They praised their children lavishly for good grades in school and for being successful at piano lessons and activities in summer camp. Sociologist Martha Wolfenstein wrote of the extent to which the American-born Jewish mother saw her home as a "launching platform," the place from which her children could take off for their own successful lives.[11] The shtetl mother had not run her home as a launching pad. The purpose of child rearing was not to equip a son or daughter to run a strong race on an endless, boundaryless track but to lead a Jewishly moral life, giving praise to God. Although immigrant-generation mothers and shtetl grandmothers had been busy household managers whose activity often placed them at the center of Jewish family life, their energy was not focused as sharply as that of the American-born Jewish mother and wife, who often prodded husband and children toward new accomplishments. Her status in the eyes of other women often depended on her having a generous, financially successful husband and children who brought *nachas.*

As husbands worked harder at making money, wives tended to take a more active role in Jewish community affairs. The wives often were joiners, club women who, when they were not busy negotiating with teachers or promoting romances for nieces and nephews, ran for office at Hadassah or other Jewish organizations and raised money for charity. In Lloyd Warner's well-known study of the social systems of American ethnic groups, the authors were surprised at the degree of civic leadership taken by second-generation Jewish women (defined by them to include those who had emigrated at age eighteen or under) in Newburyport, Massachusetts. In no other ethnic group could such activity be found. The Jewish women conducted charities in the United States as well as for Jews in Poland and Palestine, a harbinger of the extent to which philanthropy would become associated with Jewish activity in later decades for both men and women. The authors found that the women represented their families in the associational life of the Jews and also spoke for the Jewish community in such city-wide organizations as the Newburyport Health Center and the Newburyport City Community Welfare Board. Although the women established no credit cooperative of their own in Newburyport, women did so in many other cities in the 1920s.[12]

Even as they created and sustained charitable and communal organizations—orphan asylums, hospitals, homes for the aged, synagogue sisterhoods, and Zionist groups—Jewish wives, for the first time in history, took on the major share of supervising the religious education of their children. In most families, the mothers arranged for the children to attend Hebrew schools, checked on their performance, and saw to it that sons prepared for the bar mitzvah (and girls for the bat mitzvah after World War II).

Participation of wives in communal activities probably was approved by most American-born Jewish husbands as long as it did not interfere with their wives' having dinner on the table on time or result in neglect of the children. By encouraging their wives to participate in Jewish communal organizations, husbands hoped to encourage their children to identify as Jews. Precedents had long been set by Sephardi and Jewish women of German ancestry, who had founded organizations that performed *tzedakah* or other morally valuable functions. In 1893 a Jewish women's congress met for four days at the Chicago World's Fair, where they created the National Council of Jewish

Women. As Joyce Antler points out, the well-to-do German and Sephardi fathers of such women tended to give their daughters good educations and to take pride in their intellectual and organizational accomplishments.[13] They were active in the campaign to ratify the Eighteenth Amendment, granting women the right to vote, and in peace groups and other liberal organizations.

These women were different in many ways from the unmarried women of eastern European background encountered on the Lower East Side by Hutchins Hapgood. He described a certain type among eastern European Jewish women, taken by the ideals of socialism or fascinated by great literature, as "straightforward and intensely serious" young women, with traits that Hapgood thought were normally called "masculine."[14] Some of these women, as already indicated, kept up their commitments to civic, political, and intellectual activity after marriage, but most of them became too busy as mothers and wives to continue.

Such activity was not what most American-born Jewish husbands wanted in this period. Like most American middle-class husbands, they preferred wives whose dresses and hair styles would be up to date and who would serve a good meal to a boss or business partner or to his parents and carry on a pleasant conversation. Most of all, they wanted wives who would be good mothers, who would see to it that the children were healthy, well-behaved, successful in school, and at least somewhat Jewishly identified. The children wanted mothers who took care of them when they were sick, gave them money for candy, and extracted them from trouble at school but did not interfere with their freedom. It was Mom's job to exercise authority on a day-to-day basis, an increasingly difficult task given the hyperindividualism of American middle-class families.

A large majority of these mothers probably gave love and encouragement to their children, hoping that they would stay out of trouble, do reasonably well at school, and marry respectably.[15] They sought pleasure in the good behavior and achievements of their children, in the preparation of a meal well received, in maintaining clean and well-organized homes, in extended family and neighborhood relationships, and in their Jewish communal activities. They argued with their husbands, sometimes quarreled with their sisters, and, especially in the 1930s, worried about the family budget. But the majority functioned effectively without psychiatrists, antidepressant pills, or group therapy. They did not seem heroic to their own children, but such mothers often did a heroic job of raising children largely on their own. Some kept Shabbat. Many went to Friday night dinner at the homes of their parents, most of whom probably knew and acquiesced in the fact that the grandchildren played ball in the streets on Saturday morning.

Most of these women and their husbands, too, probably thought that to be a Jew it was enough to visit the parents periodically, attend the synagogues on the high holy days, celebrate Passover and perhaps Hanukkah, and pay for their sons' bar mitzvahs and Hebrew school lessons. It was difficult to find time for more Jewish observance than that and to go to baseball games and take vacations, too, while giving moral support to husbands who worked overtime to push ever harder toward success. Mothers wanted and perhaps expected recognition and gratitude for being good mothers, and sometimes they got it.

Many mothers encouraged their daughters to expect generous treatment from their husbands. It was a common pattern, according to sociologist Werner J. Cahnman, for mothers to train their daughters to look for men who were ambitious in the marketplace and capable of satisfying high material expectations.[16] Living vicariously through the success of daughters and sons to such a large extent later proved unsatisfying for many Jewish women. Their investment of enormous emotional energy in nurturing, motivating, and promoting their children led to the familiar caricature of the intrusive mothers found in so much American Jewish fiction. Herbert Gold tells, in his autobiographical *My Last Two Thousand Years*, of his mother trying to persuade him to attend college in Ohio, near home. Her recommendation was Western Reserve University, which, she told him, everyone knew was the best school in the country. "Murray's going, Stanley's going. You can have your own room at home," she promised. Also in stereotypical fashion, she adjusted to his decision to accept a scholarship at Columbia University in New York, not quite believing that they would award money to a

Jewish boy. When he finally left, his mother presented him with a package of food to take on the journey, including a jar of prunes, and Gold remarked in retrospect that "she feared anti-Semitism and constipation on the new Pennsylvania Turnpike."[17]

Despite the strings that sometimes were attached to their mothers' love, young boys usually could count on its constancy. Mothers took them shopping for new shoes or slacks, visited the teachers, made arrangements with the superintendent of the building to use an empty apartment for a party, repaired zippers, and leaned out the apartment window to call them up for dinner.

In speaking of his friends, young Bobby in S. J. Wilson's *Hurray for Me* says that he did not know all their fathers but he knew every one of their mothers. Because the center of Bobby's world was his mother, he was frightened one day when she could not walk him to school and his father was assigned as a substitute. He can't take me to school, thought Bobby. Only mothers do that. He wondered what he would talk to him about for two whole blocks. To his amazement, his father was recognized by the local tailor, barber, and policeman, who nodded to him.[18] But for American-born Jewish fathers, home often was an apartment to sleep in at night and leave in the morning. With those traditionally Jewish male tasks of moral guidance, practical instruction, and discipline for the children left almost entirely to mothers and schoolteachers in most middle-class families, the fathers of children's friends became shadowy figures seen on the margin of a youngsters' life. With what little energy was left over from work, dad might read the funnies to the kids, go to the movies with them or, when boys became of age, to the ball game. They might even play catch once in a while in the street or the playground. Several grandchildren of immigrants have written about the bond that baseball was between them and their American-born fathers, sometimes the most important one.[19]

In some families, not even baseball could connect fathers and sons. The classic fictional account of such a family appears in *Awake and Sing*, a play by Clifford Odets about a poor Jewish family struggling during the Depression in the Bronx, where the father, Myron Berger, is dependent on his son and daughter for financial support. He seems hardly ever to complete a sentence but merely repeats what his wife says. As he follows her off to bed, the son remarks, "Look at him draggin' after her like an old shoe." When her successful American businessman brother, Morty, comes to dinner, Bessie, the wife, prepares chopped liver and duck and exclaims in front of Myron that her son should be a success like the uncle. Myron pleads ineffectually with his son, "I'm not foreign-born. I'm an American, and yet I never got close to you. It's an American father's duty to be his son's friend." But Ralph, the son, retorts: "You never in your life had a thing to tell me."[20] At one point, Bessie sums up America from her perspective. Admonishing her son, she says: "Here, I'm not only the mother but also the father. First two years I worked in a stocking factory for six dollars while Myron Berger went to law school. If I didn't worry about the family, who would? . . . Without a dollar, you don't look the world in the eye. Talk from now until next year—this is life in America."[21] Jacob, the grandfather, points out: "In my day, the propaganda was for God. Now it's for success."[22] The anger of wives at husbands who do not succeed in America is reflected in a variety of ethnic-American literature. Maxine Hong Kingston, for example, tells in *Chinamen* of a woman who scolds her husband for being unemployed: "You piece of liver. You poet. You scholar. What's the use of a poet and scholar on the gold mountain?"[23]

European and Asian observers of American domestic life in the nineteenth and twentieth centuries often commented on the assertive, scolding behavior of American women. Coming from rigidly patriarchal cultures, they were quick to notice such things.[24] What they missed was how much wives' scolding had to do with their disappointments in the inability of their husbands to be more successful in providing for them and their children, compared to others they knew, a theme that recurs repeatedly in Jewish-American fiction. When Philip Roth wrote in the 1960s that his fictional Alexander Portnoy constantly saw his mother as "scolding, correcting, reproving, criticizing, fault-finding without end! filling the patriarchal vacuum!" he was referring to the weakness and passivity of his father at least as much as to her neurotic bossiness.[25] Driven by fears of failure, the father in this America Jewish family had lost his father-hood. Roth has Alexander observe that "in that ferocious and self-annihilating way in which so mary Jewish men of his generation served their families, my father served my mother, my sister, Hannah, but particularly me."[26]

Even good providers are not often presented as significant fathers in American Jewish fiction. They tend to be nonentities at home, like Mr. Patimkin in Roth's *Goodbye, Columbus*. A successful businessman who could afford to live in the suburbs, he was generous and indulgent with his children and wife, but his intellectual and physical energy centered on his business. It was at business in an unpretentious office, like so many occupied by successful Jewish small businessmen, that he came alive with orders, decisions, and arguments. There he was a force to be reckoned with. At home the children did not know him as a source of moral guidance or steady discipline. Summing up Mr. Patimkin's place in the family, his daughter's boyfriend, Neil Klugman, says: "In the entire house, I haven't seen one picture of Mr. Patimkin."[27]

Many American-born dads may have spoken more *about* their sons than *to* them. In Europe, until the late Middle Ages, many fathers would examine their sons at night or after returning from a journey by asking them what they had learned at *cheder* or how far they had come in the *Gemara*. The father would listen, perhaps correct the boy once or twice, and glow with happiness at each new intellectual achievement. A father praised his son's performance to other men at the synagogue, and it was understood that his intelligence and scholarship were a credit to his father. The same kind of boasting now took place in business districts of American cities by fathers who might not have known which subjects in school actually interested their sons most but who boasted freely that Sam was graduating third in his high school class or that Harry had been accepted at the University of Chicago.

For many American Jewish boys, the bar mitzvah signaled not the beginning of adulthood, the entrance into a sacred male bonding system, but the end of Hebrew lessons. Among the middle class the bar mitzvah increasingly became a family bash, a time to show off. Middle-class American-born Jewish parents made a huge party for what Herbert Gold called "a momentous lack of occasion."[28] It was not a total loss, as those who have read about such bar mitzvah parties know, since relatives and friends brought presents to the bar mitzvah boy in recognition of his ability to read Hebrew from a scroll and make a speech of thank you's almost by formula to his rabbi, parents, and friends. A fountain pen was a common gift, presumably because it was to be used someday in a stellar performance at high school, college, and beyond.

The significance of the bar mitzvah in an Orthodox family was still largely religious and was not usually the occasion for a major party; but the number of Orthodox Jews in America dwindled during the 1920s, 1930s, and 1940s. Until the movement of Orthodox Jews to the United States in the 1930s to escape Hitler and of survivors who came after the war, it looked as though Orthodoxy would ultimately embrace only a handful of congregations. But some Jews clung fast to Orthodoxy. Historian Deborah Dash Moore tells of Jewish families who preferred to stay in the crowded, steamy streets of the Lower East Side, close to their old synagogue, rather than move to quieter neighborhoods that did not seem Jewish enough. One man told of his family's abortive attempt to move to Brownsville in Brooklyn in 1929: "At night the street was deserted and quiet. Gentiles lived across the way; one had to walk two and three blocks to reach a store."[29] But Orthodox Jews could replicate the shtetl-like atmosphere in other neighborhoods, as shown by Solomon Poll in his study of the Hasidic community in Brooklyn's Williamsburg. Poll described a completely sex-segregated community with no televisions or radios, where the idea of a bat mitzvah seemed absurd and arranged marriages were the norm. Young boys were expected to become learned in Talmud, and divorce was almost nonexistent in this relatively insulated community.[30]

By 1941, probably more than 90 percent of all American Jews were either unaffiliated or associated with Reform or Conservative congregations, whose members broke from aspects of the old talmudic patriarchal system soon after the war by providing rituals for girls to match those of boys, the bat mitzvah for the bar mitzvah and the infant girl's naming ceremony for the *bris*, and later more sharply by ordaining female rabbis. Family seating replaced the sex-segregated system even before the war, in some Orthodox congregations in the South and West. Such changes were slight compared to the abandonment of Shabbat and regular synagogue attendance in non-Orthodox families. Yet the vast majority of American-born Jewish fathers and mothers wanted their children to remain Jews. A small minority sent them to Jewish day schools. A larger number participated in Zionist activities, and still more were active in Jewish philanthropies. For most of them in the growing middle class, raising their children with a Jewish identity meant having them attend Hebrew school to prepare for a bar mitzvah (perhaps for as little as a year), participating in cultural and athletic events at a Jewish community center, going to a predominantly Jewish summer camp, attending the synagogue on the high holy days, and sometimes having a Shabbat meal at the home of their grandparents.

Jews had found a country in which they could be involved with Judaism and Jewish communal life or not, to the extent that they wished. They had come to a society in which they could compete on reasonably fair terms with others, feel relatively free from the threat of violence, and interpret the meaning of their ancient heritage for themselves and to others. But abandonment of the old patriarchal system did not mean the end of patriarchy. That system produced one kind of father, the American system another. Generalizations about American-born Jewish middle-class fathers should not to be allowed to obscure the reality of differences among them, any more than generalizations about Jewish mothers should oversimplify their variety of personalities and behaviors in this or any period. The writer Letty Cottin Pogrebin's father tried to be both a Jewish and a modern patriarch. She writes that he pretended to be more observant than he was so that he could be a bigshot at the synagogue. At home he was an occasional playmate and constant source of instruction in all kinds of knowledge to Letty. But, as she writes about him, he was not a loving patriarch, Jewish or American.[31]

The generalization that seems least assailable is that by becoming hardworking achievers who increasingly met the measure of success established by American culture, Jewish men who grew to adulthood in this period adapted effectively to American-style patriarchy. It was only after World War II that many of the sons of these achievers, spurred in part by a feminist revolution, began to question American-style patriarchy, too.

CHAPTER 11

THE EROSION OF

PATRIARCHY, 1960–2000

IN THE LAST HALF OF THE TWENTIETH CENTURY, DRAMATIC NEW SOCIAL AND ECONOMIC CONDITIONS IN THE UNITED STATES PROPELLED AMERican Jews into the forefront of the movement to end patriarchy, but in the 1950s there were few signs of that development. Although increasingly economically successful and geographically mobile,[1] most adult Jews in the 1950s and 1960s were still far from being feminists.

In the 1950s many parents read to their children about the life of an idealized American Jewish family depicted in Sidney Taylor's *All-of-a-Kind*, a popular series of three books for Jewish children. Taylor presents a 1950s family that combines Jewish and American patriarchal ideals. The mama in these stories is always at home, patient, warm, and loving to her children and husband. She says a prayer over the Shabbat candles, and the children line up in front of the father to be blessed by him before the Shabbat meal. The father, a hardworking businessman, is able to move his family from the Lower East Side to a large apartment in the Bronx while fulfilling his major religious obligations. He loves his wife, and he tries to lighten her parental tasks. When the children become sick with scarlet fever, he shops for an entire week, and every Saturday night after Shabbat he helps his wife with the washing.[2] Although the six children, all girls, occasionally get into mischief, they show respect to their parents, as when they save pennies to buy Papa a birthday gift. When they require discipline, Mama and Papa act as one in delivering it, much as Zborowski and Herzog said that Jewish parents did in the shtetlach of Poland and Russia.

The Jewish family depicted in Sidney Taylor's books was not typical in regard to Jewish observance, even for the 1950s. In sociologist Marshall Sklare's study of Jewish life in the suburban town of "Lakeville," the average family observance of 11 practices used as indices of Jewishness was merely 2.8, compared to 5.2 for their parents, as recalled by interviewees. Only 10 percent observed 7 or more of the practices. Nineteen percent of the Jews observed none, including activities as important as lighting the candles on Friday night and fasting on Yom Kippur.[3] Although less religiously observant than the parents in Sidney Taylor's books, American Jews generally valued family connections and commitments, as several studies showed.[4] Up to the 1980s, marriage rates were high and divorce relatively infrequent, compared to those who identified themselves as white Protestants.[5] But the 1970s saw a huge outpouring of concern about the growing fragility of Jewish families.[6] Sidney Taylor's ideal Jewish family was becoming less common.

The rising anxiety of Jews about family life in the 1970s and 1980s occurred at the same time as the accelerating feminist attack on modern patriarchy, with a disproportionate number of Jewish women leading the charge. The 1990 National Population Survey of American Jews reported that nearly half of the Jewish women interviewed scored high on the feminism scale, compared to only 16 percent of non-Jewish women.[7] Moshe and Harriet Hartman, whose study of gender equality among Jews is based on data from that survey, correctly relate the rise of American Jewish feminism to the unusually strong appetite of American Jewish women for higher education. Coming from middle- and upper-middle-class families, they could afford it; coming from homes that valued education, they took advantage of the widening opportunities for women to obtain education.

Both Jewish men and women in 1990 had considerably more schooling than the white population as a whole, but the disparities for women were greater than for men. Only 18 percent of white American women had completed sixteen or more years of education, compared to nearly three times that many for Jewish women. More than five times as many women in the general white population completed less than twelve years of education. Three times the proportion of Jewish women had a B.A. or higher degree than non-Jewish white women. In professional education the gender gap was closing quickly for Jewish men and women in the thirty- to thirty-four-year-old group. By 1990, 43 percent of medical degrees granted to Jews and 40 percent of the law degrees in that group had gone to women.[8] Given their educational attainments, their effective use of contraception, and possibly their inheritance of a tradition of Jewish women who actively engaged in the marketplace, it is not surprising that married Jewish women had consistently higher rates of participation in the paid labor force than married women in the wider white U.S. population at all ages.[9] Somewhat more remarkable is that 20 percent had M.A.s and 8 percent Ph.D.s or professional degrees.[10]

Young Jewish women became professionals and managers, just as Jewish men had done a generation earlier. The 1990 National Jewish Population Survey showed that women under forty-five who had been born or raised as Jews were catching up to the men; 14 percent of them were in high status professions, compared to 22 percent of Jewish men; 14 percent of the women and 16 percent of the men held managerial positions. In the helping professions—psychotherapists, teachers, and social workers—Jewish women led Jewish men by 29 percent to 18 percent.[11]

Increasingly educated for careers, American Jewish women in the 1980s married later and had fewer children than did Protestants or Catholics.[12] A 1980 study of ninety-seven Jewish career women with three or more children showed that most of them were happy with their careers, a finding not necessarily inconsistent with the results of another study showing that Jewish mothers were more likely than non-Jews to stay at home when their children were of preschool age, interrupting their careers for a while.[13] Jewish women with young children were less likely than non-Jewish mothers to work full time, especially when children were between three and five years of age, a factor undoubtedly related to the high proportion of Jews in the middle and upper middle classes.[14] However, in a clear repudiation of the doctrine of the two separate spheres of responsibility for wives and husbands, a 1985 survey showed that only one of every three Jewish women believed that women who stay at home make better mothers than those who work outside it.[15]

That Jewish women were in the forefront of the assault on the American patriarchal system and its doctrine of the two spheres was consistent with the Jewish tradition of women as economic agents with economic rights, who often earned income to support their husbands and children. Clearly less Jewish than their grandmothers, as measured by ritual practice and other observance of Jewish laws, the granddaughters and great-granddaughters of Jewish women immigrants became leaders in the movement to break down the barriers that kept American women in general from moving into the professions, management, and business. These near descendants of the immigrant women who had organized rent strikes and meat boycotts continued in that tradition of public protest and agitation by Jewish women in the United States.[16] They also provided considerable leadership in advocating women's reproductive rights, as non-Orthodox women actively defended the right of women to choose to have an abortion, especially when the life or health of the mother was imperiled.

By the 1990s it appeared that most Jewish men were comfortable marrying women who wished to pursue careers of their own. Many of them took pride in the achievements of their daughters and wives in the educational and economic marketplaces of America. There was evidence that the more highly educated Jewish men were among those most likely to feel comfortable marrying such women. And in a 1980 study of ninety-seven Jewish career women with three or more children, the husbands most supportive of their wives' pursuing careers were married to women with M.A. and/or Ph.D. degrees. These women held relatively high-status and well-paying jobs, enabling them and their husbands to afford household help and perhaps in some cases to have more flexible work schedules than most in the paid labor force.[17]

There were several reasons that Jewish women (and perhaps men too) were disproportionately active in feminist causes. Higher education and middle-class status is certainly one of them. The tendency of Jewish parents to limit and space births is another. The disproportionate involvement of Jews in the civil rights movement and in liberal causes stressing the importance of equality in all relationships is a third. Jewishness, however attenuated and reconfigured in America, perhaps also played a part in their extraordinarily active leadership in egalitarian causes generally and in the feminist movement specifically. Only as they adapted to modern patriarchy in Europe and especially in America did Jews frown on women working outside the home. The traditional Jewish belief that women had economic and reproductive rights and that fathers could and should share responsibilities for nurturing, teaching, and representing their children (especially their sons) is clearly compatible with the modern feminist movement. Here was a case in which the historic religious and cultural inheritance of a small American minority, now largely secularized and active in wider politics, may have played a role in undermining the modern American patriarchal system.

The wider American culture, including the more secularized Jews, also had an effect on changing the relationships between Jewish women and men within traditional Judaism itself. It helped to stimulate an accelerated attack by Jewish women on the classical Jewish patriarchal model. The egalitarianism implicit in American culture pushed Judaism away from patriarchy farther than it did in Europe or anywhere else. American Protestantism, the dominant religious force in American history, had a long tradition of female religious ministers and teachers. In the seventeenth century, Anne Hutchinson had been banished from Massachusetts to Rhode Island for preaching like a man. But soon there were others to take her place. In subsequent decades women evangelists became common. Other women, like Christian Scientist Mary Baker Eddy, became founders of religious movements.

Pamela Nadell has shown how Jewish women in America pioneered as teachers of Judaism in Sunday school and supplementary schools in the nineteenth century, and how the coeducational emphasis in American education affected assimilating Jews, particularly in the new Reform congregations, some of which actually began the practice of confirmation of girls as well as boys. Cincinnati's Reform rabbi Isaac Mayer

Wise pushed for an expansion of women's role in the synagogue in the middle of the nineteenth century. Women joined the choir in his congregation, boys and girls were confirmed together, and girls read the Torah publicly in the synagogue. Other Reform rabbis and Jewish women took up the cause of gender equality within Judaism. New organizations, such as the National Council of Jewish Women and Hadassah, held forums on the role of women in American Judaism. After the turn of the century, with the formation of the American Jewish Congress and the American Jewish Committee, they played active roles in both organizations. In the 1920s several women agitated to become rabbis, but it was not until 1972 that the Reform Hebrew Union College ordained the first American woman rabbi.[18]

The Reconstructionist Rabbinical College included women from the time it opened in 1968, ordaining its first woman rabbi in 1974. The most important male bonding system in Jewish civilization had been breached; it did not take long for women to make up 40 percent of the entering classes of the Reform Hebrew Union College or for women to take over pulpits in Reform and Reconstructionist congregations. The pressure to produce women rabbis and cantors mounted steadily within the Conservative movement in the 1970s and 1980s. Its Rabbinical Assembly ruled in 1973 that women could be counted for a minyan, and ten years later nearly 60 percent of the Conservative congregations were calling women to read the Torah. Then, on October 24, 1983, by a vote of 34 to 8, the Assembly approved the ordination of women. In 1985 the first woman was ordained as a Conservative rabbi, and two years later the Conservative Jewish Theological Seminary graduated its first female cantor.[19]

In the last two decades of the century, women rabbis played a major role in transforming prayer books and creating new rituals to reflect the equality of women and men.[20] An increasing number of women became instructors in rabbinical schools and took leadership positions, particularly in the Reform and Reconstructionist colleges. The enthusiasm of Reform congregants for having women participate in religious life equally with men may have helped to spur a growth in adherents. Between 1970 and 1990 the number of Reform congregations grew from 700 to 950, while the number of Conservative congregations decreased from 850 to 800.[21]

Feminist pressures within Judaism also affected the Orthodox, whose numbers, while generally underestimated, dwindled from somewhere around 11 percent to 6 or 7 percent of all American Jews between 1970 and 1990, before beginning to rise again. In 1970 the study of Talmud by Orthodox women was unusual, but in the 1980s and 1990s many of them began to study rabbinic Judaism's classic texts. Women's prayer groups emerged in the *tefillah* (prayer) movement. A confederation of about twenty-five such groups emerged in the early 1990s. They sought out *halakhot* (laws) that were compatible with their feminism and also created new rituals and prayers. The bat mitzvah, virtually unheard of among the Orthodox in the early 1970s, had become the norm.[22] One feminist Orthodox leader, Blu Greenberg, asked in 1993: "Is now the time for Orthodox women rabbis?"[23] In 1997 an Orthodox Sephardic congregation in Berkeley, California, conducted its entire Rosh Hashannah and Yom Kippur services with men and women sitting together.[24] A growing but still small number of Orthodox Jews asked whether women could be counted to form a minyan.[25]

More than one thousand Orthodox feminists met in New York City in 1997 for the first international conference on Orthodoxy and feminism. Some came with heads uncovered and wore pants; others wore long skirts and wigs, including a few Hasidic women. When Professor Tamar Ross came to the podium, her female students rose to honor her in a way that generations of young male scholars had honored their teachers.[26] She was an example of Jewish women "entering the sacred realm," and making a considerable contribution to it.[27] In a volume edited jointly by a Conservative and an Orthodox scholar, the contributors relied on traditional texts to argue that women could and should have a much more active role within the framework of the law. One issue was how to interpret the freedom of women to perform those mitzvot from which women are exempt. The *Shulkhan Arukh* said that women were obligated to study only those laws that pertain to them. But many contemporary Orthodox women, and some men, argue that women can perform commandments on a voluntary basis, and some Orthodox women have begun to put on the tallit and the tefillin daily.

Judith Hauptman, associate professor of Talmud at the Conservative Jewish Theological Seminary, concludes that there are ample talmudic precedents regarding the role of women in religious life to sanction a flexible interpretation of law to accommodate such changes.[28] Support for that position comes from some Orthodox rabbis, too. Rabbi Avraham Weiss, a professor at Yeshiva University's Stern College for Women, finds classical rabbinic support for the proposition that women are not excluded from the public performance of Jewish ritual. He writes that the right of women to experience the holding, touching, and kissing of the Torah has a clear basis in *halakhah*.[29] Blu Greenberg goes beyond Weiss in arguing that there are precedents within the Jewish tradition for bringing women to a position of equality. As an Orthodox feminist, Greenberg asks why any of the Talmud should remain off limits for study by women when the Torah and Mishnah are not forbidden to them. She also challenges rabbinic scholars to search within halakhah, as did their predecessors, for solutions to blatant injustices against Orthodox Jewish women, most notably the requirement that a husband write and deliver a bill of divorce to his wife in order for a marriage to be terminated.[30]

Debate on the role of women in Orthodoxy was heightened in the 1990s when the great talmudic scholar Rav Yosef Dov Soloveitchik approved the teaching of Talmud to the young girls attending the Maimonides elementary and high schools in Boston under his jurisdiction and when the late charismatic Lubavitcher rebbe, Rabbi Schneerson, asserted that all women were capable of learning the oral law and could do so on a voluntary basis.[31] But other Orthodox rabbis, including Hasidim, believe that even women's prayer groups are prohibited.[32]

The issue of prayer groups was not nearly as controversial as the question of ordaining rabbis. Rabbi Norman Lamm, president of Yeshiva University, a progressive among the Orthodox in most matters, including prayer groups, approved of the admission of large numbers of Jewish women to the Yeshiva medical and law schools but would not allow their ordination as rabbis. Yeshiva University was ready to contribute to the erosion of American-style modern patriarchy, but it still defended the essentials of the classical rabbinic patriarchal paradigm. The other branches of Judaism disagreed. By the fall of 1992, about 280 women had been ordained as rabbis by Reform, Reconstructionist, and Conservative rabbinical seminaries.[33] But Orthodox girls still were not called to read the Torah in the synagogue on the day of the bat mitzvah, a position defended by Tamar Frankiel, a feminist who became Orthodox and who writes that she does not feel a need to be called to the Torah. Why would she want to do men's mitzvot, she asks. The major women of the Torah are more real than pagan goddesses, Frankiel writes; they are "great in their feminine spiritual achievements" without performing the *mitzvot* of men.[34]

Many modern Jewish women have chosen Orthodoxy, even with its prescribed differences between men and women in the sacred realm, because it meets their spiritual needs and, according to some of them, leads to a genuine partnership within the family. Interviews with 150 newly Orthodox women, 120 of whom had earned at least a bachelor's degree, find most of them arguing that adherence to the Torah enables them to control many aspects of their lives by being "able to make demands on men as husbands and fathers in ways they believe less possible in the secular world."[35] Child care was part of the daily responsibility of these men, even the lawyers and doctors. On Shabbat they took the older children to the synagogue and spent the entire day with their families, sometimes modifying their own work schedules or changing careers to do it; and almost three quarters of the women reported that their husbands did the big weekly grocery and meat shopping.[36] The enthusiasm of these women may be unrepresentative of Orthodox wives as a whole, particularly since this group appears to be relatively well off financially. Reports from other sources on wife abuse and desertion by Orthodox husbands indicate that some Orthodox marriages are far from satisfactory.[37]

Whether or not Orthodox Jewish men share in parental and domestic responsibilities more than other Jewish men of the same income and occupational backgrounds is an open question, since there are no data on the subject. But there is no doubt that the movement for gender equality has changed the lives of women and men in Orthodox communities. Three studies of Orthodox communities, published in 1962, 1972, and 1979, show just how rapid some of these changes have been. Solomon Poll's 1962 study of Williamsburg found that dating was unknown; marriages were arranged. In 1962 it was not expected that wives would prepare for a career, and husbands did virtually no housework.[38] In the study of the Satmar Hasidic community in Williamsburg published ten years later, marriageable young men and women were permitted to get to know each other in semiprivate circumstances before deciding they wanted to marry. Husbands were reported to be doing some housework and sharing with their wives in making important family decisions much more than in earlier times.[39]

In the third study, reported seven years later, this time on the Orthodox of Boro Park, Brooklyn, women were expected to be intellectual companions to their husbands, who were not only sharing in housework but changing their children's diapers.[40] Young Orthodox women went to evening courses at Brooklyn College while their husbands baby-sat, something that would have been highly unlikely in the 1950s. Egon Mayer, the author of the Boro Park study, concluded: "Since much of the educational experience of young men and women, especially in secular subjects, is identical, it should hardly be surprising to find that their expectations for personal esteem, gratification, and even occupational achievement have grown more alike"[41]

The Orthodox women who argue that it is the Talmud's patriarchal system that makes Jewish men into good husbands and fathers raise the essential question posed in this book: Under what conditions will men be motivated to invest their time and energy in being fathers without the incentives of patriarchy? Although many books were written in the 1990s on the importance of fathering, empirical research specifically on Jewish fathers was virtually nonexistent. In an annotated bibliography of the hundred most important articles on Jewish families written between 1970 and 1982, only one dealt with fathering.[42]

Will Jewish fathers in Reform, Conservative, and Reconstructionist communities who are less involved in ritual life at home and in leadership roles in the synagogue find that their moral authority as fathers has been undermined at home? One commentator, Rabbi Clifford E. Librach, thinks so, arguing that "as the egos of Jewish men have been marginalized in the distribution of synagogue power and honors, the foundation of the commitment to this way of life [as religious teachers] has collapsed."[43] Conservative rabbis have also noticed that it is mothers who are bringing children to services on Shabbat or festivals. Jack Wertheimer, provost of the Jewish Theological Seminary, believe that men are voting with their feet in terms of synagogue attendance and "allowing women to serve as [religious] role models for their children."

Concern about the feminization of Judaism has also drawn attention from Reform rabbis, one of whom asserted that "the great, unspoken crisis facing modern Judaism, is the disengagement of men in large numbers."[44] Sylvia Barack Fishman has observed that allowing women to be counted in the minyan has made it more difficult to attract men. Fishman cites Conservative rabbi Richard M. Yellin, who points out that Jewish survival in the past depended not on Jewish warriors or businessmen but on the piety of Jewish fathers and husbands. The Jewish patriarchal paradigm, in short, provided survival just as Yahweh promised. Yellin seems to be arguing that it will not be possible to get rid of patriarchy without reducing the quality of Jewish fathering.[45]

All other things being equal, observing Shabbat is likely to help Jewish men be engaged fathers, but one does not have to be Orthodox to do that. On major holidays in Conservative, Reform, and Reconstructionist synagogues, one sees young fathers, with babies slung over their backs or against their chests, called up to the *bimah* (dais) along with their wives by a female rabbi to read from Torah. There is no solid research on what kind of fathers these men make the rest of the year, but at such times they seem totally engaged and quite comfortable carrying infants while listening to a female rabbi or a woman president of the congregation.

It is even possible that there is a growing renewal of commitment to fathering by many Jewish men, going beyond that of their fathers and grandfathers in America. In the twentieth century, tens of thousands of Jewish fathers left the teaching of their children to schoolteachers and the popular culture, and discipline to Mom, concentrating on providing clothes, food, allowances, vacations, and bar and bat mitzvah parties for their children. In one 1966 study of American Jewish wives, several of them talked of their marriages as partnerships, but they meant something quite different from what many contemporary Jewish women mean by the same term. As one of the 1966 women put it: "Ours is a partnership. I run the home; he runs the office." Roles were complementary, not shared. Now, given access to higher education and opportunities for using their abilities in the paid labor force, many Jewish women are asking husbands to share in domestic responsibilities on a more equal basis.[46]

The weak father, the "it's only father" father, is a creature of modernity, particularly in the United States, and not of Jewish tradition. That tradition does not prevent males from diapering babies, preparing food, or cleaning the refrigerator; many aspects of it encourage them to nurture, teach, and discipline their children. Many women seek such men to be fathers for their children, but a central question of family life remains: Why should males, who contribute such infinitesimal biological energy to the production of a child, commit themselves to being devoted husbands and fathers without the enormous satisfaction that comes from membership in an exclusive male bonding system that puts men only, as in the case of the Jews, in a special relationship to God? Under the traditional Jewish patriarchal paradigm, it is a fraternity in which only they read the Torah in the synagogue, only they became rabbis, and only they, in an act of putting on the tefillin every morning, speak to Torah with these loving words: "I will betroth thee to myself forever. I will betroth thee to myself in righteousness and in kindness, in justice and mercy. I will betroth thee to myself in faithfulness."

The old system worked to protect family stability against its most threatening, destabilizing forces: male lust and rebellious sons. But the old system, like that of traditional patriarchal systems in other modern democratic societies, is eroding under rapidly changing economic and social circumstances and the understandable and valid desire of women to apply their talents, interests, and passions in the worlds of religion and work as the spiritual and intellectual equals of men. Whether most men will become loving and devoted husbands and fathers, strengthening families without the incentives of exclusive male bonding systems, is unknown. Many Jews and other upper middle class men in economically advanced democratic societies may be in the forefront of a movement to create a new paradigm of partnership parenting without patriarchy, a possibility explored more generally in the final chapter.

BEYOND PATRIARCHY?

HEN I FINISHED WRITING *FAMILY MAT-
TERS* (1972), I WAS DISTURBED ABOUT THE
CLASH OF WHAT SEEMED TO ME TO BE
two moral imperatives: the right of women to be equal to men in the
choices they make regarding their public lives and the right of infants
and children to receive continuity of authoritative, loving care from
their parents or other adults whom they perceive to be responsible for
them. In short, patriarchy should end; motherhood and fatherhood
should be major responsibilities for anyone who has a child.

Several facts already were evident: Women were moving increasingly
into positions of equality with men in many public roles; some men
were beginning to take on more responsibility for the care of children,
although the pace of change was slow; many men were leaving the responsibilities of fatherhood altogether; extended family care for children was diminishing; deficits in authoritative, loving care for infants
and children were growing; and children were increasingly at risk for
problems ranging from obesity to suicide.

As told in the Prologue, I became particularly interested in the role
that fathers play in promoting the well-being of children. Thus began
my inquiry into the relationship between incentives for postbiological
fathering and patriarchy in the evolution of hominids and later in many
cultures. What I found about the relationship of human nature to fathering and male dominance is reported briefly in chapter 1: Human
males are alone among male primates in making a substantial investment in postbiological fathering for their own biological offspring;

they are alone in entering into long-term pair bonds with the mothers of those offspring; the engagement of human males in continuing to be fathers well beyond the act of procreation probably results from adaptations by adult hominids to maximize the survival of unusually dependent offspring; and finally, male dominance is universal among the other primates, except for the bonobos, and theories that posit the dominance of males among hominids rest on plausible inferences from the evidence.

Although I found that patriarchy is deeply embedded in all cultures, no theory explaining its universality or its origins demonstrates its inevitability. This is not to say that hominid adaptations that favored a pronounced sexual dimorphism in *Homo sapiens*, compared to other primates, are not or will cease to be a major determinant of the different roles played by men and women in families. As sociologist Alice S. Rossi concluded in 1984, even before the recent flood of work in biological anthropology, there is "mounting evidence of sexual dimorphism from the biological and neurosciences" that men on the average are predisposed to behavior quite different from that of women.[1] But there is no genetic code for patriarchy. Sexual dimorphism is not necessarily the enemy of sexual equality, especially under conditions where education is available to women on a basis of equality with men in an information-service economy; and when women have control over the number of children they will have, and mothers and infants no longer routinely die in the birthing process. Under those circumstances, as already seen, the erosion of patriarchy is already under way. I believe that the evidence suggests that sexual dimorphism and an enlarged investment by fathers in postbiological parenting are compatible, although, as discussed later, mothers are likely to continue to make more of an investment in caring for infants and small children than fathers do.

Paradoxically, the story of the Jews, as outlined here, in their revision of the generic patriarchal paradigm, reinforces my belief that patriarchy is not inevitable. The paradox lies in the fact that the Jews evolved a tight religiously based patriarchal culture; but the main lesson from the story is that Jews revealed the human capacity for radical cultural change regarding the relationship of fathering to patriarchy. In their beginnings, at least from what we know, the peoples who later became the Jews thought of women as chattel and, as in patriarchies generally, often abused them. After they united around a religious insight of one God as the source of all life and developed Torah rules for ethical living, they practiced a radically different and distinct patriarchy, particularly after their defeat by the Romans in 70 C.E. and their dispersion. The Jewish patriarchal model persisted through the late Middle Ages. From the nineteenth century on, particularly in the United States, most people who called themselves Jews modified the Jewish patriarchal paradigm and substituted for it a modern model within which Jewish men competed and succeeded. Finally, during the last four decades of the twentieth century, many Jews, especially Jewish women, played leading roles in attacking the modern patriarchal system in a movement calling for sexual equality in public roles, plus partnerships in parenting at home.

Although the story of the Jews shows the human capacity for major cultural change, resistance to ending patriarchy will continue to come from many quarters, including those men and women who are sincerely concerned about the deficits in child care that sometimes result when mothers enter the full time paid labor force. Patriarchy will not be ended because of ideological arguments, as experience in Communist countries makes clear. Communism, according to its proponents, would end bourgeois patriarchy. Women would have equal access to high-status positions and remunerative income. They would no longer be slaves to the capitalist nuclear family. But patriarchy was deeply entrenched in the cultures of Russia and China, the two most powerful of all Communist nations. In 1969, on a lecture tour in Russia and Ukraine, I learned that whenever any kind of job became predominantly women's work, even that of physician, it was downgraded in status and salary. Fifteen years later, on a lecture tour of universities in China, I visited a major clothing factory, where I learned that work was segregated by sex and that women performed the less well paid and less respected tasks.

Japan is probably the best example of cultural resistance to feminist ideology in the face of some of the same conditions that gave rise to feminism in the United States, western Europe, and other modern democratic countries. Despite those changes, the Japanese have layers of cultural resistance to overcome before coming close to toppling patriarchy.[2] But access to education, jobs in a high tech service economy, and control over reproduction are spurring Japanese feminists to attack patriarchy.[3]

When patriarchal cultures are religiously based, then resistance to feminist arguments is particularly intense, even if those religiously based patriarchies function in modern societies, such as the Mormons, Hutterites, Amish, and Hasidic Jews in the United States. But those patriarchies are also affected to some degree by the factors that gave rise to the modern feminist movement to begin with, such as equal access for women with men to secular education, as seen in chapter 11 regarding modern Orthodox Jews.

The fight to defend patriarchy is particularly militant in several Muslim countries, where religious leaders defend it as God's will. When Ayatollah Khomenei came to power in Iran in 1979, he proclaimed the code requiring Muslim women to cover their arms, legs, hair, and *zina* (enticing parts).[4] When the fundamentalist group, the Taliban, gained ascendancy in Afghanistan, it acted quickly to tighten enforcement of its view of the Islamic social code, particularly the taboos that ban women from working in other than domestic occupations and require all females beyond puberty to cloak themselves from head to toe.[5] Girls were not permitted to go to school or to leave their homes unless accompanied by a close male relative. Some who violated that rule were whipped, beaten, and at times killed. After Algeria's Islamic insurgents ordered all women to veil themselves in 1995, a recalcitrant sixteen-year-old high school student who walked to class without a head scarf was killed by the militants. Between 1992 and 1995, fifty women were murdered in Algeria for working alongside men or wearing Western dress.[6]

A less violent but still militant example of resistance to change is the strong opposition of the ultra-Orthodox men in Israel to women's efforts to invade traditionally exclusive male responsibilities and privileges. When, in 1989, approximately forty women tried to hold morning prayers at the Western Wall, they were attacked by ultra-Orthodox men and forced to flee after police fired tear gas to disperse the attackers. The Western Wall, the holiest site in Judaism, was no place for women to pray, thought these ultra-Orthodox men, who do not believe that women should be permitted to carry a Torah scroll.[7] But there are Orthodox Jews who are working to enlarge women's rights, as seen in chapter 11; there also are religious Muslims who are working toward the same goal.

Educated, upper-middle-class Malaysian women have been in the forefront of an international group of Muslim women who have been promoting a feminist agenda. The women argue that they find no contradiction between their "desire to be strong, independent modern women" and their desire "to be good Muslims."[8] In some Muslim countries, such as the tiny oil kingdom of Qatar, where the undersecretary of education in 1998 was a woman, an increasing number of women were working side by side with men, although in deference to Muslim tradition most of them wore veils on the job. Patriarchy and polygyny still prevail in Qatar, along with the social segregation of females. Classes at the university are not mixed. Women often cloak themselves from head to ankle. Yet education and access to such positions as professor or bank manager are now open to women.[9]

In portions of the world where large numbers of people live at or close to subsistence level, the spread of feminist consciousness and an equal rights movement is confined primarily to a growing but still relatively small number of university-educated women and focused on issues of neglect of and brutality toward women. Those in the forefront of the movement for women's rights—the most educated—are also most likely to postpone marriage or do without husbands altogether. In Kenya, where one third of the students at Nairobi University are women, the proportion of twenty- to twenty-four-year-old women who had never married jumped from 24 percent in 1984 to 32 percent five years later. One self-employed woman interviewed in her well-equipped apartment told a Western reporter: "At least our African grandfathers looked after their women . . . but now the average man might contribute to the rent but use the rest for mistresses and beer."[10] In the Ivory Coast in 1996, a university-educated woman led a campaign against the practice of sexual harassment in the workplace and the entrenched customs of multiple wives, mistresses, and concubines.[11] Women from dozens of countries met in Beijing in September 1995 at the United Nations Fourth World Conference on Women and asserted that a woman's right to make sexual decisions free of coercion or violence must be protected. The woman who called it "a major step forward in defining human rights" was correct, although it was a step taken more than two thousand years ago in Judaism.[12]

Much of the world still does not recognize women's sexual rights, as discussed in chapter 3. Domestic male violence also is commonly sanctioned. It continues to exist in Israel, where it appears to have risen in the 1990s, despite the Torah's prohibition of it.[13] As a result of what appears to be an increase in battering among Orthodox women, many of them launched a publicity effort in 1996 to reach out to victims of domestic abuse. These religious women, including nurses, lawyers, teachers, and social workers, decided to expose the myth that Jewish men never abuse their wives. But social workers acknowledged that the incidence was still relatively low for Jews, compared to the general population. A task force of women developed rabbinic training seminars for religious leaders to help them deal with the problem, indicating support among men in the community for exposing it.[14]

It is not accidental that some of the most militant resistance to the sexual equality movement in the United States has occurred in the armed forces. Through some combination of hominid adaptations and subsequent cultural conditioning, males everywhere have tended to think of themselves as protectors of their females and children. It would be extraordinary if the protector-warrior male bonding systems that have been so important to men could be ended without meeting opposition. The best-publicized resistance to the end of male bonding privileges in the 1990s came in the reaction of many young men to the government's insistence that women be admitted to the Virginia Military Institute and the Citadel, two previously all-male military preparatory institutions. When a female visitor from the *Washington Post* visited VMI, many of the young men there were incensed. One of them stripped off his clothes and marched along the second floor mezzanine naked, to the cheers of his classmates, in order to get his point across that she was not welcome. Another carried a "Keep Women Out" sign.[15] Within the armed services, the sexual harassment of females by males has been a continuing, serious problem.[16]

Young men in close physical proximity to women often will be sexually aggressive toward them, and in many poor communities such behavior is exacerbated by the men's feelings of powerlessness. In 1993 two female students at different alternative high schools in Brooklyn were beaten by their boyfriends because, according to the author of the story, the young women went back to school and had jobs, whereas their boyfriends found it difficult to obtain employment. Bob Herbert of the *New York Times* wrote: "In a typical situation, the girl will go to school, then go to work, then pick up the children from whoever has been watching them, and then go home. The boy friend will want sex. The girl will explain that she's tired . . . or maybe she has homework . . . the boy friend will go berserk, calling her every degrading name he can think of, accuse her of seeing someone else, and beat her."[17] These young men are, inexcusably, using physical power perhaps to express feelings of diminished cultural power in relationships with these young mothers. The explanation for their behavior is undoubtedly complex. In any case, the young women are likely to raise their children without any real help from the young fathers, who, to one degree or another, flee from fatherhood.

To go beyond patriarchy without dooming many children to a fatherless childhood has already proved extremely difficult, especially in many poor communities in America, where being unable to provide for or protect one's family is a spur to leaving fatherhood altogether. The pattern, often found among African American women and Puerto Ricans and other Latin Americans, of raising children without their biological fathers present is an old story for poor ethnic groups in America. It resembles the situation of Irish Catholic women in the inner cities of the Northeast during the last half of the nineteenth century, when nearly four million Irish arrived in the United States. Mothers became super-mothers, survivors who had to be fathers and mothers both, sometimes even to their nominal husbands, whose male ancestors often had been substantially stripped of paternal authority during nearly eight hundred years of brutal English rule.

English attempts at cultural genocide and impoverishment of the Irish provoked patterns of response typical of other groups in similar situations. Many Irish Catholic women decided not to marry at all.[18] Some of those who married remained with husbands for religious reasons, men who were fathers in name only. In the middle and late nineteenth centuries in the United States, unemployment and poverty as well as alcoholism and other illnesses made many Irish Catholic men in America more of a burden to their wives than an asset in raising children. The children, particularly when there were many of them, suffered from father absenteeism, as reflected in the data recording their high rates of illness, school leaving, and petty crime.[19]

The best-known contemporary example of fleeing fatherhood has occurred among African Americans. Three hundred years of slavery and caste, during which black men were rendered largely powerless, had substantially undermined paternal authority by the time of the great migration of rural southern blacks to major cities in the South and especially to the North (close to four million between 1915 and 1970). As with the Irish Catholics, mothers became super-mothers, learning to depend more and more on themselves and on female relatives. The situation of African American mothers is much better known than that of Irish Catholics because it is contemporary. Whereas most Irish Americans are now solidly in the middle class, African Americans experience poverty far out of proportion to their numbers. In recent years the incentives for black women to do without husbands have increased, partly because of welfare but also because young black women have been more employable than poor young black men.[20]

That women can raise children without husbands has been proved by Irish Americans, African Americans, and many others, especially when they can get help from extended family members. In many Italian and Mexican villages it has been customary for men to be away for long periods of time to work. In one such village in Italy, the mothers teach their children, decide on the amount of their daughters' dowries, and make nearly all decisions for their families.[21] When men are taken away by work or war, women usually struggle to help their children survive. A group of Muslim women whose husbands were killed in Srebeninca in 1995 told an interviewer that their lives were empty without their husbands, the only meaning coming from their desperate attempts to save their children and to keep the memories of their husbands alive.[22] In a Kurdish village where men had been forcibly removed by Iraqi soldiers, their wives, now responsible for managing family life, spoke of their husbands to their children as heroes and as fathers.[23] The emotional attachment of the children to those men, dead or missing, probably remained strong for them most of the time, as it does for the absent Italian, Mexican, and other fathers who work for long periods of time far from home. It is not so much the physical absence of a father as the father's psychological and emotional truancy that makes children feel fatherless. In the United States, absentee fathers often, but not always, give the impression that they are uninterested fathers.

In addition to militant resistance and flight from fatherhood, there is a third pattern of response by males to the erosion of patriarchy. The Southern Baptist Convention of the nation's largest Protestant denomination, called in June of 1998 to end father truancy. Fathers should, they said, "provide for, protect and lead" their families. The Southern Baptists' president explained that the resolution was a response to "a time of growing crisis in the family," and asked for a much greater commitment on the part of men to being good fathers and husbands. But the resolution also asserted that a woman should "submit herself graciously" to her husband's leadership, a declaration justified by references to the New Testament, such as the passage in Ephesians that compares the authority of husbands over wives to that of Christ ruling the church (Eph. 5:22–33).[24]

Before the Southern Baptists made their declaration, the Nation of Islam and the movement known as the Promise Keepers emphasized the importance of restoring responsible fathering through benign patriarchal rule. Although there are many differences between the two groups, besides the fact that members of the Nation of Islam are Black Muslims and the Promise Keepers includes Christians of all colors, what they have in common is that large groups of men come together for public national confession that goes something like this: "We have been bad patriarchs. We have neglected our responsibilities as leaders. Sometimes we have been bad fathers, and there are occasions when we even have abused our power badly by hurting our wives emotionally and physically. We turn our backs on those failures and now pledge to be good Muslim and Christian patriarchs. With the power to rule must come the responsibility for being caring, nurturing husbands and fathers. We will be devoted fathers and loving, kindly and faithful husbands, and we will be in charge."[25] As the Promise Keeper leader, Bill McCartney, asserted, "When there is a final decision that needs to be made . . . the man needs to take responsibility."[26]

Many women in the Nation of Islam and those married to Promise Keepers understandably give testimony to their appreciation for the respect shown them by their husbands. The trade-off is an ancient one. Women hope to obtain husbands they can rely on to be good fathers to their children; men obtain wives who acknowledge the male right to power and leadership, at least in public. That many women think the bargain is reasonable, or at least livable in comparison to alternative options, is hardly surprising. They do not want husbands who keep girlfriends or visit prostitutes. Nor do they believe that polygyny is a valid solution for a perceived shortage of reliable marriage partners, as an increasing number of women apparently do in Utah: A 1998 report indicated that in fifty years there had been a tenfold increase in the number of women living in polygynous families, reaching about 2 percent of the state's population.

The abuse of women within polygynous relationships, one reason for the near-abandonment of polygyny by Jews in talmudic times, is also reported to be on the increase. Female advocates of polygyny point out that it provides women a sisterhood of co-wives and an opportunity to pursue their own interests and careers, in addition to strong fathers. On the other side, many ex-wives from polygynous marriages agree with one of them who said: "Once you threw out the religion, all of us women realized that it was made for the benefit of men."[27] That many men still want marriages in which they are clearly dominant is indicated by the increase in recent years of the international mail order bride business, in which agencies routinely describe potential brides as "faithful, devoted, unspoiled . . . raised to be servants for men . . . derives her basic satisfaction from serving and pleasing her husband."[28]

Perhaps the most ambitious attempt in the twentieth century to end patriarchy as a system of privilege took place on the secular kibbutzim of Israel from the 1930s to the 1960s. When sociologist Melford Spiro first studied the kibbutzim in 1951, women claimed that they had been emancipated from the burden of child rearing and from dependency on their husbands. The key to their emancipation was to be free from the responsibilities of infant care through the infants' and children's houses, where youngsters slept overnight and were cared for by specialized caregivers. Now, women reasoned, they could share in public roles equally with men, driving tractors, serving in the army, and managing the kibbutz. Twenty-five years after his first visit, Spiro found that the children of the original revolutionary kibbutzniks were moving back to traditional ideas in the areas of marriage, family, and sex roles. Mothers rebelled against giving up so much responsibility and control to others in raising their children. They wanted the freedom and equality that emancipation from tasks of nursing and child rearing might give them, but as mothers they also wanted to be in charge of what happened to their children. Eventually, nearly all of the kibbutzim abandoned the idea of the infants' house.

The results were a surprise and a disappointment to Spiro, who began his work as a cultural determinist interested in observing the influence of culture on human nature and then discovered that he was observing what he called the influence of human nature on culture.[29] After conducting different experiments in role playing and fantasy play by boys and girls on the kibbutz, Spiro decided, against his ideological preference, that powerful biological, prehistorical factors probably explained the retreat to gender role differentiation.[30] Did role differentiation mean a retreat to patriarchy for these women? Not according to their own testimony. Even though men tended to hold positions of greater power on the kibbutz than their wives did, the women have come to believe that sexual equality does not mean sharing equally in all roles. This view was held in another study of six kibbutzim reported by

Spiro, showing that *sabra*-born (native-born) women rejected the assumption that equality with males means becoming like them A great majorities of both male and female *sabras* in the six kibbutzim agreed that sexual equality remains a primary characteristic of the kibbutz, in practice as well as an ideal.[31]

There is an obvious connection between patriarchy in the public realm and patriarchy in family life. Most modern women in democratic societies want full equality in work, politics, and religion. They also know how difficult it is to be an effective parent without having a partner in parenting in the fathers of their children. Adult caregivers, mainly parents, must nurture, teach, protect, and provide for children. Someone must represent them to the outside world until they are young adults, and someone must manage the households in which they live.

Men who may be willing to yield to the moral imperatives of equality in the public realm may be reluctant to take on more as caregivers of children and as household managers. In the United States, mothers still tend to be largely responsible for child care and housework, although many chores customarily done by males—repairing the car, cleaning the cellar or the garage, paying the insurance bills—are not usually thought of as housework.[32] However, an increasing number of fathers in intact families have become involved in day-to-day caregiving chores in recent years, compared to decades past. One study showed that in 1977 men put in only 30 percent as much time on household chores as women did, compared to 75 percent in 1997. Working fathers in such families were spending 2.3 workday hours caring for and doing things with their children, a half hour more than the average reported in a Department of Labor survey two decades earlier.[33]

James A. Levine, director since 1981 of the Fatherhood Project, found that "there [still] is a mismatch in the young women's and men's views," at colleges and universities, of who will take care of children and who will work for money. Levine is a leader in what could loosely be called a growing movement for fatherhood beyond patriarchy.[14] Levine and many of his colleagues, having amassed data to show that men feel conflict between work and family more than had previously been thought, conclude that the major obstacle to men's becoming involved fathers is an unfriendly workplace. The Fatherhood Project works on strategies to support the involvement of men in the lives of their children, mainly by trying to get the workplace to be more supportive. One vehicle for the movement was the magazine *Modern Dad*, which appeared first in 1995 and ceased publication in 1997. Edited by a woman, it urged men to "get up and get involved" as fathers.[35] Not surprisingly, more subscriptions were bought by women for their sons, husbands, and sons-in-law than by their primary target male audience. "We tried to appeal to the masculine side of men with articles on things like tools and lawn care," wrote the editor, "while at the same time we were undeniably trying to appeal to the feminine side of men with articles on bonding with their babies or dealing with the death of a baby."[36]

Biological anthropologists and evolutionary psychologists might be expected to cast a skeptical eye on ambitions for such a magazine or even on the idea of partnership parenting if that rests on the assumption that men will be as interested as women in the care of infants and small children. Many would hold the view that it took millions of years of evolution to bring about the sexual dimorphism that leads human females to be more nurturing than males and males to be more aggressive than females. Yet many men have shown a desire for the teaching and nurturing aspects of fatherhood, according to David Blankenhorn and his colleagues, who interviewed 250 parents in eight states. The male respondents accepted the view that fatherhood "means fathers teaching children a way of life" and used such words as "instilling," "advising," "teaching," "setting an example," and "preparing."

Blankenhorn seems, without any reference to the talmudic patriarchal paradigm, to be calling for a reinvention of the classical rabbinic Jewish father. He wants the norms to say: "I am a man because I cherish my wife and nurture my children."[37] Several studies show that blood pressure, heart rate, and galvanic skin responses of men and women are the same when they hear babies crying in discomfort.[38] Those physiological reactions reveal that at least some fathers care at a deep, visceral level about the well-being of their infants. But they do not necessarily mean that most males will be sufficiently motivated to spend less time and energy competing in some aspect of life outside the family in order to share equally with their wives in the care of infants and small children. Fathers in intact families are spending more time in child care and housework than they did just three or four decades ago, perhaps more than twice as much for the parents of young children.[39] If the culture becomes increasingly supportive of such behavior, an increasing number of men probably will engage in it without the patriarchal incentives that in the past have motivated fathers to be teachers and nurturers. In an ambitious attempt at social engineering in Norway, the government in 1998 introduced regulations to its equal rights law to promote preferential treatment for men in jobs such as child care, preschool and primary school teaching, and child welfare, to encourage a change in children's views of gender roles.[40] To judge from the kibbutz experience, the government may fail to accomplish its objectives, even as it discriminates against women, who may be excluded from jobs they want and for which they are qualified.

My inquiry has led me to conclude that a successful assault on patriarchy as a system of power and privilege does not depend on the obliteration of gender role differences in domestic life, although it is clearly related to the willingness of males to invest energy in the continuing loving care of their children. The end of patriarchy is a moral imperative toward which we should work in the spiritual, economic, political, and domestic realms of life. It will mean families and workplaces in which men and women truly respect each other. It will also mean that women and men will be free to be nurturing parents.

Sociologist Judith Wallerstein reports from her research and that of others what everyday observation confirms: most mothers and their babies are tied "by a thousand and one biological and psychological strands" that fathers do not experience. The father may really love the baby and want to share more in its upbringing, but sometimes his wife does not want him to (a significantly higher percentage of kibbutz women than men wanted to end the infants' house). The father has not experienced pregnancy nor the demands of nursing. Because her biological energy investment in the production of a child overwhelms his, most mothers would be expected to feel a more intense bond with their infants than most fathers do.[41] But we are not dealing with an iron law of biology, and there are and will continue to be exceptions to that generalization.

We are in the midst of a revolution in relations between men and women regarding sex roles, and that has caused great confusion, perhaps especially for males who are trying to figure out how to respond.[42] The future of parenting by true partnership on a basis of equality will be shaped by hundreds of millions of negotiations between men and women as they sort out their own understanding of the responsibilities they have toward each other and toward their children. The end of patriarchy as a system of power and privilege may find many women wanting to spend more time on child care than their husbands do, as Spiro found on the kibbutz, where the kibbutzniks claimed that patriarchy is over. However any given couple allocates child care roles, the end of patriarchy would mean that women and men will be able to pursue their interests and negotiate their differences on an equal footing under the law and cultural sanctions. That is taking place now in an increasing number of middle-class families, particularly in the economically advanced democratic countries. Aka men, as discussed in chapter 2, take care of infants in exchange for the vital economic contributions of their wives, who collect fruits and caterpillars and hunt small animals.[43] Perhaps the Aka spouses can be compared in this regard to a growing number of young husbands and wives who work at home in start-up family businesses. But the Aka did not abandon patriarchy. No society ever has, yet.

One study in Cambridge, Massachusetts, reveals the conditions that might be most favorable to partnership parenting without patriarchy. In research regarding professional parents, both mothers and fathers made strong efforts to make special time to play with and teach their children.[44] Both presumably had achieved some recognition in the world of work; between them, they were able to provide for supplemental caregivers. As educated upper-middle-class men and women, they probably had already embraced the ideology of partnership parenting; as professionals, they may have had some control over their work schedules. But neither the vast majority of the world's people nor even the vast majority of Americans are parents in such conditions. It is under those conditions that men are likely to be soccer dads, Cub scout den leaders, fathers who change their children's diapers and read to their children as well as teach and discipline them, without requiring patriarchal incentives. It is much easier for fathers to be lovingly involved in their children's care when they are reasonably well off and respected in their work, especially if they have some control over their schedules.

The story of the Jews, taken to the end of the twentieth century in the United States, shows that many middle-class Jewish men have abandoned patriarchal norms and practices and, like the professional parents in Cambridge, appear to be ready for partnership parenting. Perhaps it helps many of them, even those who do not have a close knowledge of Judaism, that their religion provides a rationale for men to be as nurturing as women by emphasizing that a genderless God is mother and father to the children of Israel. Feminist biblical scholar Phyllis Trible sees the Jewish ideal as having both males and females lift infants close against their cheeks and take children in their arms, "with reins of kindness, with leading strings of love," according to the prophet Hosea (11:1–4).[45] Jewish patriarchs were rewarded by being made the cultural custodians of what was most valuable to Jews. Their patriarchy may have made them, on the average, more affectionate, responsible husbands and fathers than others, but it was patriarchy nonetheless. In teaching their sons what was most sacred to their covenanted people, they saw their own immortality.

An increasing number of men have shown that they do not have to believe they are rulers over their wives in order to link their immortality to what they see in their children's faces and behavior. Fathers who are not needed as protectors of and providers for females and who no longer have the power to control them must gain their sense of esteem and significance in other ways than through patriarchy. In the end, the deepest, longest-lasting sense of significance that most men and women achieve will be in the response of their children and grandchildren to the love and the values that they teach. That is the hope for a world of committed, engaged fathers without the incentives of patriarchy.

Beyond Patriarchy?

By beginning a radical change in relations between men and women more than two thousand years ago, the Jews demonstrated the human capacity for major cultural change in a relationship that appears to have deep biological roots. It was a reform of great magnitude but not as profound as the one that would bring men and women to a new paradigm of partnership parenting without patriarchy. What would that paradigm look like? Since patriarchy is not programmed by biology, it would mean the end of special power and privileges for males as a class. Clearly, it would not and could not mean the end of evolution-based sexual dimorphism. Those differences do not support a simplistic view of partnership that insists on men and women necessarily having the same roles as nurturers of infants and small children. But true partnership would give full recognition to the rights of women to make choices as individuals to the extent that their economic situation permitted it, choices that were consistent with their special biological and psychological qualities as they experience them. At such a time we will have moved beyond patriarchy.

Whether men and women in fact move beyond patriarchy to fulfill a vision of partnership parenting that is rewarding for both sexes and provides a continuity of authoritative, loving care by adults for children who perceive those adults as responsible for their well-being is one of the most important questions to be faced in the twenty-first century.

NOTES

1. In 1910, only 5 percent of white American women worked outside the home. The *Ladies Home Journal* and other women's magazines consistently reinforced women's expressed preference to work only at household management and child rearing. In 1938, 75 percent of the American population disapproved of a married woman's earning money if her husband was capable of supporting her. Even in 1946, after large numbers of women had been in the paid labor force during the war, a *Fortune* magazine survey found that both men and women believed that homemaking was a full-time job (which in many families it was). They also believed that homemakers had more interesting jobs than women who worked outside the home, a result perhaps of the kinds of jobs that were open to women—and to most men, too—and because war-weary men and women hungered for a return to domesticity. Forty-six percent of the men and 49.5 percent of the women said that "only women who have to support themselves should have an equal chance with men for jobs in business and industry." See Robert L. Griswold, *Fatherhood in America* (New York: Basic Books, 1995), 188.

   By 1978, only 26 percent of the American population, men and women, disapproved of married women's earning money even if their husbands were able to support them. But only 34.1 percent of women with children under three years were in the labor force in 1975. By 1990, 53 percent of all American women with children under the age of one year were in the paid labor force (68 percent of the college graduates); and by 1997, 67.8 percent with children under three worked full-time, as did 72.3 percent with children aged three to five. See Erik Eckholm, "Finding Out What Happens When Mothers Go to Work," *New York Times*, 6 October 1992. Census data are reported in the *New York Times*, 23 August 1998.

2. "Why Fathers Count: The Crisis: Two out of Every Five Kids in America Do Not Live with Their Real Fathers. It Makes a Huge Difference." *U.S. News and World Report*, 27 February 1995. The story opened with the hyperbolic and unscientific claim that "Dad is destiny . . . more than virtually any other factor, the biological father's presence in the family will determine a child's success and happiness."

3. Sarah McLanahan and Gary Sandefur, *Growing Up with a Single Parent: What*

Hurts, What Helps (Cambridge, Mass.: Harvard University Press, 1994). In the United States, young males seem to be particularly at risk for death or incarceration. At age twenty-five, the odds that a white male will live out the year are 561 to 1, compared to 1,754 to 1 for white females; for blacks, the comparative odds are 311 to 1 for males and 943 to 1 for females. See Warren Farrell, *The Myth of Male Power: Why Men Are the Disposable Sex* (New York: Simon & Schuster, 1994), 30. The vulnerability of adolescent boys is particularly striking. From ages ten to fourteen the suicide rate of boys is twice as high as for girls; from fifteen to nineteen, four times as high; and from twenty to twenty-four, six times as high (p. 81).

1. THE BIOLOGICAL ORIGINS OF PATRIARCHY?

1. I learned to take biology with great seriousness and to respect the power of Darwinian explanations for human behavior from scholars with whom I worked in the early 1970s at the Social Studies Curriculum Project at Education Development Center, then in Cambridge, Massachusetts. I owe a large debt of gratitude to Irven DeVore and Robert L. Trivers, both of whose works affected my thinking. DeVore had already co-edited, with R. B. Lee, *Man the Hunter* (Chicago: Aldine, 1968), and Trivers had written his seminal article "Parental Investment and Sexual Selection," which can be found in *Sexual Selection and the Descent of Man, 1871–1971*, ed. B. Campbell (Chicago: Aldine, 1972).

Other, earlier influential works include George P. Murdock, *Our Primitive Contemporaries* (New York: Macmillan, 1934); Margaret Mead, *Male and Female* (New York: William Morrow, 1949); Robert Ardrey, *The Territorial Imperative: A Personal Inquiry into the Animal Origins of Property and Nations* (New York: Atheneum, 1966); Ashley Montague, *The Natural Superiority of Women*, rev. ed. (New York: Macmillan, 1968); Lionel Tiger, *Men in Groups* (New York: Random House, 1969); Judith M. Bardwick, *Psychology of Women: A Study of Biocultural Conflicts* (New York: Harper & Row, 1971); Alison Jolly, *The Evolution of Primate Behavior* (New York: Macmillan, 1972).

I read most of these before the publication of my own book *Family Matters* (New York: Random House, 1972), which summed up what I had learned to that point. See the section "Equality? Biology and Culture," pp. 126–44.

Since that time, there has been an explosion of research in sociobiology, biological anthropology, and evolutionary psychology. See E. O. Wilson, *Sociobiology: The New Synthesis* (Cambridge, Mass.: Belknap Press, 1975); and R. B. Lee and I. DeVore, eds., *Kalahari Hunter-Gatherers* (Cambridge, Mass.: Harvard University Press, 1976). More recently, see J. H. Barkow, L. Cosmides, and J. Tooby, *The Adapted Mind: Evolutionary Psychology and the Generation of*

Culture (Oxford: Oxford University Press, 1992); David M. Buss, *The Evolution of Desire: Strategies of Human Mating* (New York: Basic Books, 1994); M. Daly and M. Wilson, *Sex, Evolution, and Behavior* (Boston: Willard Grant, 1984); J. R. Krebs and N. B. Davies, *An Introduction to Behavioural Ecology* (Oxford: Blackwell Scientific Publications, 1987); Robert Wright, *The Moral Animal* (New York: Vintage Books, 1994).

2. See Sherwood L. Washburn and C. S. Lancaster, "The Evolution of Hunting," in *Man the Hunter*, ed. R. B. Lee and I. DeVore (Chicago: Aldine, 1968); Catherine Milton, "Primary Diets and Gut Morphology: Implications for Hominid Evolution," in *Food and Evolution: Toward a Theory of Human Food Habits*, ed. Marvin Harris and Eric B. Ross (Philadelphia: Temple University Press, 1987); Robert L. Trivers, "The Evolution of Reciprocal Altruism," *Quarterly Review of Biology* 46 (1971): 35–57; and Martha Tappen, "Savannah Ecology and Natural Bone Deposition: Implications for Early Hominid Site Formation, Hunting, and Scavenging," *Current Anthropology* 36 (1995).

3. See Richard W. Wrangham, James Holland Jones, Greg Laden, David Pilbeam, and NancyLou Conklin-Britten, "The Raw and the Stolen: Cooking and the Ecology of Human Origins," *Current Anthropology* (December 1999): 567–94.

4. On the bonobos, a primate species that lives in the humid forests south of the Zaire river, see Frans B. M. deWaal, "Bonobo Sex and Society," *Scientific American* (March 1995): 82–88; Randall L. Susman, ed., *The Pygmy Chimpanzee: Evolutionary Biology and Behavior* (New York: Plenum Press, 1984); Takayoshi Kano, *The Last Ape: Pygmy Chimpanzee Behavior and Ecology* (Stanford, Calif.: Stanford University Press, 1992); and Frans B. M. deWaal, *Peacemaking Among Primates* (Cambridge, Mass.: Harvard University Press, 1989).

The bonobos, which, like hominids, do not have estrus, appear to be constantly engaged in sex of one kind or another. DeWaal argues that nuclear families probably are incompatible with the diverse use of sex found in bonobos. They do not have nuclear families, and indeed they do not have patriarchy. Bonobo society appears to be female-centered and in some ways female-dominated (the highest ranking males of a bonobo community tend to be the sons of important females); but sex with anyone, at any time, in any way, also appears to be incompatible with their longevity as a species. The species has an unusually low rate of reproduction, and there is considerable doubt about its ability to survive, according to deWaal. In any case, the bonobos have nothing like the human family. As deWaal points out, human family life implies paternal investment, which is unlikely to develop unless males can be reasonably certain that they are caring for their own, not someone else's, offspring.

5. Richard Wrangham and Dale Peterson, *Demonic Males: Apes and the Origin of*

Human Violence (Boston: Houghton Mifflin Co., 1996). In pair-bonding mating strategies there was an implicit trade-off or compact. The fact that hominid females did not form female alliances made them dependent on male power. See particularly pp. 124, 125, 241, 242. The theory that human mating strategies evolved through the efforts of hominid females to avoid sexual harassment is identified mainly with the work of Sarah L. Mesnick, "Sexual Alliances: Evidence and Evolutionary Implications," in *Feminism and Evolutionary Biology: Boundaries, Intersections and Frontiers,* ed. P. A. Gowaty (Lexington, Ky.: Chapman & Hall, 1997). For a survey of the literature on the evolution of patriarchy, see Helen E. Fisher, *Anatomy of Love: The Natural History of Monogamy, Adultery and Divorce* (New York: W. W. Norton & Co., 1992), and *The Sex Contract: The Evolution of Human Behavior* (New York: William Morrow, 1982). See also Barbara Diane Miller, ed., *Sex and Gender Hierarchies* (Cambridge: Cambridge University Press, 1993); Patricia Adair Gowaty, "Evolutionary Biology and Feminism," *Human Nature* 3 (1992): 217–49; Adam Kuper, *The Chosen Primate: Human Nature and Cultural Diversity* (Cambridge, Mass.: Harvard University Press, 1994); and Barbara B. Smutts, "The Evolutionary Origins of Patriarchy," *Human Nature* 1 (1995): 1–32.

In a review of the sociobiological argument for the evolution of patriarchy, sociologist Cynthia Fuchs Epstein challenges the idea that male dominance arose because of the long period of dependence of the human infant and the early modes of obtaining food in hunter-gatherer societies (*Deceptive Distinctions: Sex, Gender, and the Social Order* [New Haven, Conn.: Yale University Press, Russell Sage Foundation, 1988], 60–64). But Epstein does not question what she calls the "near-universality" of patriarchy and indeed does not suggest another explanation for what is in fact the universality of patriarchy (p. 70).

6. For an emphasis on the importance of sexual dimorphism in *Homo sapiens,* see Weston LaBarre, *The Human Animal* (Chicago: University of Chicago Press, 1954). Also see his foreword to Melford E. Spiro's *Gender and Culture: Kibbutz Women Revisited* (Durham, N.C.: Duke University Press, 1979), where he emphasizes the sexual dimorphism of *Homo sapiens* and the dependency of human infants on learning as an explanation for the evolutionary adaptation of human mating strategies and male-female divisions in reproduction and child care.

2. PATRIARCHY AND CULTURAL FATHERHOOD

1. J. J. Bachofen, *Das Mutterrecht* (Basel: B. Schwab, 1897); Robert Briffault, *The Mothers* (New York, 1927; repr. New York: University Library, 1953); Kathleen

Gough, "The Origin of the Family," *Journal of Marriage and the Family*, 33(4) (November 1971): 760–71.

2. Susan Starr Sered, *Priestess, Mother, Sacred Sister: Religions Dominated by Women* (New York: Oxford University Press, 1994).

3. Cynthia Fuchs Epstein, *Deceptive Distinctions: Sex, Gender, and the Social Order* (New Haven, Conn.: Yale University Press, Russell Sage Foundation, 1988), 70. Also see Frances Dahlberg, ed., *Woman the Gatherer* (New Haven, Conn.: Yale University Press, 1981).

4. See Steven Goldberg, *The Inevitability of Patriarchy* (New York: William Morrow & Co., 1973); Gerda Lerner, *The Creation of Patriarchy* (New York: Oxford University Press, 1986); and Sherry Ortner, "Is Female to Male as Nature Is to Culture?" in *Women, Culture and Society*, ed. Michelle Zimbalist Rosaldo and Louise Lampher (Stanford, Calif.: Stanford University Press, 1974).

5. Monica Wilson, *Good Company: A Study of the Nyakyusa Age-Villages* (London, New York: Oxford University Press, 1951).

6. Stuart A. Queen and Robert W. Habenstein, "The Polyandrous Toda Family," chap. 2 in *The Family in Various Cultures*, 3rd ed. (New York: J. B. Lippincott Co., 1967).

7. Stuart A. Queen and Robert W. Habenstein, "The Polygynous Baganda Family," chap. 4 in *The Family in Various Cultures*, 3rd ed. (New York: J. B. Lippincott Co., 1967).

8. Ibid.

9. Leo W. Simmons, ed., *Sun Chief: The Autobiography of a Hopi Indian* (New Haven, Conn.: Yale University Press, 1942), 81–84. This account is an oversimplified version of an extremely complicated and long ceremony. A later series of ceremonies inducting young men into Hopi manhood is described in chapter 8, "The Making of a Man."

10. R. Mugogatheru, *Child of Two Worlds: A Kikuyu's Story* (New York: Frederick A. Praeger, 1964).

11. Barry S. Hewlett, "Husband-Wife Reciprocity and the Father-Infant Relationship among Aka Pygmies," in *Father-Child Relations: Culture and Biosocial Contexts*, ed. Barry S. Hewlett (New York: Aldine and Digruyter, 1992), 172.

12. Vishvajit Pandya, "Gukwelon One: The Game of Hiding Fathers and Seeking Sons among the Ongee of Little Andaman," in Barry S. Hewlett, ed., *Father-Child Relations: Culture and Biosocial Contexts* (New York: Aldine and Digruyter, 1992), 267, 269, 270.

13. S. C. Dube, *Indian Village* (New York: Harper & Row, 1967).

14. Ivan Chen, trans., "The Twenty-Four Examples of Filiopiety," in *The Book of Filial Duty* (London: John Murray, 1908), 31–60.

15. There is an extensive literature on the influence of Confucianist thought on

Chinese family and sexual relations. See Herlee G. Creel, *Chinese Thought from Confucius to Mao Tze-Tung* (Chicago: University of Chicago Press, 1953); Wolfram Eberhard, *Guilt and Sin in Traditional China* (Berkeley: University of California Press, 1967); Francis L. K. Hsu, *Under the Ancestors' Shadow: Kinship, Personality and Social Mobility in China* (Stanford, Calif.: Stanford University Press, 1971); Francis L. K. Hsu, *Americans and Chinese: Passage to Differences*, 3rd ed. (Honolulu: University of Hawaii Press, 1981); William Kessen, ed., *Childhood in China* (New Haven, Conn.: Yale University Press, 1975); and Jan Myrdal, *Report from a Chinese Village* (New York: Pantheon Books, 1965).

3. PATRIARCHY AS A SYSTEM OF POWER

1. John Ward Anderson and Molly Moore, "The Burden of Womanhood," *Washington Post National Weekly Edition*, 22–28 March 1993.
2. Bruce Porter, "I Met My Daughter at the Wuhan Foundling Hospital," *New York Times Magazine*, 11 April 1993, 24–34. For a larger picture of the role of women in Chinese society, see Roxanne Weithe and Margery Wolf, *Women in Chinese Society* (New York: Stanford University Press 1975); Marilyn Young, *Women in China* (Ann Arbor: University of Michigan, 1973); and Caty Curtin, *Women in China* (New York: Pathfinder Press, 1975).
3. Ian Hogbin, *The Island of Menstruating Men: Religion in Wogeo, New Guinea* (London: Chandler Publishing Co., 1970).
4. Rigoberta Menchú, *An Indian Woman in Guatemala*, ed. and introduced by Elizabeth Burgos-Debray (New York: Verso, 1984), 10, 12, 14, 214.
5. Richard Gambino, *Blood of My Blood* (Garden City, N.Y.: Doubleday, 1974). Also see Charlotte G. Chapman, *Milocca: A Sicilian Village* (London: Allen & Unwin, 1973), 107; Ann Cornelisen, *Women of the Shadows: The Wives and Mothers of Southern Italy* (Boston: Little, Brown, 1976).
6. J. K. Campbell, *Honour, Family and Patronage: A Study of Institutions and Moral Values in a Greek Mountain Community* (New York: Oxford University Press, 1964), 280.
7. Luigi Barzini, *The Italians* (New York: Atheneum, 1964), 200.
8. Campbell, *Honour, Family and Patronage*, 153.
9. Ibid., 60–61, 62, 63.
10. S. C. Dube, *Indian Village* (New York: Harper & Row, 1967), 142, and Edward Rice, *Mother India's Children* (New York: Pantheon Books, 1971).
11. Robert B. Edgerson, *The Fall of the Ashanti Empire: The Hundred Year War for Africa's Gold Coast* (New York: Free Press, 1994).

12. Jane Perlez, "Women's Work Is Never Done: Not by Masai Men," *New York Times*, 2 December 1991.
13. Nathaniel C. Nash, "Bolivia Is Helping Its Battered Wives to Stand Up," *New York Times*, 30 March 1990.
14. The accounts from the Mbuti and !Kung Sfan are discussed in Richard Wrangham and Dale Peterson, *Demonic Males: Apes and the Origin of Human Violence* (Boston: Houghton Mifflin Co., 1996), 122–24, and Marjorie Shostak, *Nisa: The Life and Words of a !Kung Woman* (New York: Vintage Books, 1998).
15. Marvin Harris, *Cows, Pigs, Wars and Witches: The Riddles of Culture* (New York: Vintage Books, 1978), 76–78.
16. Campbell, *Honour, Family and Patronage*, 66.
17. Nicole Umemoto, "Like a Moth Chasing the Fire: An HIV/AIDS Analysis of Urban Men in Myanmar," unpublished, Yangon, Myanmar, 1998, 54–65. As one of the men said, "In our Myanmar tradition, women are to be ruled over by their husbands, to be attentive to serve their husband as the master and head god of the house."
18. Maynard H. Merwine, "How Africa Understands Female Circumcision," *New York Times*, 24 November 1993.
19. Diana M. Cahn, "Lifting the Ancient Bedouin Veil of Secrecy," *The Jerusalem Post*, 3 July 1993, international edition. For a scholarly review of the practice, see Hanny Lightfoot-Klein, *Prisoners of Ritual: An Odyssey into Female Genital Circumcision in Africa* (Binghamton, NY: Harworth Press, 1989).
20. Campbell, *Honour, Family, and Patronage*, 186, 187, 275, 276. Campbell tells of a father who, in 1948, discovered that his daughter was pregnant by a man who refused to marry her. First, he took her to a secluded place, shot her with a pistol, and sank her body in the sea. Later he killed the seducer, removing his body in the same way, an action that was praised by the villagers. Women found that their honor depended on the reputation that the community gives them concerning their behavior in relation to sex.
21. Ibid., 275–77.
22. Nicholas D. Kristof, "Asian Childhoods Sacrificed to Prosperity's Lust: Children for Sale," *New York Times*, 14 April 1996.
23. James Brooke, "Rapists in Uniform: Peru Looks the Other Way," *New York Times*, 29 April 1993.
24. "We Are Mehinaku" (Washington, D.C.: Public Broadcasting Service, 1981), script, p. 7. Also see Thomas Gregor, *Mehinaku: The Drama of Daily Life in a Brazilian Indian Village* (Chicago: University of Chicago Press, 1987), and Robert F. Murphy, "Social Structure and Sex Antagonism," in *Peoples and Cultures of Native South America*, ed. Daniel Gross (Garden City, N.Y.: Natural History Press, 1973).

4. YAHEWH'S INCENTIVES FOR TAMING MALES

1. There are many stories in the Bible for which there is no historical evidence that tell of sexual chaos and violence by men against women among the early Israelites. Reuben, the son of Israel (Jacob), rapes his father's concubine (Gen. 35:21, 22). Earlier, when Jacob's two sons, Simeon and Levy, learn that She-chem the Hivite loved their sister Dinah, carried her off, and had sex with her, they fell upon the town and pillaged it, killing all the males and taking from the Hivites their flocks, cattle, donkeys, and whatever was in the town and the countryside. "They carried off all their riches, all their little children and their wives, and looted everything to be found in their houses." Jacob's only complaint to his sons was that they had put him in bad odor with the people of the land, the Canaanites and the Perizzites (Gen. 34: 1–31).

2. In this book, I frequently use the customary term *God* to signify the transcendent, nameless, imageless, timeless source of all. In Exodus, when God first appears to Moses, the prophet asks Yahweh what he should tell the sons of Israel if they ask for the name of God. The answer came: "I Am who I Am." This frmula in the third person becomes "he is," which frequently is translated as Yahweh. My own preference is for the less familiar term Hashem, which defies absolutely any definition and best preserves the essential mystery of the Eternal Source. For the sake of readers who are largely unfamiliar with Hashem, I will use "God or "Yahweh."

3. Leo G. Perdue, Joseph Blenkinsopp, John J. Collins, and Carol Myers, *Families in Ancient Israel* (Louisville, Ky., Westminster John Knox Press, 1997).

4. Carol Myers, *Discovering Eve: Ancient Israelite Women in Context* (New York: Oxford University Press, 1988), 180, 187, 190. Gerda Lerner also believes that as Jewish tribes moved from confederacy to statehood there probably was a gradual restriction of women's public and economic roles and an increase in the regulation of their sexuality. Lerner finds confirmation in this view in "the excessive language of censure of women's 'whoring in prophets' so that whoring becomes a metaphor for the evils of a bad society." Gerda Lerner, *The Creation of Patriarchy* (New York: Oxford University Press, 1986), 177.

5. John J. Collins, "Marriage, Divorce, and Family in Second Temple Judaism," in Perdue et al., *Families in Ancient Israel*, 104–49.

6. See Shaye J. D. Cohen, *From the Maccabees to the Mishna* (Philadelphia: Westminster Press, 1987), 20–24, for a summary of the major changes that took place in the transition from a temple cult to a universal religion. Also see Gösta W. Ahlström, *Who Were the Israelites?* (Winona Lake, Ind.: Eisenbrauns, 1986).

7. Louis Finkelstein, *Akiba: Scholar, Saint and Martyr* (New York: Atheneum, 1970), viii.

5. THE SANCTIFICATION OF LUST

1. I. B. Singer, "The Spinoza of Market Street," in *The Spinoza of Market Street and Other Stories* (New York: Avon Books, 1958), 24.
2. Flavius Josephus, *The Works of Flavius Josephus, Containing Twenty Books of the Jewish Antiquities, Seven Books of the Jewish War, and the Life of Josephus Written by Himself,* trans. William Whiston (Philadelphia: Lippincott, Grambo & Co., 1850), 2:515.
3. Matt Ridley, *The Red Queen: Sex and the Evolution of Human Nature* (New York: Penguin Books, 1993), 193–282. Ridley surveyed the work of several anthropologists and came to the decisive conclusion that men of high status everywhere had multiple sexual partners, but he did not look at the Jews. His survey leans heavily on several articles by Laura L. Betzig and on her book *Despotism and Differential Reproduction: A Darwinian View of History* (New York: Aldine, Hawthorne, 1986).

   For another well-written, easily accessible account of the subject, see Helen E. Fisher, *Anatomy of Love: The Natural History of Monogamy, Adultery, and Divorce* (New York: W. W. Norton & Co., 1992). Fisher claims that some Chinese emperors copulated with over one thousand women, carefully routed through the royal bedroom when they were most likely to conceive. In the T'ang Dynasty of China (618–906 C.E.), the golden age of Chinese civilization, careful records were kept of dates of menstruation and conception in the harem to allow the emperor to copulate with the most fertile concubines.
4. This discussion of the Jewish approach to sexuality in marriage relies on the work of many authors, several of whom should be mentioned at the outset. David Biale's *Eros and the Jews: From Biblical Israel to Contemporary America* (New York: Basic Books, 1982) is a superb work of scholarship on an extremely complicated subject. Biale points out that Jews were affected from time to time by ascetic ideals found in Greco-Roman and Christian cultures. He found the ascetic strain in the Hasidic movement of the eighteenth and nineteenth centuries and even in Zionism and Jewish socialism. But Biale would support the basic theme here. Whatever minority tendencies Jews had toward sexual asceticism or toward licentiousness, from the Talmud until the late Middle Ages sexual fidelity was the general practice as well as the norm within a religiously sanctioned view that sexual desire was sanctified within marriage.

   Also see Rachel Biale, *Women and Jewish Law: The Essential Texts, Their History, and Their Relevance for Today* (New York: Schocken Books, 1995), and Daniel Boyarin, *Carnal Israel: Reading Sex in Talmudic Culture* (Berkeley: University of California Press, 1993). Boyarin, a talmudic scholar, makes an imaginative effort to reconcile Orthodox *halakhic* strictures on women within the religious community with his feminism. Blu Greenberg, an Orthodox woman, takes the same approach to the attempt to reconciling *halakhah* with feminism in *On Women and Judaism: A View from Tradition* (Philadelphia: The Jewish Publication Society of America, 1996). See also another Orthodox writer, Tamar Frankiel, *The Voice of Sarah: Feminine Spirituality in Traditional Judaism* (New York: HarperCollins, 1990), particularly chap. 2, on womanhood and sexuality, where she repeats the consensus view that Judaism evolved a positive attitude toward sexuality so that intense sexuality and intense spirituality are not mutually exclusive.

Another source for the overall approach that sex is positive and holy when confined to marriage and should be joyous, too, can be found in Maurice Lamm, *The Jewish Way in Love and Marriage* (New York: Harper & Row, 1980). Lamm writes that the key concept in understanding Jewish love and marriage is *yichud*, which means "together." It is a mutual relationship, implying intimacy, such as the love one has for a spouse. It connotes sustained love and sex within the framework of marriage. He believes that there is talmudic authority for the view that "not intercourse alone is a religious command, but all forms of intimacy by which a man rejoices with his wife" (p. 23). There is no question, according to Lamm, of the positive view of sex in marriage.

Also see David M. Feldman, *Marital Relations, Birth Control and Abortion in Jewish Law* (New York: Schocken Books, 1968); see especially chapters 4 and 5.

5. Feldman, *Marital Relations*, 21–26.

6. Ibid., 63–65.

7. R. Biale, *Women and Jewish Law*, 130, 131.

8. Lamm, *The Jewish Way*, 136.

9. D. Biale, *Eros and the Jews*, 96.

10. R. Biale, *Women and Jewish Law*, 140. Biale thinks that the *Iggeret Ha-Kodesh* may have been written by a kabbalist, Joseph ben Abraham Gikatilla (1248–1325), but it could easily have been written by Nahmanides.

    David Biale also points to Gikatilla, who was a close friend of Moses de Leon, the author of the *Book of Splendor*, the *Zohar*, at the end of the thirteenth century. D. Biale, *Eros and the Jews*, 110.

11. D. Biale, *Eros and the Jews*, 103.

12. R. Biale, *Women and Jewish Law*, 142.

13. D. Biale, *Eros and the Jews*, 78.

14. R. Biale, *Women and Jewish Law*, 144. Here we have an explicit example of the sexual agency of women. It is the wife who is being advised on how to conduct foreplay. In one respect, a sexual double standard that favors women is set up. *Halakhah* has virtually nothing to say on lesbianism, and it is mentioned in the Talmud only twice, without any punitive aspect to it. Although it is considered licentious, lesbianism does not constitute an act of promiscuity, which would disqualify a woman from marriage to a priest. It must have

existed. Maimonides expresses his opposition to it but acknowledges that there is no commandment prohibiting it (see p. 195).

15. Lamm, *The Jewish Way*. See chap. 2, "Romantic Love and the Jewish Concept of Love," on the Jewish concept of love for the Isaac and Jacob examples.

16. Many of these stories are interpreted from a woman's perspective in Frankiel, *The Voice of Sarah*.

17. *Selected Poems of Judah Halevi*, ed. Heinrich Brady (New York: Arno Press, 1973). For examples of sensual love poems, see pp. 65, 159, 160.

18. D.Biale, *Eros and the Jews*, 117.

19. Ibid., 131.

20. Ibid., 78.

21. Those rabbis had many biblical passages to rely on in their opposition to the strict segregation of the sexes, including Gen. 29:7, 24:13; Exo. 2:16; Ruth 2: 3, 7, 9, 14; Exo. 32:22; Deut. 31:12; Josh. 8:35.

22. These circumstances are described variously in Exo. 15:20; Judg. 16:27, 22:21; Jer. 31:12; Judg. 11:34; 1 Sam. 18:6; Judg. 4:4–8, 18; 2 Sam. 14:2–4; 1 Kings 19:2, 21: 8; Judg. 4:8, 18, 9:53.

23. Louis M. Epstein, *Sex Laws and Customs in Judaism* (New York: Ktav, 1948), 13–15. On Christian doctrine, see Matt. 5:28: "Whosoever looketh on a woman to lust after her hath committed adultery with her in his heart."

24. D. Biale, *Eros and the Jews*, 78, 92, 115. Maimonides' view was quite different from that of the talmudic rabbi Judah the Hasid, who advised: "Your wife should dress and adorn herself like a fruitful vine so that your lust will become inflamed like a fire and you will shoot semen like an arrow."

25. R. Biale, *Women and Jewish Law*, 3. Also see Norman Lamm, *A Hedge of Roses* (New York: Philipp Feldheim, 1966). Lamm, a modern Orthodox rabbi, writes: "Family purity represents . . . the joyous affirmation of life and the abhorrence of death and suffering. The institution of the *mikvah*, through the symbol of the waters, offers the possibility of a magnificent beginning for human life in love with life" (p. 89).

26. D. Biale, *Eros and the Jews*, 115.

27. R. Biale, *Women and Jewish Law*, 132, 133.

28. Greenberg, *On Women and Judaism*, 118.

29. L. Epstein, *Sex Laws and Customs*, 128.

30. Ibid., 108.

6. PATRIARCHS WHO DEPEND ON WIVES

1. Rachel Biale, *Women and Jewish Law: The Essential Texts, Their History, and Their Relevence for Today* (New York: Schocken Books, 1995), 62.

2. Nikos Kazantzakis, *Zorba the Greek* (New York: Simon & Schuster, 1953), 13.

In the motion picture, Zorba, played by Anthony Quinn, gives his answer as follows: "Am I not a man? And is not a man stupid? So, I'm married. Wife, children, house, everything. The full catastrophe!"

3. Avie Goldberg, "Family and Community in Sephardic North Africa: Historical and Anthropological Perspectives" (manuscript), 26, 27.

4. David M. Feldman, *Marital Relations, Birth Control and Abortion in Jewish Law* (New York: Schocken Books, 1968), 41.

5. Louis J. Newman, ed., *The Talmudic Anthology* (New York: Behrman House, 1945), 538–40.

6. Aviva Cantor, *Jewish Women/Jewish Men: The Legacy of Patriarchy in Jewish Life* (San Francisco: Harper, 1995), 130.

7. Newman, *Talmudic Anthology*, 272.

8. Adapted and translated by Florence Ayscough, *Chinese Women: Yesterday and Today* (Boston: Houghton Mifflin, 1967), 242–45. The contrast between the ideal Jewish wife in the Torah paradigm and the ideal Confucianist wife may have a lot to do with the fact that the Chinese wife married into a clan. The bride was brought as a gift from the son to his parents in gratitude; thus, she was taken into the bridegroom's household much as an indentured servant would be. The mother-in-law had almost final authority over her daughter-in-law. The son continued to direct his love toward his parents, not his new wife. In Precept 6 of the seven precepts, the ideal woman asks the important question as to how she can "gain the hearts of father-in-law and mother-in-law" and concludes that nothing is equal in importance to "the imperative of obedience" to them (pp. 246, 247). The rabbis, however, took the view that once a man marries he must direct his love toward his wife, which fits in a nuclear family much more effectively than in a clan household.

9. Cantor, *Jewish Women/Jewish Men*, 115, 116.

10. Tamar Frankiel, *The Voice of Sarah: Feminine Spirituality in Traditional Judaism* (New York: HarperCollins, 1990), 10.

11. Sylvia Barack Fishman, "Soldiers in an Army of Mothers: Reflections on Naomi and the Heroic Biblical Women," chap. 5 in Judith A. Kates and Gail Twersky Reimer, eds., *Reading Ruth* (New York: Ballantine Books, 1994), 277.

12. Louis M. Epstein, *The Jewish Marriage Contract* (New York: Jewish Theological Seminary of America, 1927), 100.

13. Montefiore Loewe, ed., *Rabbinic Anthology* (Philadelphia: The Jewish Publication Society of America, 1963), 509.

14. R. Biale, *Women and Jewish Law*, 203–18.

15. Moses Maimonides, *The Guide for the Perplexed*, trans. M. Friedlander (New York: Dover Publications, 1956), 15.

16. R. Biale, *Women in Jewish Law*, 37.
17. Cantor, *Jewish Women/Jewish Men*, 115, 116.
18. Newman, *Talmudic Anthology*, 545.
19. L. Epstein, *The Jewish Marriage Contract*, 277–78. For a discussion of the *ketubah* as a charter for women's rights, see also Maurice Lamm, *The Jewish Way in Love and Marriage* (New York: Harper & Row, 1980), 200; Feldman, *Marital Relations*; and Blu Greenberg, *On Women and Judaism: A View from Tradition* (Philadelphia: The Jewish Publication Society of Americas, 1996), 131–33.
20. Material on divorce and the *agunah* issue can be found in Feldman, *Marital Relations*; Lamm, *The Jewish Way*, 200; L. Epstein, *The Jewish Marriage Contract*; and Greenberg, *On Women and Judaism*.
21. Rabbi Akiba is cited in R. Alcalay, ed., *Words of the Wise* (Jerusalem: Masada Press, 1970), 313.
22. For a discussion of the paucity of historical scholarship on Jewish family life, see Paula E. Hyman, "Perspectives on the Evolving Jewish Family," in Steven M. Cohen and Paula E. Hyman, eds., *The Jewish Family: Myths and Reality* (New York: Holmes & Meier, 1986), 3–13.
23. Sondra Henry and Emily Taitz, *Written Out of History: Our Jewish Foremothers*, rev. ed. (Fresh Meadows, N.Y.: Biblio Press, 1983), 32–34.
24. Shlomo Dov Goitein, *The Family*, vol. 3 in Goitein, *A Mediterranean Society: The Jewish Community of the Arab World as Portrayed in the Documents of the Cairo Geniza* (Berkeley and Los Angeles: University of California Press, 1978), a book on Jewish family life in the Mediterranean basin from the tenth to the thirteenth century, which is devoted entirely to the Jewish family in Sephardic communities. An easily accessible review of the Cairo documents can be found in Henry and Taitz, *Written Out of History*, 71–76.
25. Henry and Taitz, *Written Out of History*, 76–79. Also see Jacob Katz, *Tradition and Crisis: Jewish Society at the End of the Middle Ages* (New York: Schocken Books, 1961; reprint 1971), 135–56; and Jacob R. Marcus, ed., *The Jew in the Medieval World: A Source Book, 315–1791* (New York: Atheneum, 1972), 389–94, 399–401 for stories of some independent women.
26. Edward Fram, *Ideals Face Reality: Jewish Law and Life in Poland, 1550–1655* (Cincinnati, Ohio: Hebrew Union College Press, 1997), 79, 80.
27. The story about Glückel of Hameln, told in many sources, can be found in Jay David, *Growing Up Jewish* (New York: William Morrow & Co., 1969), 15–22. For those who want a translation of the original, see *The Memoirs of Glückel of Hameln (1646–1724) written by Herself*, trans. and ed. Beth-Zion Abrahams (New York: Thomas Yoseloff, 1962).
28. Israel Abrahams, *Jewish Life in the Middle Ages* (New York: Atheneum, 1969), 88.

29. Ibid., 84, 87. Jewish men also accepted wives who took responsibility for making decisions for their family and managing businesses, as Glückel did.
30. Nahum N. Glatzer, ed., *The Judaic Tradition* (Boston: Beacon Press, 1969), 202.
31. Cantor, *Jewish Women/Jewish Men*, 106.
32. Ibid., 107, 108.
33. Greenberg, *On Women and Judaism*, 63.
34. Ellen M. Umansky and Dianne Ashton, *Four Centuries of Jewish Women's Spirituality: A Source Book* (Boston: Beacon Press, 1992), 133. See Abrahams, *Jewish Life in the Middle Ages*, 54. Also see Henry and Taitz, *Written Out of History*, 87. Henry and Taitz tell about Eva (Hava) Bacharach, who was an expert in rabbinical and biblical writings; Rebecca Tiktiner, who probably lived in Prague or Poland about 1520 and died around 1550 and who wrote a book on religion and ethics; and Mary Mizrachi, wo ran a yeshiva (see pp. 87–109).
35. Henry and Taitz, *Written Out of History*, 59.

7. TO TEACH THE CHILDREN DILIGENTLY

1. Louis J. Newman, ed., *The Talmudic Anthology*, (New York: Behrman House, 1945) 124.
2. *Sayings of the Fathers*, trans. and commentary by Joseph H. Hertz (New York, Behrman House, 1945), 101–3.
3. Newman, *Talmudic Anthology*, 124.
4. Michael Medved, "You Must Remember This: Jewish Men and Jewish Memory," *Sh'ma: A Journal of Jewish Responsibility* 20 January 1995, 3.
5. Newman, *Talmudic Anthology*, 70.
6. Ibid.
7. Solomon Ganzfried, *Code of Jewish Law (Kitzur Shulkhan Aruk. A Compilation of Jewish Laws and Customs)*, trans. Hyman E. Goldin (New York: Hebrew Pub. Co., 1927), 1:92.
8. Nahum N. Glatzer, *The Jewish Reader* (New York: Schocken Books, 1946), 119.
9. Ibid., 214. In other places, the Talmud reverses the order of importance. The rabbi answered the question as to whether a father or a mother should be attended to first when both request a drink of water and replied that the father comes first "because both you and your mother have a duty of honoring him." Abraham Cohen, *Every Man's Talmud* (New York: Schocken Books, 1975), 181.
10. Newman, *Talmudic Anthology*, 71.
11. Philip Ariès, *Centuries of Childhood* (New York: Vintage Books, 1962). According to Ariès, Europeans did not pay much attention to the stages of life of children.

12. Ivan G. Marcus, *Rituals of Childhood: Jewish Acculturation in Medieval Europe* (New Haven, Conn.: Yale University Press, 1996), 1–19. Maimonides is quoted on p. 19.

13. Ibid., 43.

14. Ibid., 31.

15. Israel Abrahams, ed., *Hebrew Ethical Wills* (Philadelphia: The Jewish Publication Society of America, 1948), 1:80.

16. Ibid., 1:322.

17. Shlomo Dov Goitein, *The Family*, vol. 3 in Goitein, *A Mediterranean Society: The Jewish Community of the Arab World as Portrayed in the Documents of the Caio Geniza* (Berkeley and Los Angles: University of California Press, 1978), 225, 226.

18. Ibid., 224.

19. Abrahams, *Hebrew Ethical Wills*, xxii.

20. Ibid., 36, 41, 42, 44, 48.

21. Jack Riemer and Nathaniel Stampfer, eds., *Ethical Wills: A Modern Jewish Treasury* (New York: Schocken Books, 1983), 5.

22. Abrahams, *Ethical Wills*, 116.

23. Ibid., 57, 61, 79.

24. Ibid., 123.

25. Ibid., 305.

26. Newman, *Talmudic Anthology*, 124.

27. Abrahams, *Hebrew Ethical Wills*, 281.

28. Ibid., 170.

8. CONTINUITY AND CHANGE IN EUROPE

1. Judah Goldin, "The Period of the Talmud," chap. 3 in vol. 1, *The Jews: Their History, Culture and Religion*, ed. Louis Finkelstein (New York: Harper & Brothers, 1949), vol. 1, chap. 3, pp. 170, 171.

2. Louis Wirth, *The Ghetto* (Chicago: University of Chicago Press, 1956), 30.

3. Ibid., 119.

4. Jacob Katz, *Tradition and Crisis: Jewish Society at the End of the Middle Ages* (New York: Schocken Books, 1961; reprint, 1971), 7.

5. Wirth, *The Ghetto*, 57.

6. David Biale, "Childhood, Marriage and the Family in Eastern European Jewish Enlightenment," chap. 4 in *The Jewish Family: Myths and Reality*, ed. Steven M. Cohen and Paula E. Hyman (New York: Holmes & Meier, 1986), 46, 47.

7. Ibid., 48–53.

8. Paula E. Hyman, *Gender and Assimilation in Modern Jewish History: The Roles and Representation of Women* (Seattle: University of Washington Press, 1995), 70–78.

9. Susan A. Glenn, *Daughters of the Shtetl: Life and Labor in the Immigrant Generation* (Ithaca, N.Y.: Cornell University Press, 1990), 13.

10. D. Biale, "Childhood," 46, 47; Marion A. Kaplan, "Priestess and Hausfrau: Women and Tradition in the German-Jewish Family," chap. 5 *in The Jewish Family: Myths and Reality*, ed. Steven M. Cohen and Paula E. Hyman (New York: Holmes & Meier, 1986).

11. Isaac Leib Peretz, "Lonely," in *The Book of Fire* (New York: Thomas Yoseloff, 1960), 324.

12. Isaac Leib Peretz, in *The Book of Fire* (New York: Thomas Yoseloff, 1960), 242; I. B. Singer, "The Destruction of Kreshev," in *The Spinoza of Market Street* (New York: Farrar, Straus and Cudahy, 1962), 182. In "The Destruction of Kreshev," the morning after Lise's wedding night her mother "found her daughter hiding under the quilt and too ashamed to speak to her. . . . It took a good deal of coaxing before Lise would permit her mother to examine the sheets, and indeed there was blood on them. 'Mazel tov, daughter,' the mother exclaimed. 'You are now a woman and share with us all the curse of Eve.'" We get the same response in Peretz's story "Uncle Shachne and Aunt Yachne." Chava won't get out of bed. She lies in bed with her face covered. Uncle Shachne and Aunt Yachne plead with her to get up: "At last a thin, frightened voice came from under the bedclothes: 'I am ashamed!'"

13. Mark Zborowski and Elizabeth Herzog, *Life Is with People: The Culture of the Shtetl* (New York: Schocken Books, 1962), 286, 287.

14. D. Biale, "Childhood."

15. I. B. Singer, "The Destruction of Kreshev," in *The Spinoza of Market Street* (New York: Avon Books, 1970), 187.

16. I. B. Singer, *The Manor* (New York: Farrar, Straus and Giroux, 1967).

17. I. B. Singer, *The Estate* (New York: Farrar, Straus and Giroux, 1969).

18. I. B. Singer, "Short Friday," in *Short Friday* (Philadelphia: Jewish Publication Society, 1945), 240.

19. Jacob R. Marcus, "Solomon Maimon in Poland," in *Jew in the Medieval World: A Source Book, 315–1791* (New York: Atheneum, 1972), 344.

20. Other proverbs that indicate the power of wives to determine the course of a marriage are "A woman makes of her husband what she will"; "As much as the wife is a queen, so much will her husband be king"; "A mother is a cover—she hides her children's faults and her husband's vices"; "Women persuade to good or to evil, but they always persuade"; "A comely wife is half a livelihood." For these and others in Yiddish, see Ignatz Bernstein and B. W. Segal, eds., *Yudishe shprikhverter un redensorten* (Warsaw: J. Kaufmann, 1908).

21. Ruth Rubin, ed., *Jewish Folk Songs* (New York: Oak Publishers, 1965), 22.
22. Zbrowski & Herzog, *Life Is with People*, 131.
23. Ibid., 132.
24. Shalom Aleichem, "Eternal Life," in *A Treasury of Yiddish Stories*, ed. Irving Howe and Eliezer Greenberg (New York: Viking Press, 1954), 151.
25. I. B. Singer, *Yoshe Kalb* (New York: Harper & Row, 1965), 139.
26. Sol Gittleman, *From Shtetl to Suburbia: The Family in Jewish Literary Imagination* (Boston: Beacon Press, 1978), 46.
27. Ibid., 90.
28. Marcus, "Ten Commandments for the Married Woman before 1620," in *The Jew in the Medieval World*, 444. Many Yiddish books were written for women. This one has a chapter on marriage in which a queen is giving her daughter in marriage to a young king and provides instructions embraced in the form of ten rules. The essence of the instruction is that she should not get angry with her husband or cross him in any way. "Try to have his meals ready at the proper time . . . try to be thrifty and careful with your husband's money . . . don't be anxious to know his secrets . . . don't expect of him anything that he considers difficult . . . don't make him jealous in any way; don't like his enemies, and don't hate his friends . . . don't be contrary with him."
29. Gittleman, *From Shtetl to Suburbia*, 67.
30. Hanan Jayalti, ed., *Yiddish Proverbs* (New York: Schocken Books, 1963), 91.
31. ChaeRan Y. Freeze, "Making and Unmaking the Jewish Family: Marriage and Divorce in Imperial Russia, 1850–1914" (Ph.D. diss., Brandeis University, 1997), 42.
32. Ibid.
33. Ibid., 65.
34. Ibid., 112.
35. Ibid., 266.
36. Ibid., 268, 269.
37. Ibid., 5.
38. Ibid., 235.
39. Ibid., 288.
40. Moses Leib Lilienblum, "The Sins of My Youth," in *The Golden Tradition: Jewish Life and Thought in Eastern Europe*, ed. Lucy S. Dawidowicz (Boston: Beacon Press, 1967), 127. The ideas of the *haskalah* first shook Lilienblum from his Orthodox moorings. He resented the fact that he had only been trained in Talmud as a young man and had not received a practical education. He resented his arranged marriage as well, and he sought meaning in movements that freed him from Orthodox constraints.
41. I am indebted to ChaeRan Y. Freeze for bringing a copy of Pauline Wenger-

off's manuscript to my attention. Pauline Wengeroff, "A Grandmother's Memoirs: Images from the Cultural History of the Jews in Nineteenth Century Russia," p. 372.

42. Copies of these documents were made by ChaeRan Y. Freeze, several of which were shown to me.

43. Zbrowski and Herzog, *Life Is with People*, 38.

44. Isaac Leib Peretz, "Mendel Braines," in *The Book of Fire* (New York: Thomas Yoseloff, 1960), 231–32.

45. Isaac Leib Peretz, "The Messenger," in *Stories and Pictures*, trans. Helena Frank (Philadelphia: The Jewish Publication Society of America, 1906), 106.

46. In a memoir by Benjamin M. Laikin, *Memoirs of a Practical Dreamer* (New York: Bloch Publishing Co., 1970), Laikin writes that his mother's tasks
. . . were heavier than those of the rest of the family. The male members took care of the horses, but it was mother's job to take care of the cows, to feed them and milk them. The men in the family felt that such work was beneath their dignity. We always had lots of wood in the yard, but here again it was not considered a man's job to haul wood into the house, so that too was mother's chore. In addition, she had to do the cooking, the cleaning, dishwashing, and the laundry. She also had to sew clothing for the younger children, repair the clothing of the older ones and, in her spare time, knit socks for the entire family. During the winter months Mother had to pluck feathers for pillows, prepare filling for the pillow cases for my sister's dowry, and also knit woolen gloves and woolen socks for the men in the family, since it was very cold at the mill. She had other chores and was never surprised at the demands made of her. One day my father came from the mill and said: "Kraineh, I have just bought a wagon full of buckwheat, and I need another 25 rubles." Without a word, my mother put a kerchief on her head and went out to arrange a *"gemilut khessed,"* a short term interest-free loan. (pp. 42, 43)

47. Mary Antin, *The Promised Land* (Boston: Houghton Mifflin Co., 1911), 34.

48. Isaac Leib Peretz, "The Outcast," in *The Book of Fire* (New York: Thomas Yoseloff, 1960), 430. Sholom Aleichem wrote often and poignantly about the pampering of boy children, who were constantly praised for intellectual achievements. One father listens with pride to his son explain how far he has gotten in his studies. Glowing with happiness, he proclaims him a jewel. See Sholom Aleichem, "Home for Passover," in *Collected Stories of Sholom Aleichem* (New York: The Modern Library, 1956), 98. Sons were given choice bits of food, sung to, and turned to by mothers for advice as they got older (Aleichem, "I'm Lucky I'm an Orphan," *Collected Stories*, 266). Fathers praised their sons as thinking, intelligent members of the human race, often

praising each intellectual success (Aleichem, "The Lottery Ticket," *Collected Stories*, 361).

49. I. B. Singer, "Yentl, the Yeshiva Boy," in *Short Friday* (New York: Schocken Books), 132.

50. Frieda Forman, et al., eds., *Found Treasures: Stories by Yiddish Women Writers* (Toronto: Second Story Press, 1994).

51. Ibid., 160.

52. Antin, *Promised Land*, 93.

53. Ibid., 41.

54. Puah Rakowski, "A Mind of My Own," in *The Golden Tradition: Jewish Life and Thought in Eastern Europe*, ed. Lucy S. Dawidowicz (Boston: Beacon Press, 1967), 392.

55. Zborwski and Herzog, *Life Is with People*, 291.

56. Maurice Samuel, *The World of Shalom Aleichem* (New York: Vintage Books, 1943), 313.

9. IMMIGRANTS AND THEIR CHILDREN, 1880–1920

1. L. Fuchs, *Family Matters* (New York: Random House, 1972), 40–43.

2. For a brief review of this period, see Gerald Sorin, *A Time for Building: The Third Migration, 1880–1920* (Baltimore: Johns Hopkins University Press, 1992), 1–11.

3. Nancy Cott, *The Bonds of Womanhood: "Woman's Sphere" in New England, 1780–1835* (New Haven, Conn.: Yale University Press, 1977), pp. 200–1; Carl N. Degler, *At Odds: Women and the Family in America from the Revolution to the Present* (New York: Oxford University Press, 1980).

4. Leon Kobrin, "The Tenement House," in *The New Country*, ed. Henry Goodman (New York: Yiddischer Kultur Farband, 1961), p. 27. It was not just New York where the Jews lived in poverty. That was true in any of the big East Coast cities of the United States and Chicago, too. Isaac M. Fein described how the immigrants suffered terribly from poverty in Baltimore, where desertion was also common. See Isaac M. Fein, *The Making of an American Jewish Community* (Philadelphia: The Jewish Publication Society of America, 1971). It was also true in Buffalo, where Selig Adler described the severe overcrowding in the William Street ghetto in an "atmosphere in which there were no decent play outlets for children, [where] many youngsters got into trouble." Selig Adler and Thomas E. Connolly, *From Ararat to Suburbia* (Philadelphia: The Jewish Publication Society of America, 1960), 160–223, 224.

5. Michael Gold, *Jew without Money* (New York: Avon, 1972), 5.

6. William Dean Howells, *Impressions and Experiences* (New York: Harper & Brother, 1896), 127–49.
7. Abraham Cahan, *The Rise of David Levinsky* (New York: Harper & Row, 1917), 95.
8. See Jack Riemer and Nathaniel Stampfer, eds., *Ethical Wills: A Modern Jewish Treasury* (New York: Schocken Books, 1983). See also Jacob Rader Marcus, ed., *Documents of American Jewish Life* (Northvale, N.J., J. Aronson, 1990); see esp. "This I Believe."
9. Harry Golden, preface to *The Spirit of the Ghetto*, by Hutchins Hapgood (New York: Schocken Books, 1965), 18.
10. Hutchins Hapgood, *The Spirit of the Ghetto* (New York: Schocken Books, 1965), 22.
11. Ibid., 26, 27.
12. Saul Bellow, *Herzog* (New York: Viking Press, 1964), 147.
13. Ludwig Lewisohn, *The Island Within* (Philadelphia: The Jewish Publication Society of America, 1968), 16.
14. Herbert Gold, *Fathers* (New York: Random House, 1966), 125.
15. Mary Antin, *The Promised Land* (Boston: Houghton Mifflin Co., 1911), 17, 18.
16. Anzia Yerzierska, *Bread Givers* (New York: Doubleday: Page & Co., 1925), p. 15.
17. Ibid., 45, 46.
18. Ibid., 48.
19. Ibid., 265. The theme of deep resentment against husbands whose piety gets in the way of their making a living recurs in other Jewish immigrant fiction, as in Isaac Raboy, *Nine Brothers* (New York: Yiddisher Kultur Farband, 1968). By the end of the book, around 1908 or 1909, the wife, Reizi, controls what little money the family has and runs the household, but she bitterly resented her husband, Chaim, for spending so much time in the synagogue. In her eyes, her husband had become a bum, hanging around with loafers at the synagogue "who were nobodys themselves and no good to anyone else either" (p. 197).
20. Henry Roth, *Call It Sleep* (New York: Avon Books, 1962).
21. Henry Roth, interview by Yossi Melman, *Jerusalem Post*, 24 September 1994, international ed.
22. Budd Schulberg, *What Makes Sammy Run?* in *The Literature of American Jews*, ed. Theodore L. Gross (New York: Free Press, 1973), 237.
23. Cahan, *Rise of David Levinsky*, 96–97.
24. Harry Roskolenko, "America, the Thief," in *The Immigrant Experience: The Anguish of Becoming American*, ed. Thomas C. Wheeler (Baltimore: Master Deed, Penguin Books, 1971), 152.
25. Richard Brown, "Two Baltic Families Who Came to America: The Jacobsons

and the Kruskals, 1870–1970," *American Jewish Archives* 24:(1) (April 1972), 68–69.

26. Jonathan D. Sarna, ed. and trans., *People Walk on Their Heads: Moses Weinberger's "Jews and Judaism in New York"* (New York: Holmes and Meier Publishers, 1981).

27. Susan A. Glenn, *Daughters of the Shtetl: Life and Labor in the Immigrant Generation* (Ithaca, N.Y.: Cornell University Press, 1990), 77. A wonderful semi-fictional account of the process by which many immigrants assimilated to the new norms of husband-wife relationships can be found in Charles Angoff's *In the Morning Light*. Angoff writes: "But once Moshe began to work on the Sabbath, he became tolerant of many things in America" (p. 16). Angoff goes on to tell how Moshe and his three brothers went into business and how, with their success, Moshe changed his attitude toward husband-wife relationships. Mottel and his wife, Bassel, had owned a candy store. Mottel sold it and went into manufacturing. Bassel no longer helped her husband, and they moved to a better neighborhood, where her life changed. He wanted her to have nice clothes and furs, and he wanted her to join women's organizations. Even though she did not pressure him for these things, he still wanted them to live in what he considered the American way. Charles Angoff, *In the Morning Light* (New York: Beachurst Press, 1952), 307, 559.

28. Angoff, *In the Morning Light*, 15–16.

29. Hapgood, *Spirit of the Ghetto*, 7, 8.

30. Thomas Kessner, *The Golden Door: Italian and Jewish Immigrant Mobility in New York City 1880–1915* (New York: Oxford University Press, 1977), 61.

31. Ibid., 64, 65, 70.

32. Judith E. Smith, *Family Connections: A History of Italian and Jewish Immigrant Lives in Providence, Rhode Island, 1900–1940* (Albany: State University of New York Press, 1985), 31, 48.

33. Jacob Alfred Kutzik, "Social Basis of American Jewish Philanthropy" (Ph.D. diss., Brandeis University, 1967).

34. Glenn, *Daughters of the Shtetl*, 66.

35. Elizabeth Ewen, *Immigrant Women in the Land of Dollars: Life and Culture on the Lower East Side, 1890–1925* (New York: Monthly Review Press, 1985), 39, 40, 87, 101–3.

36. Howard Simons, *Jewish Times: Voices of the American Jewish Experience* (Boston: Houghton-Mifflin Co., 1988), 8.

37. Angoff, *In the Morning Light*, 215. For comparable memories see Sydelle Kramer and Jenny Masur, eds., *Jewish Grandmothers* (Boston: Beacon Press, 1976). Many immigrant fathers worked so hard that they had little time for anything else. A classic example appears in Bernard Malamud's *The Assistant*,

where it is learned that Morris Buber worked in his store fifteen to sixteen hours a day, seven days a week, for twenty-two years. He was honest and a good provider. No one expected him to know Torah. Bernard Malamud, *The Assistant* (New York: Farrar, Straus & Cudahy, 1957).

38. Alfred Kazin, "A Walker in the City," in *Jewish-American Literature: An Anthology*, ed. Abraham Chapman (New York: Mentor Book, New American Library, 1974), p. 249.

39. Paula E. Hyman, *Gender and Assimilation in Modern Jewish History: The Rules and Representation of Women* (Seattle: University of Washington, Press, 1995), 42.

40. Ibid., 26, 27, 39–48.

41. Ibid., 118.

42. Isaac Metzker, ed., *A Bintel Brief* (Garden City, N.Y.: Doubleday & Co., 1971), 109–10.

43. Ibid.

44. Maxine S. Seller, "Defining Socialist Womanhood: The Woman's Page of the *Jewish Daily Forward* in 1919," *America Jewish History* 76(4) (1987): 414–38.

45. Adler and Connolly, *From Ararat to Suburbia*, 227; and Fein, *Making of an American Jewish Community*, 153. One reason for the spike in the Jewish desertion rate was that spouses were often separated for as much as three or four years, since men came to the United States before their wives.

46. Metzker, *Bintel Brief*, 83–84.

47. Richard F. Shepard and Vicki Gold Levi, eds., *Live and Be Well: A Celebration of Yiddish Culture in America from the First Immigrants to the Second World War* (New York: Ballantine Books, 1982), 64–66.

48. H. Simon, *Jewish Times*, 133. See also Robert Rockaway, *But He Was Good to His Mother: The Lives and Crimes of Jewish Gangsters* (Jerusalem: Geffen House, 1983); Jenna Weissman Joselit, *Our Gang: Jewish Crime and the New York Jewish Community, 1900–1940* (Bloomington: University of Indiana Press, 1983); and Rich Cohen, *Tough Jews: Fathers, Sons and Gangster Dreams* (New York: Simon & Schuster, 1998).

49. Shepard and Levi, eds., *Live and Be Well*, 50, 51.

50. Hapgood, *Spirit of the Ghetto*, 44, 45.

51. Irving Louis Horowitz, *Daydreams and Nightmares: Reflections on a Harlem Childhood* (Jackson: University Press of Mississippi, 1990), 34.

52. Bella Spewack, *The Streets: A Memoir of the Lower East Side* (New York: The Feminist Press at the City University of New York, 1995). Later, Kate Simon, daughter of immigrants in the Bronx, held onto the moving trolleys alongside her brothers. Kate Simon, *Bronx Primitive* (New York: Harper & Row, 1982).

53. Budd Schulberg, *What Makes Sammy Run?* (New York: Random House, 1941), p. 244.

54. Antin, *Promised Land*, xx.

55. K. Simon, *Bronx Primitive*, 36.

56. Irving Howe, *World of Our Fathers* (New York: Harcourt Brace Jovanovich, 1976), 181.

57. Jerome Weidman, "My Father Sits in the Dark," in *My Father Sits in the Dark and Other Selected Stories* (New York: Random House, 1961), 367–71. In *History of the Jews of Los Angeles*, Max Vorspan and Lloyd Gartner tell of the bewilderment of many Jewish immigrant fathers. One of them says: "I am a father and I am trying to set good ideals. As soon as the boy leaves home, the influences tend to tear those down, so what can I do? We have a religious atmosphere in our home, but outside there are anti-religious tendencies, even." Max Vorspan and Lloyd Gartner, i (Los Angeles: Huntington Library, 1970), 147.

58. Horowitz, *Daydreams and Nightmares*, 35.

59. Cahan, *Rise of David Levinsky*, 490.

60. Meyer Levin, *The Old Bunch* (New York: Viking Press, 1937), 16.

61. H. Simons, *Jewish Times*, 106.

62. Allon Schoener, *Portal to America: The Lower East Side, 1870–1925* (New York: Holt Rinehart & Winston, 1967), 255–56.

63. H. Roth, *Call It Sleep*, 507.

64. Sarna, *People Walk on Their Heads*, 76, 77.

65. Antin, *Promised Land*, 186.

66. Alfred Kazin, *A Walker in the City* (New York: Harcourt Brace Jovanovich, 1951), 17–18.

67. Saul Bellow, *The Adventures of Augie March* (New York: Viking Press, 1953), 31.

68. Cahan, *Rise of David Levinsky*, 491.

69. Morris Raphael Cohen, *A Dreamer's Journey: The Autobiography of Morris Raphael Cohen* (Boston: Beacon Press, 1949), 84–85.

70. Jacob Riis, "The Children of the Poor," in *The Poor in Great Cities*, ed. Robert A. Woods, et al. (1896; reprint, London: Arno Press, 1971), 102.

71. Kessner, *The Golden Door*, 97, 98.

72. Kazin, "Walker in the City," *Jewish American Literature*, 241.

73. H. Roth, *Call It Sleep*, p. 284.

74. Neil M. Cowan and Ruth Schwartz Cowan, *Our Parents' Lives: Jewish Assimilation in Everyday Life* (New Brunswick, N.J.: Rutgers University Press, 1989), 89.

75. Abraham Cahan, *The Education of Abraham Cahan*, ed. Leon Stein (Philadelphia: The Jewish Publication Society of America, 1969), 240.

76. Morris Hillquit, "The Birth of Jewish Unions," in *Autobiographies of American Jews*, ed. Harold U. Sibolow (Philadelphia: The Jewish Publication Society of America, 1965), 81.

77. George Kranzler, *Williamsburg: A Jewish Community in Transition* (New York: Philipp Feldheim, 1961), 24.

78. Schoener, *Portal to America*, 133–34.

79. For a review of how Jews co-opted American culture in order to sustain interest in Judaism, see Jenna Weissman Joselit, *The Wonders of America: Reinventing Jewish Culture, 1880–1950* (New York: Hill and Wang, 1994).

80. Sam Levinson, "Everything but Money," in *Growing Up Jewish*, ed. by Jay David (New York: William Morrow & Co., 1969), 236, 237.

81. Roskolenko, "America, the Thief," 175.

82. Alfred Kazin, "A Walker in the City," in *Growing Up Jewish*, ed. Jay David (New York: William Morrow & Co., 1969), p. 255.

83. Hapgood, *Spirit of the Ghetto*, 29.

84. Andrew R. Heinz, *Adapting to Abundance: Jewish Immigrants, Mass Consumption, and the Search for American Identity* (New York: Columbia University Press, 1990). Heinz persuasively argues that the lure of consumption hastened the decline of traditional Judaism.

10. THE AMERICANIZATION OF FATHERS, 1920–1960

1. Neil M. Cowan and Ruth Schwartz Cowan, *Our Parents' Lives: Jewish Assimilation in Everyday Life* (New Brunswick, N.J.: Rutgers University Press, 1989), 235.

2. Henry L. Feingold, *A Time for Searching: Entering the Mainstream, 1920–1945* (Baltimore: Johns Hopkins University Press, 1992), 139.

3. Ibid., 142.

4. Ibid., 126.

5. Ibid., 145, 152, 153.

6. Paula E. Hyman, *Gender and Assimilation in Modern Jewish History: The Roles and Representation of Women* (Seattle: University of Washington Press, 1995), 105, 106.

7. Cowan and Cowan, *Our Parents' Lives*, 239.

8. Riv-Ellen Prell, *Fighting to Become Americans: Jews, Gender, and the Anxiety of Assimilation* (Boston: Beacon Press, 1999). See chap. 3, "Consuming Love: Marriage and Middle Class Aspirations."

9. Quotd in Hyman, *Gender and Assimilation*, 123.

10. A detailed analysis of differences in sexual behavior among the three major religious groups, as found in the *Kinsey Report on American Males*, appears in Louis A. Berman, *Jews and Intermarriage* (New York: Thomas Yoseloff, 1968). In every age group with the educational level of thirteen years or more,

Jews had a higher median frequency of sexual intercourse, within the married group only.

11. Martha Wolfenstein borrowed from Margaret Mead the idea of the American family as a "launching pad." See Martha Wolfenstein, "Two Types of Jewish Mothers," in *Childhood in Contemporary Cultures*, ed. Margaret Mead and Martha Wolfenstein (Chicago: University of Chicago Press, Phoenix ed., 1963), 438.

12. Lloyd W. Warner and Leo Srole, *The Social Systems of American Ethnic Groups* (New Haven, Conn.: Yale University Press, 1945) esp. pp. 113, 114. On women's loan societies, see Shelley Y. Tenenbaum, *A Credit to Their Community: Jewish Loan Societies in the United States, 1880–1945* (Detroit: Wayne State University Press, 1993), 84–90.

Mary McCune, "Social Workers in the *Muskeljudentum*: 'Hadassah Ladies,' 'Manly Men,' and the Significance of Gender in the American Zionist Movement, 1912–1928," *American Jewish History* 86 no. 2 (1998) 135–65. Also see Faith Rogow, *Gone to Another Meeting: The National Council of Jewish Women, 1893–1993* (Tuscaloosa: University of Alabama Press, 1993); Linda Gordon Kuzmack, *Women's Cause: The Jewish Women's Movement in England and the United States, 1881–1993* (Columbus: Ohio State University Press, 1990); Joyce Antler, *Journey Home: Jewish Women in the American Century* (New York: Free Press, 1997). Studies reported on in the next chapter show that Jewish women's organizational activity and leadership were nothing short of phenomenal, in Jewish and non-Jewish causes.

These were outlets for energetic, capable women whose grandmothers and great-grandmothers may have run small businesses in eastern Europe. In America, middle-class women found many barriers to participating in the paid labor force and often embraced the view that that was no place for a woman. See Alice Kessler-Harris, *Out to Work: A History of Wage-Earning Women in the United States* (New York: Oxford University Press, 1982).

13. Joyce Antler's *Journey Home* is a fine chronicle of the history of the achievements of American Jewish women. The most prominent of these women was Emma Lazarus, who at the age of seventeen wrote a volume of poems that her father, in sharp contrast to Mary Antin's father, printed privately with great pride.

14. Hutchins Hapgood, *The Spirit of the Ghetto* (New York: Schocken Books, 1965), 83.

15. One study of Jewish mothers in the period emphasizes their attempts to keep their children with them and to invest enormous emotional energy in their upbringing. See S. Barv, *Jewish Family Solidarity* (Vicksburg, Miss.: Nogales Press, 1940).

16. Werner J. Cahnman, "Intermarriage against the Background of American Democracy," in *Intermarriage and Jewish Life: A Symposium* (New York: Hertzl Press and Jewish Reconstructionist Press, 1963), 173–208.
17. Herbert Gold, *My Last Two Thousand Years* (New York: Random House, 1972), 13. Probably the most widely known of all neurotic, intrusive Jewish mothers is Sophie Portnoy in Philip Roth's *Portnoy's Complaint* (New York: Bantam Books, 1969). Sophie thinks of everything and takes care of everything and reminds her son Alex of it. When he rejects her food at one point, she takes it personally and asks Alex to tell her what horrible things she and her husband have done to be treated so badly.

    A mother in Daniel Fuchs's novel *Homage to Blenholt* listens in on her daughter's telephone conversations and grills her like a detective interrogating a suspect. Her son Max tries desperately to win her approval by succeeding in ways she endorses. See Daniel Fuchs, *Homage to Blenholt* (New York: Avon Books, 1972). The tradition extends into the 1950s with Mrs. Patimkin, who is unstrung after discovering a diaphragm in her daughter Brenda's bedroom, wondering what she, the mother, could have done to deserve such treatment (Philip Roth, *Goodbye, Columbus* [Boston: Houghton Mifflin Co., 1959]), and into the 1960s with *Portnoy's Complaint*.
18. S. J. Wilson, *Hurray for Me* (New York: Crown Publishers, 1964), 212–17.
19. Roger Kahn takes that point of view in *The Boys of Summer* (New York: Harper & Row, 1972). Also see Gerald Green's novel *To Brooklyn with Love* (New York: Triton Press, 1967). A great many kids growing up in the 1930s and 1940s in Brooklyn and the Bronx, like Albert Abrams in his fictional account set in Brownsville in 1934, found baseball to be the essence of Americanism and yet a way to make connections with their fathers.
20. Clifford Odets, "Awake and Sing," in *The Literature of American Jews*, ed. Theodore L. Gross (New York: Free Press, 1973), 153.
21. Clifford Odets, "Awake and Sing," in *Six Plays of Clifford Odets* (New York: Grove Press, 1966), 95.
22. Ibid., 71, 95, 153.
23. Maxine Hong Kingston, *Chinamen* (New York: Alfred A. Knopf, 1980), 248.
24. L. Fuchs, *Family Matters* (New York: Random House, 1972). See chap. 3, "On Being Female in America."
25. P. Roth, *Portnoy's Complaint*, 45.
26. Ibid., 7.
27. P. Roth, *Goodbye, Columbus*, 42. Comedians and sociologists mirrored this general approach to the decline of fathers in their work. "For sociologists and comics, Jewish patriarchy had fallen on hard times, producing a family out of kilter." Prell, *Fighting to Become Americans*, 163.

28. Herbert Gold, *My Last Two Thousand Years* (New York: Random House, 1972), 89. For a historian's view, see Jenna Weissman Joselit, *Wonders of America: Reinventing Jewish Culture* (New York: Hill and Wang, 1994), 102–5.
29. Deborah Dash Moore, *At Home in America: The Second Generation New York Jews* (New York: Columbia University Press, 1981), 58.
30. Solomon Poll, *The Hasidic Community of Williamsburg* (New York: The Free Press of Glencoe, 1962), 31–57. For a more detailed examination of changes in Hasidic families, see William Shaffir, "Persistence and Change in the Hasidic Family," chap. 13 in *The Jewish Family: Myths and Reality*, ed. Steven M. Cohen and Paula E. Hyman (New York: Holmes & Meier, 1986).
31. Letty Cottin Pogrebin, *Deborah, Golda and Me: Being Female and Jewish in America* (New York: Crown Publishers, 1991). See chap. 3, "One Man, Two Fathers."

II. THE EROSION OF PATRIARCHY, 1960–2000

1. Edward S. Shapiro, *A Time for Healing: American Jewry since World War II* (Baltimore: Johns Hopkins University Press, 1992), 99, 155–56, 233. The GI Bill of Rights had an enormous impact on the rate of Jewish college attendance. By 1967, 62 percent of the native-born Jews in New York City had attended college, and an astonishing one of four had some postgraduate education. For an analysis of the data, see Jack Elinson, Paul Haberman, and Cyrelle Gell, *Ethnic and Educational Data on Adults in New York City, 1963–64* (New York: School of Public Health and Administrative Medicine, Columbia University, 1967).

The penchant of Jews for higher education and their occupational mobility were accompanied by a sharp drop in birthrates. Given the opportunity for success, they made sure to concentrate their resources on fewer children. See Sidney Goldstein and Calvin Goldscheider, *Jewish-Americans: Three Generations in a Community* (Englewood Cliffs N.J.: Prentice-Hall, 1968), 135–36.

On the movement of Jews to warm weather cities, see Deborah Dash Moore, *To the Golden Cities* (New York: Free Press, 1994), a fascinating study on continuing and changing Jewish sensibilities and issues around identity for this period.
2. Sidney Taylor, *All-of-a-Kind* (New York: Dell Publishing Co., 1951).
3. Marshall Sklare and Joseph Greenblum, *Jewish Identity on the Suburban Frontier: A Study of Group Survival in the Open Society* (New York: Basic Books, 1967), 55. According to Sklare and Greenblum, native-born American Jews spent less time socializing with their relatives than their parents did.

4. Robert Winch, Scott Greer, and Rae Lesser Blumberg, "Ethnicity and Extended Familialism in an Upper-Middle-Class Suburb," *American Sociological Review* 32 (April 1967): 267; Sklare and Greenblum, *Jewish Identity*, 251–52; and Hope Jensen Leichter and William E. Mitchell, *Kinship and Casework* (New York: Russell Sage Foundation, 1967), 217, 241. Another study showed that Jews were closer to their parents than non-Jews and had the happiest marriages and fewest divorces. See Judson T. Landis, "Religiousness, Family Relationships, and Family Values in Protestant, Catholic and Jewish Families," *Marriage and Family Living* 22 (November 1960), pp. 341–47.

The closeness to parents, so suffocating in much of American Jewish literature of the period, appears to have been a factor in the success of third- and fourth-generation American Jews. Parents often were achievement machines. See Benjamin B. Ringer, *Edge of Friendliness: A Study of Jewish-Gentile Relations* (New York: Basic Books, 1967), 71–72. But not only were results in achievement high, but it appears from studies of the period that Jewish mental health levels were relatively high, compared to non-Jews. See Zena Smith-Blau, "A Comparative Study of Jewish and Non-Jewish Families in the Context of Changing of American Family Life")paper presented at the American Jewish Committee conference, Consultation on the Jewish Family and Jewish Identity, New York, April 1972). The so-called neurotic mothers of the period, according to Blau, were strongly ego-supporting for their children. Also see a major study in New York that showed Jews to have much less mental health impairment in all socioeconomic classes. They were less inclined to self-impairing types of behavior, such as suicide or alcoholism. They used services extensively, but they had less serious impairment. See Leo Srole and Thomas S. Langner, et al., *Mental Health in the Metropolis: The Midtown Manhattan Study* (New York: McGraw-Hill, 1962), 305, 306, 315. The stereotype of the highly protective Jewish mother may have been generally valid. But their overprotective behavior—rating high on affection, too—did not lead to serious mental impairment.

Also see Fred Strodtbeck, "Family Interaction, Values and Achievement," in *The Jews*, ed. Marshall Sklare (Glencoe, Ill.: Free Press, 1958), 147–65, confirming the general pattern of stronger marriages, tighter kinship relationships, and greater stability in Jewish families than among Protestants and Catholics. For more of the same, see Gerhard Lenski, *The Religious Factor* (Garden City, N.Y.: Doubleday & Co., 1963), 212–59.

5. On Jewish divorce rates, see P. Hyman, "Perspectives on the Evolving Jewish Family," 223, in *The Jewish Family: Myths and Reality*, ed. Steven M. Cohen and Paula E. Hyman (New York: Holmes and Meier, 1986). Goldstein and Goldscheider, *Jewish-Americans*, 103, found that almost three quarters of

Jewish males over fourteen were married, compared to two thirds of the total white male population. While 2.6 percent of all white males were divorced or separated, only 0.5 percent of the Jewish population was divorced or separated (data taken from the 1960 census). On the closing of Jewish divorce rates with those of Gentiles, see Steven Bayme, "A National Perspective" (paper presented at a workshop on strategies for strengthening the Jewish family, New York, American Jewish Committee, May, 1989), 22.

6. In the 1970s and 1980s many conferences were held and articles and essays written on changes in American Jewish family life. Included among those in the 1970s were Gerald Bubis, "The Modern Jewish Family," *Journal of Jewish Communal Service* (spring 1971): 240; Lawrence Fuchs, "The Jewish Father, for a Change," *Moment* (September 1975): 45–50; Manheim S. Shapiro, "Changing Life Styles and the Jewish Family," *Congress Monthly* (September 1975): 14–21; Gerald S. Berman, "The Adaptable American Jewish Family: An Inconsistency in Theory," *Jewish Journal of Sociology* (June 1976): 5–16; Gershon Kranzler, "The Changing Orthodox Jewish Family," *Jewish Life* (summer-fall 1978): 23–36; Gladys Rosen, "The Impact of the Women's Movement on the Jewish Family," *Judaism* (spring 1979): 160–68; Chaim I. Waxman, "The Centrality of Family in Defining Jewish Identity and Identification," *Journal of Jewish Communal Service* (summer 1979): 353–59. In the early 1980s the following appeared: Chaim I. Waxman, "The Impact of Feminism on American Jewish Communal Institutions," *Journal of Jewish Communal Service* (fall 1980): 73–79; Steven Martin Cohen, "The American Jewish Family Today," *American Jewish Yearbook* (1982):, 136–54; Gerald Bubis, "The Jewish Family Confronts the 80s," *Baltimore Jewish Times* (December 26, 1980): 42–45; Chaim I. Waxman, "The Family and the American Jewish Community on the Threshold of the 1980s: An Inventory for Research and Planning," in *Understanding American Jewry*, ed. Marshall Sklare (New Brunswick, N.J.: Rutgers University Press, 1982), 163–85; Andrew J. Cherlin and Carin Celebuski, *Are Jewish Families Different?* (New York: American Jewish Committee, William Petschek National Jewish Family Center, 1982); Norman Linzer, "The Jewish Family: Authority and Tradition in Modern Perspective," *Journal of Jewish Communal Service* (winter 1982): 132–43. The American Jewish Committee established the William Petschek National Jewish Family Center in 1979 for the purpose of encouraging studies, conferences, and programs to help promote cohesive Jewish families.

7. Sylvia Barack Fishman, *A Breath of Life: Feminism in the American Jewish Community* (New York: Free Press, 1993), 109, 110. Leading Jewish feminists included Betty Friedan, Shulamith Firestone, Susan Brownmiller, Andrea Dworkin, Robin Morgan, and Letty Cotton Pogrebin. See Shapiro, *Time for*

Healing, 245–47. Also see Moshe Hartman and Harriet Hartman, *Gender Equality and American Jews* (Albany: State University of New York Press, 1966), 15–16, 169, 291–92, 294, 297. The National Jewish Population Survey provided a wealth of data for both Fishman and particularly for the Hartmans. The survey represented 6.8 million Jewish individuals living in 3.2 million households with at least one Jewish member. The selection process in determining respondents finally yielded 1,800 of them, ages eighteen and over. Adding household members, the total was 3,020.

8. Hartman and Hartman, *Gender Equality*. These data and much more are reported on pp. 30–42. In the 1990s, more than three times as many Jewish women graduated from college as non-Jewish white women. Joyce Antler, *Journey Home: Jewish Women in the American Century* (New York: Free Press, 1997), 3.

9. Hartman and Hartman, *Gender Equality*, 80.

10. Fishman, *Breath of Life*, 70, 71.

11. Hartman and Hartman, *Gender Equality*. See chap. 4, "Occupational Achievement of American Jewish Men and Women," esp. pp. 118, 121, 128–31.

12. See Hartman and Hartman, *Gender Equality* (p. 133), which provides data from the 1990 National Jewish Population Survey showing that Jewish professional men and women had a mean of 1.4 children, with the mean age at birth of first child at 26.3.

13. American Jewish Committee Institute of Human Relations, *For the Jewish Family: Goals, Programs, Accomplishments, 1979–1986* (New York: American Jewish Committee Institute of Human Relations, 1986), 7. See also Barry Chiswick, "Labor Supply and Investment in Child Quality: A Study of Jewish and Non-Jewish Women," *Contemporary Jewry* 9 (1988): 35–61, and Bayme, "National Perspective," 20.

14. Hartman and Hartman, *Gender Equality*, 95–101.

15. Shapiro, *Time for Healing*, 245.

16. See Seymour and Eleanor Lerner, "Jewish Involvement in the New York City Women Suffrage Movement," *American Jewish History* 70 (4) (1981); Charlotte Baum, Paula Hyman, and Sonja Michel, *The Jewish Woman in America* (New York: Dial Press, 1976); Paula E. Hyman, "Immigrant Women and Consumer Protest: The New York Kosher Meat Boycott of 1902," *American Jewish History* 70 (1) (September 1980).

17. Linda Gordon Kuzmack and George Salomom, *A Study of Ninety-Seven Jewish Career Women* (New York: National Jewish Family Center of the American Jewish Committee, Institute of Human Relations, 1980), 15.

18. Pamela S. Nadell, *Women Who Would Be Rabbis: A History of Women's Ordination, 1889–1985* (Boston: Beacon Press, 1998), 13–38, 48–50, 59. It was outside

the strictly religious area that Jewish women's leadership in Jewish communal activity was most pronounced, according to Marshall Sklare's study of Jews in suburbia, *The Jews: Social Patterns of an American Group* (Glencoe, Ill.: Free Press, 1958), 255. More than four women in ten regularly participated in organizational activities, and one fourth were office holders or board members. The women took the lead in many organizations designed to influence social policy and affect the lives of others (p. 258).

19. Shapiro, *Time for Healing*, 176, 177; Nadell, *Women Who Would Be Rabbis*, 200–13.

20. Debra Orenstein, ed., *Life Cycles: Jewish Women on Life Passage and Personal Milestones* (Los Angeles: Jewish Lights Publishing, 1994).

21. Walter Ruby, "Reform v. Conservative: Who's Winning?" *Moment* (April 1996), 32.

22. Debra Nussbaum Cohen, "Women Carving New Place in Orthodox Judaism," *Jewish Bulletin of Northern California*, 1 September 1995, 1–11.

23. Blu Greenberg, "Is Now the Time for Orthodox Women Rabbis?" *Moment* (December 1993).

24. Ronnie Caplane, "Another First in Berkeley: Egalitarian Sephardic Services," *Jewish Bulletin of Northern California*, 26 September 1997.

25. Fishman, *Breath of Life*, 157–67.

26. Peter Steinfels, "Beliefs," *New York Times*, 22 February 1997. Also Debra Nussbaum Cohen, "Orthodox Feminist Conference Draws More than Seven Hundred in New York," *Northern California Jewish Bulletin*, 28 February 1997.

27. Susan Grossman and Rivka Haut, eds., *Daughters of the King: Women in the Synagogue* (Philadelphia: The Jewish Publication Society of America, 1993).

28. Judith Hauptman, *Re-reading the Rabbis: A Woman's Voice* (New York: Westview/HarperCollins, 1997).

29. Avraham Weiss, *Women at Prayer: A Halakhic Analysis of Women's Prayer Groups* (Hoboken, N.J.: Ktav, 1990), xiv, 30, 63, 98.

30. Greenberg, *On Women and Judaism: A View from Tradition* (Philadelphia: The Jewish Publication Society of America, 1996), x, 6, 7, 47.

31. The citation for Soloveitchik is from Weiss, *Women at Prayer*, 63; the citation for Schneerson is from Fishman, *Breath of Life*, 193.

32. Alan J. Yuter, "Women's Prayer Groups and the *Halakhic* Process," *Sh'ma: A Journal of Jewish Responsibility* (4 April 1997), 1.

33. Fishman, *Breath of Life*, 201.

34. Tamar Frankiel, *The Voice of Sarah: Feminine Spirituality in Traditional Judaism* (New York: HarperCollins, 1990), xi, 3.

35. Debra Renee Kaufman, *Rachel's Daughters: Newly Orthodox Jewish Women* (New Brunswick: N.J.: Rutgers University Press, 1993), 13, 114.

36. Ibid., 92.
37. Fishman, *Breath of Life*, 35, 36.
38. Solomon Poll, *The Hasidic Community of Williamsburg* (New York: Free Press of Glencoe, 1962), 52, 53.
39. Israel Rubin, *Satmar: An Island in the City* (Chicago: Quadrangle Books, 1972), 106, 115.
40. Egon Mayer, *From Suburb to Shtetl: The Jews of Boro Park* (Philadelphia: Temple University Press, 1979), 80.
41. Ibid., 80.
42. L. Fuchs, "Jewish Father"; David Singer, comp., *Focus on the American Jewish Family: A Select Annotated Bibliography, 1970–1982* (New York: American Jewish Committee, Institute of Human Relations, 1984). In addition to intermarriage, the articles frequently dealt with fertility and divorce.
43. Clifford E. Librach, "The Eclipse of Jewish Men," *Sh'ma: A Journal of Jewish Responsibility* (20 January 1995): 6, 7.
44. Gary Rosenblatt, "Will Men Become an Unusual Species in the Synagogue?" *Northern California Jewish Bulletin*, 24 July 1988, p. 22. The Reform rabbi quoted is Jeffrey Salkin of Port Washington, N.Y.
45. Fishman, *Breath of Life*, 209. The original article comes from Richard M. Yellin, "A Philosophy of Masculinity: One Interpretation," *Conservative Judaism* 32(2) (winter 1979): 89–94.
46. Gwen Gibson and Barbara Wyden, *The Jewish Wife* (New York: Peter H. Wyden, 1969), 71. In this study of 200 Jewish wives in the greater New York, Los Angeles, Chicago, and Philadelphia areas—mostly in middle- and upper-middle-class neighborhoods—and of 200 non-Jewish wives in the same neighborhoods, it was found that Jewish husbands and wives had significantly more interaction with each other regarding the husbands's business activities and more frequently than non-Jews. They also discussed matters concerning discipline of the children, relatives, sex, and the wife's daily activities more than others did.

EPILOGUE: BEYOND PATRIARCHY?

1. Alice S. Rossi, "Gender and Parenthood," *American Sociological Review* 49 (February 1984): 1.
2. Fewer than one in ten Japanese managers is a woman, even less than in Mexico. In 1996 only 2.3 percent of the members of Japan's lower house of Parliament were women, compared to 10.9 percent in the United States, putting Japan far down on a list of 161 countries for which such statistics are kept. Nicholas D.

Kristof, "Japan Is a Woman's World Once the Front Door Is Shut," *New York Times*, 19 June 1996.

3. The trend line for greater economic independence for women in Japan is clear, as reflected in an increase in the share of twenty-five- to twenty-nine-year-old Japanese women who are unmarried, from 18.1 percent in 1970 to 48 percent in 1995. Steven Butler, "Japan's Baby Bust," *U.S. News and World Report*, 5 October 1958, 43.

In addition, access to effective birth control has sharply reduced the number of children born to the average Japanese woman, from 4.5 in the years following World War II to 1.53 in 1990 and to 1.39 in 1997. Maternal deaths during pregnancy have fallen dramatically during the same period, and the life span of Japanese women has gone from an average of 49.6 years in 1938 to 81.9 in 1990. One study showed that women spent considerably less time in food shopping, meal preparation, and other domestic work in 1989 than in 1959. Because of objective conditions, women are beginning to show much greater independence, even in Japan. One survey, published in 1993, found that 41 percent of single women agreed that "women should not necessarily get married if they can get along on their own." Sumiko Iwao, *The Japanese Woman: Traditional Image and Changing Reality* (Cambridge, Mass.: Harvard University Press, 1993), 26, 31, 45, 63.

4. Carla Makhalouf, *Changing Veils* (Austin: University of Texas Press, 1979). Also see Patricia Jefferey, *Fogs in a Well: Indian Women in Purdah* (London: Zed Press, 1979). In parts of the Middle East, even the slightest immodesty in a woman can bring loss of honor to her husband, father, or brother.

5. John F. Burns and Steve LeVine, "How Afghans' Stern Rulers Took Hold," *New York Times*, 31 December 1996.

6. Geraldine Brooks, "A Well-Founded Fear," *New York Times*, 7 March 1995.

7. "Hasidim Attack Women at Prayers," *New York Times*, 21 March 1989.

8. Zainah Anwar, as quoted by Seth Mydans, "Blame Men, Not Allah, Islamic Feminists Say," *New York Times*, 10 October 1996.

9. Douglas Jehl, "In Changing Islamic Land, Women Savor Options," *New York Times*, 20 July 1997.

10. Jane Perlez, "Elite Kenyan Women Avoid a Rite: Marriage," *New York Times*, 3 March 1991.

11. Howard W. French, "For Ivory Coast Women, New Battle for Equality," *New York Times*, 6 April 1996.

12. Seth Faison, "Women's Meeting Agrees on Right to Say No to Sex," *New York Times*, 11 September 1995.

13. Janet Silver Ghent, "Domestic Violence," *Jewish Bulletin of Northern California*, 7 August 1998, 1, 48.; Natalie Weinstein, "In Bay Area, Safe Haven

Eludes Some Jewish Women," *The Jewish Bulletin of Northern California*, 7 August 1998, 1.

Some reports indicate that as many as 40,000 victims of abuse reached emergency wards, 2,000 of whom filed charges or sought refuge in shelters. A good portion of the increase probably is attributable to the use of alcohol by men from the former Soviet Union. Some of it was perpetrated by Ethiopian male immigrants. Whatever the causes, even among those who inherit a tradition highly critical of men who abuse their wives, the practice exists. A report on battering in the San Francisco area shows that American Jewish women have not escaped the affliction. Attributable to the strains of immigration, battering appears to come disproportionately from newcomers from the former Soviet Union and cultures where Judaism had almost died out and in which domestic violence was common.

14. Sarah Blustain, "Orthodox at Turning Point on Domestic Violence," *Forward*, 29 December 1995.

15. Peter Baker, "An All-Male Bastion Fights Its Marching Order to Admit Women," *Washington Post National Weekly Edition*, 12–18 February 1990, 34.

16. Timothy Egan, "Sexual Conflict in Army Can Be Undisciplined," *New York Times*, 15 November 1997.

17. Bob Herbert, "Battered Girls in School," *New York Times*, 24 November 1993; also see Jane Gross, "Where 'Boys Will Be Boys' and Adults Are Befuddled," *New York Times*, 29 March 1993.

18. Partly because they did not want to take a chance on marrying Irish men, a great many Irish women emigrated on their own. Janet A. Nolan, *Ourselves Alone: Women's Immigration from Ireland, 1885–1920* (Lexington: University Press of Kentucky, 1989).

19. The literature on Irish family life and the stresses on fathers over several hundred years is extensive. See Andrew M. Greeley, *That Most Distressful Nation* (Chicago: Quadrangle Books, 1972), and *The Irish-Americans* (New York: Harper & Row, 1981); Oscar Handlin, *Boston's Immigrants* (New York: Atheneum, 1972). Works of fiction and long memoirs tell the story of the weakening of Irish fathers and the consequences to children. A recent Pulitzer Prize–winning account is Frank McCourt's autobiography, *Angela's Ashes*, a dramatic story of the decline of Irish male authority, although the McCourt children survived and transcended extremely difficult beginnings. Frank McCourt, *Angela's Ashes* (New York: Scribner, 1996).

20. Rates of desertion by Jewish men were a relatively short-lived phenomenon, which ended as Jews gained access to decent jobs in America. The story of the Irish, while detailed in a considerable amount of scholarship in fiction, is much less well known today than that of African Americans. Most Irish Americans are now solidly in the middle class. African American fathers were absent in

only 20 percent of black families in 1880, compared to 65 percent in 1995. By 1980, four times as many black families as white families were headed by women, and five times the number of black babies were born to unmarried mothers, compared to white babies.

For a history of fatherlessness in the African American community, see E. Franklin Frazier, *The Negro Family in the United States*, rev. and abridged ed. (Chicago: University of Chicago Press, 1966). Also see John Dollard, *Caste and Class in a Southern Town* (Garden City, N.Y.: Doubleday & Co., 1957); Hortense Powdermaker, *After Freedom* (New York: Atheneum, 1967); Kenneth B. Clark, *Dark Ghetto* (New York: Harper & Row, 1965); Lee Rainwater and William C. Yancey, eds., *The Moynihan Report and the Politics of Controversy* (Cambridge, Mass.: MIT Press, 1967). And for ways in which black mothers compensated for fatherless households, see Carol Stack, *All Our Kin* (New York: Harper & Row, 1975), and Andrew Billingsley, *Black Females in White America* (Englewood Cliffs, N.J.: Prentice-Hall, 1968).

21. Ann Cornelisen, *Women of the Shadows: The Wives and Mothers of Southern Italy* (Boston: Little, Brown, 1976).

22. Mike O'Connor, "Muslim Widows in Bosnia Try to Rebuild Lives without Men," *New York Times*, 13 July 1996.

23. Mary Ann Smothers Bruni, "The Zhinan," *World View* (fall 1996): 14.

24. Gustav Niebuhr, "Southern Baptists Declare Wife Should Submit to Her Husband," *New York Times*, 10 July 1998.

25. Gustav Niebuhr, "Rally Taps Men's Desire for Sense of Community," *New York Times*, 5 October 1997; Michael Janofsky, "Women, on the Rally's Edge, Mirror Divided View of Group," *New York Times*, 5 October 1997; Laurie Goodstein, "Women and the Promise Keepers: Good for the Gander, but the Goose Isn't So Sure," *New York Times*, 5 October 1997.

26. "Promise Keepers: Men Have Dropped the Ball," *U.S.A. Today*, 1 October 1997.

27. James Brooke, "Utah Struggles with a Revival of Polygamy," *New York Times*, 12 August 1998.

28. Eddy Meng, "Mail-Order Brides: Gilded Prostitution and the Legal Response," *University of Michigan Journal of Law Reform* 28(1) (fall 1994): 207.

29. Melvin E. Spiro, *Gender and Culture: Kibbutz Women Revisited* (Durham, N.C.: Duke University Press, 1979), 6–58.

30. Ibid., 103.

31. Ibid. For a discussion of the reality of sexual equality, see pp. 46–60. The study of the six *kibbutzim* in 1976 showed that 45 percent of the Israeli-born women on them preferred family sleeping over the infants' house, compared to only 37 percent of the men.

32. According to a national study by the Families and Work Institute, in households

where only the husband works, the wife does 94 percent of the cooking and 93 percent of the child care. Where both parents work, the wife's share dips only to 80 percent of the cooking and 70 percent of the child care. See Douglas Martin, "For Many Fathers, Roles Are Shifting," *New York Times*, 20 June 1993, 20, national Sunday edition.

Another study, put out by Michigan's Institute for Social Research in 1999, showed that whereas dads were spending about one third as much time as mothers in caring for kids in the late 1990s, they were spending as much as 65 percent on weekdays and 87 percent on the weekends. Fathers in intact, two-parent families more than doubled their share of child care in the past twenty years. Of course, 42 percent of U.S. children were not in intact families by 1998. See the report in Marilyn Elias, "Today's Daddies Make More Room for Child Care," *U.S.A. Today*, 10 June 1999.

33. Carol Lawson, *New York Times*, 16 May 1991.

34. James A. Levine and Todd L. Pittinsky, *Working Fathers: New Strategies for Balancing Work and Family* (New York: Addison Wesley, 1997). Also see Ronald F. Levant, *Masculinity Reconstructed: Changing the Rules of Manhood at Work, in Relationships, and in Family Life* (New York: Dutton, 1995); and Andre C. Willis, ed., *Faith of Our Fathers: African-American Men Reflect on Fatherhood* (New York: Dutton, 1996).

In addition to the Fatherhood Project, there is an academic organization, The National Center on Fathers and Families, which collects and disseminates research on fathers. There is also a membership group for people who run fatherhood programs, the National Practitioners' Network on Fathers and Families, bringing fathers together on issues of common concern. An advocacy group, the Center on Fathers, Families and Public Policies, monitors the legal issues that poor fathers face. An Institute for Responsible Fatherhood and Family Revitalization conducts programs in several cities. There are several government- and foundation-financed programs that are attempting to put fathers back into the lives of poor children. The focus on the poor is an appropriate response to the fact that only about 5 percent of the nation's three million welfare families in 1998 reported having a father in the home and that almost 70 percent of the women on welfare were unmarried when they had their first child.

35. *Modern Dad*, October/November 1995, 1.

36. Elisa Kronish, letter to author, 9 July 1999.

37. David Blankenhorn, *Fatherless America* (New York: Basic Books, 1996), 218, 225.

38. Levine and Pittinsky, *Working Fathers*, 19, 20.

39. Ibid., 26, 41.

40. *Boston Globe*, 19 July 1998, 16.
41. Judith S. Wallerstein and Sandra Blakeslee, *The Good Marriage: How and Why Love Lasts* (Boston: Houghton Mifflin, 1995), 72–77.
42. The most pessimistic view of what is happening to males comes from Warren Farrell, *The Myth of Male Power: Why Men Are the Disposable Sex* (New York: Simon & Schuster, 1994). Also see Griswold, *Fatherhood in America* (New York: Basic Books, 1995), and Blankenhorn, *Fatherless America*. Others include David D. Gilmore, *Manhood in the Making: Cultural Concepts of Masculinity* (New Haven, Conn.: Yale University Press, 1990), which argues that societies in conflict depend on males trained to be hunters and soldiers who are willing to give themselves up to protect the group; Jerrold Lee Shapiro, *The Measure of a Man: Becoming the Father You Wish Your Father Had Been* (New York: Delacorte Press, 1993), which acknowledges the erosion of authoritative fathering and pleads for men to take a more active role in raising children; David Popenoe, *Life without Father* (New York: Martin Kessler Books, Free Press, 1996); Henry B. Biller, *Fathers and Families: Paternal Factors in Child Development* (Westport, Conn.: Auburn House, 1993); Samuel Osherson, *Finding Our Fathers: The Unfinished Business of Manhood* (New York: Free Press, 1986) (Osherson did a longitudinal study of 370 men who graduated from college in the mid-1960s that stressed the importance of the relationship of fathers to sons, particularly those between the ages of three and five); Martin O'Connell, *Where's Papa? Father's Role in Child Care* (Washington, D.C.: Population Reference Bureau, 1995); and E. Antony Rotondo, *American Manhood: Transformations in Masculinity from the Revolution to the Modern Era* (New York: Basic Books, 1993).
43. Barry S. Hewlett, ed., *Father-Child Relations: Culture and Biosocial Contexts* (New York: Aldine and Digruyter, 1992), 162–64.
44. Sarah Harkness and Charles M. Super, "The Cultural Foundations of Fathers' Roles: Evidence from Kenya and the United States," chap. 9 in *Father-Child Relations: Culture and Biosocial Contexts*, ed. Barry S. Hewlett (New York: Aldine and Digruyter, 1992), 195–209.
45. Phyllis Trible, "Depatriarchalizing in Biblical Tradition" in *The New Jewish Woman: New Perspectives*, ed. Elizabeth Koltun (New York: Schocken Books, 1976), 219.

INDEX

Index

Index

Islam, 45, 56, 156–57; Nation of, 161–62
Island Within, The, 107
Israel: ancient, 31–33, 43, 48–49, 51, 59–61; modern, 163–64
Italy, male protection of families in, 23
Ivrim (early Hebrews), 31–33

Jacobson, Isaac, 110
Jael (biblical figure), 61
Japan, women in, 155–56
Jefferson, Thomas, 102
Jerusalem, 32, 35, 36, 84
Jewish Daily Forward, 106, 114–15
Jewish families and family life, 87, 93, 95–97, 103, 140–41. *See also* families and family life; fathers, Jewish; Jewish patriarchal paradigm
Jewish fathers. *See* fathers, Jewish
Jewish marriage. *See* marriage, Jewish
Jewish patriarchal paradigm: characteristics of, 29, 66, 69, 78–79; 86; decline of in America, 102, 120–26; and the diaspora, 84–85; fatherhood, incentives for, 150–51; fathers as teachers, 75, 78, 86, 144, 148, 150–51; and gender equality, 144, 154–55; husband and father type, 38–39, 50, 69; males, acceptance by, 36–38; males, special importance of, 67–69; and marriage, 43–44, 55–69; modification of generic patriarchy, 2–3, 33–37, 43–44, 61, 153–54; origins of, 33–35; and sexuality, 43–44; and upward mobility in America, 107; women, protections under rabbinic law, 61–64. *See also* marriage, Jewish; fathers, Jewish; patriarchy, generic; partiarchy, modern
Jewish religious scholarship: in America, 107–13, 120–21, 123, 130, 138; by children, 71, 75–76; decline in importance, 93, 120–21; exclusion of women from, 67–69, 97–99; and Jewish survival in the diaspora, 40–41, 84–85; and marriage, 56–57; by Orthodox women, 146; and secular

education, 87, 123; support for by women, 86, 88, 96–97, 109–11; women excluded from, 68, 97–99. *See also* Gemara, Mishnah, Talmud
Jewish survival, 38–41, 84–85, 150
Jewish traditions and religious observance: in America, 106–11, 138–41, 144–49; in eighteenth- and nineteenth-century Europe, 83–100; obligations of Jewish males, 67–69, 71–72, 149–50; women and religious courts, 62; women's responsibility for, 113–14, 132, 134, 143–50
Jews: in America before 1900, 103; educational attainments in America, 112, 141–42; entrepreneurship in America, 128; expulsion from European countries, 84; occupations in America, 112, 128, 142; segregation and integration of western Europe, 83–84, 86–87
Judah ibn Tibbon, 76–77
Judaism, 87, 103, 107, 130, 138, 144–49
Judith (biblical figure), 60

Karo, Joseph, 52–53, 62
Kazin, Alfred, 113, 122, 125
Kenya, women in, 18, 26, 157
ketubah (marriage contract), 63–64, 94
kibbutzim and gender roles, 163–64
Kikuyu (Kenya), 18, 26
Kingston, Maxine Hong, 136

labor force, women in. *See* women, work force participation; women, Jewish, occupations and work force participation
Latin America, 23, 159–60
Letter of Holiness (*Iggeret Ha-Kodesh*), 47, 89
Levin, Meyer, 119
Levinson, Sam, 124
Lewisohn, Ludwig, 107
Lilienblum, Moses Leib, 94
Luria, Solomon, 61–62

Index

Index

Rabad (Abraham ben David of Posquieres), 47
Rakowski, Puah, 99–100
rape, 27–28, 36
Rashi (eleventh-century rabbi), 48, 68
Rebecca (biblical figure), 60
Reconstructionist Judaism, 145
redemption of the son (*pidyon ha-ben*), 67, 72
Reform Judaism, 87, 107, 138, 144–49
reproductive strategies, 7–9
respect due parents, 74–75, 100
Rise of David Levinsky, The, 106, 109, 119, 121
roles of men and women. *See* gender roles and gender equality
Roskolenko, Harry, 109, 124
Ross, Tamar, 146
Roth, Henry, 109
Roth, Philip, 136–37
Russian Pale, 87
Ruth (biblical figure), 60

Sarah (biblical figure), 59–60
Sarakatsani, Greece, 23–24, 26
Schneerson, Rabbi, 147
scholarship and upward mobility in traditional cultures, 20
Schulberg, Bud, 109
segregation of the sexes, 23, 50–51, 157
sensuality tradition in Judaism, 50–53, 89
separation of church and state, 110
Sephardim, 84
settlement houses, 116
Seven Precepts for Women, 59
sexual dimorphism and gender equality, 154
sexuality and sexual behavior: female, control of, 25–26; of Jewish women in America, 130–31; and Judaism, 42–54; male, 25; in Myanmar (Burma), 25; and partnership parenting, 165–66; in Sarakatsani, Greece, 23–24, 26; and women in

ancient Israel, 60; in Yiddish fiction, 89–90
Shabbat, 95–97, 107, 113, 120, 124, 134, 148
shalom bayit (family peace), 56–57, 90, 92–93, 96
Shapira, Miriam, 68–69
shekhinah (the felt presence of God), 49–50
shtetl life, 87, 95–97
Shulamit, Queen, 61
Shulkhan Arukh, 52–53, 62, 73, 89, 146
Simon, Kate, 118
Singer, Isaac Bashevis, 89–91
single parenthood: 1–2, 115–16, 159–51
Slave, The, 90
socialism, 87–88, 125
socialization of males, 15, 17, 27–28
Soloveitchik, Rav Yosef Dov, 147
Song of Songs, 89
Spewak, Bella, 117
status of women: in America, 101–2, 104, 111–14, 127; in China, 20; in Christian Europe, 45–46; Jewish (*see* women, Jewish, status and legal protections); in Mesopotamia, 15; in Muslim countries, 156; in the Third World, 157–58
Streets, 117
success. *See* achievement and failure in America
Sun Chief (Hopi Indian), 17
synagogues, importance of in diaspora, 39, 84–85

Talmud ("study" or "learning"), 34–36, 71, 84. *See also* Jewish religious scholarship
Taylor, Sidney, 140–41
teaching, caregiving, and nurturing by males, 164–68; and American Jews, 106–7, 135, 139, 144; and feminism and gender equality, 144, 164–65; in Jewish tradition and religious activities, 38–39, 75–78, 86, 144, 148, 150–